LEARNING ABOUT LANGUAGE ASSESSMENT: DILEMMAS, DECISIONS, AND DIRECTIONS

Kathleen M. Bailey
Monterey Institute of International Studies

Paul J. Firth, Editorial Assistant

A TeacherSource Book

Donald Freeman
Series Editor

Heinle & Heinle Publishers
I(T)P An International Thomson Publishing Company

Pacific Grove • Albany • Bonn • Boston • Cincinnati • Detroit • London
Madrid • Melbourne • Mexico City • New York • Paris
San Francisco • Tokyo • Toronto • Washington

The publication of *Learning about Language Assessment: Dilemmas, Decisions and Directions* was directed by members of the Newbury House ESL/EFL Team at Heinle & Heinle:

Erik Gundersen, Editorial Director
Bruno R. Paul, Marketing Director
Kristin M. Thalheimer, Production Services Coordinator
Thomas Healy, Developmental Editor
Stanley J. Galek, Vice President and Publisher/ESL

Also participating in the publication of this program were:

Project Manager, Designer, and Compositor: Imageset Design/Mary Reed
Manufacturing Coordinator: Mary Beth Hennebury
Associate Market Development Director: Mary Sutton
Cover Designer: Ha D. Nguyen

Heinle & Heinle is a division of International Thomson Publishing, Inc.

Manufactured in the United States of America

TWE Scoring Scale is reprinted by permission of Educational Testing Service, the copyright owner. However, the test questions and any other testing information are provided in their entirety by Heinle & Heinle. No endorsement of this publication by Educational Testing Service should be inferred.

Bailey, Kathleen M.
   Learning about language assessment: dilemmas, decisions, and directions / Kathleen M. Bailey.
        p.   cm. — (TeacherSource)
   Includes bibliographical references and index.

   ISBN 0-8384-6688-5
   1. Language and languages — Ability testing.   I. Title
II. Series.
P53.4.B35   1998
418'.0076 — dc21   97-30858
                                                                                     CIP

15 14 13 12 11 10

TABLE OF CONTENTS

Dedication

This book is dedicated to my colleagues at the Monterey Institute of International Studies—particularly those who have influenced my thinking about assessment: Gary Buck, Cherry Campbell, Martha Clark Cummings, Lynn Goldstein, John Hedgcock, Ruth Larimer, Christine Pearson Casanave, Peter Shaw, Michaele Smith, Marya Teutsch-Dwyer, Jean Turner, Leo van Lier, Alex Vogel, and Devon Woods.

It is also dedicated to my colleagues in the Language Testing Research Colloquium. Although they may not find all of their ideas reflected here, I have learned a great deal from them over the years, and have fond memories of the times we have shared. I'd especially like to offer one more "Rebel Yell" for Michael.

Y también el Capítulo 11 está dedicado a los tres pescadores del barquito, a la gente del pueblito al sur de Puerto Vallarta, al taxista, y a la joven doctora, quienes nos ayudaron en aquel día horrible del "agua mala." Muchísimas gracias, amigos del camino.

Thank You

The series editor, authors and publisher would like to thank the following individuals who offered many helpful insights throughout the development of the *TeacherSource* series.

Linda Lonon Blanton	University of New Orleans
Tommie Brasel	New Mexico School for the Deaf
Jill Burton	University of South Australia
Margaret B. Cassidy	Brattleboro Union High School, Vermont
Florence Decker	University of Texas at El Paso
Silvia G. Diaz	Dade County Public Schools, Florida
Margo Downey	Boston University
Alvino Fantini	School for International Training
Sandra Fradd	University of Miami
Jerry Gebhard	Indiana University of Pennsylvania
Fred Genesee	University of California at Davis
Stacy Gildenston	Colorado State University
Jeannette Gordon	Illinois Resource Center
Else Hamayan	Illinois Resource Center
Sarah Hudelson	Arizona State University
Joan Jamieson	Northern Arizona University
Elliot L. Judd	University of Illinois at Chicago
Donald N. Larson	Bethel College, Minnesota (Emeritus)
Numa Markee	University of Illinois at Urbana Champaign
Denise E. Murray	San Jose State University
Meredith Pike-Baky	University of California at Berkeley
Sara L. Sanders	Coastal Carolina University
Donna Sievers	Garden Grove Unified School District, California
Leo van Lier	Monterey Institute of International Studies

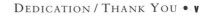

ACKNOWLEDGMENTS

I am grateful to a number of people who made it possible for me to write this book during the crazy summer of 1996.

As always, I start with heartfelt thanks to my partner, Les Zambo, who cooked, poured coffee or wine (depending on the time of day), and helped me learn a new computer system.

The series editor, Donald Freeman, was kind enough to include me in the project in the first place; he also gave me feedback on the early chapters and encouragement along the way. As we have worked together on many projects over the past five years, I have come to appreciate Donald's vision, intellect, and wit. I am thrilled to have a book in his series.

As with all the volumes in the TeacherSource series, the touchstone in this book is found in the "Teachers' Voices" section of each chapter. I am extremely grateful to the teachers who shared with me their dilemmas, their creativity, and their reflections: Michelle Bettencourt, Pat Bolger, Beckie Chase, Melinda Erickson, Tim Hacker, John Hedgcock, Peter Hicks, Christine Houba, Leo van Lier, Ellie Mason, Pete Rogan, Maricel Santos, Peter Shaw, and Diane Williams.

My mom, Char McMillan, helped me check the reference list, and my dad, Harry McMillan, kept the coffee coming and didn't bug me, even when he was stuck on his crossword puzzle. My friend Jennifer Tuman came back into my life just in time to proofread the manuscript.

While I was writing this book I moved out of my house and office, from California to Hong Kong. The manuscript was written during four long car trips and seven round trips on airlines, and while I recuperated from minor surgery. It was written in three offices, in three houses, in six hotels, in five airports, and in the cocktail lounges at three golf courses. The extent to which the manuscript is coherent and readable is largely a function of the work done by my friend and editorial assistant, Paul Firth. His word-processing and layout skills, his careful reading of the prose, the questions he raised, and the fact that he caught errors in my handling of the statistics have all made this a much better book than it would have been without him. I am deeply indebted to Paul and his family for the time he spent on this project.

PREFACE

Driving just south of White River Junction, the snow had started falling in earnest. The light was flat, although it was mid-morning, making it almost impossible to distinguish the highway in the gray-white swirling snow. I turned on the radio, partly as a distraction and partly to help me concentrate on the road ahead; the announcer was talking about the snow. "The state highway department advises motorists to use extreme caution and to drive with their headlights to ensure maximum visibility." He went on, his tone shifting slightly, "Ray Burke, the state highway supervisor, just called to say that one of the plows almost hit a car just south of Exit 6 because the person driving hadn't turned on his lights. He really wants people to put their headlights on because it is very tough to see in this stuff." I checked, almost reflexively, to be sure that my headlights were on, as I drove into the churning snow.

How can information serve those who hear or read it in making sense of their own worlds? How can it enable them to reason about what they do and to take appropriate actions based on that reasoning? My experience with the radio in the snow storm illustrates two different ways of providing the same message: the need to use your headlights when you drive in heavy snow. The first offers dispassionate information; the second tells the same content in a personal, compelling story. The first disguises its point of view; the second explicitly grounds the general information in a particular time and place. Each means of giving information has its role, but I believe the second is ultimately more useful in helping people make sense of what they are doing. When I heard Ray Burke's story about the plow, I made sure my headlights were on.

In what is written about teaching, it is rare to find accounts in which the author's experience and point of view are central. A point of view is not simply an opinion; neither is it a whimsical or impressionistic claim. Rather, a point of view lays out what the author thinks and why; to borrow the phrase from writing teacher Natalie Goldberg, "it sets down the bones." The problem is that much of what is available in professional development in language-teacher education concentrates on telling rather than on point of view. The telling is prescriptive, like the radio announcer's first statement. It is emphasizes what is important to know and do, what is current in theory and research, and therefore what you—as a practicing teacher—should do. But this telling disguises the teller; it hides the point of view that can enable you to make sense of what is told.

The TeacherSource series offers you a point of view on second/foreign language teaching. Each author in this series has had to lay out what she or he believes is central to the topic, and how she or he has come to this understanding. So as a reader, you will find this book has a personality; it is not anonymous. It comes as a story, not as a directive, and it is meant to create a relationship with you rather than assume your attention. As a practitioner, its point of view can help you in your own work by providing a sounding board for your ideas and a metric for your own thinking. It can suggest courses of action and explain why these make sense to the author. And you can take from it what you will, and do with it what you can. This book will not tell you what to think; it is meant to help you make sense of what you do.

The point of view in **TeacherSource** is built out of three strands: **Teachers' Voices**, **Frameworks**, and **Investigations**. Each author draws together these strands uniquely, as suits his or her topic and more crucially his or her point of view. All materials in **TeacherSource** have these three strands. The **Teachers' Voices** are practicing language teachers from various settings who tell about their experience of the topic. The **Frameworks** lay out what the author believes is important to know about his or her topic and its key concepts and issues. These fundamentals define the area of language teaching and learning about which she or he is writing. The **Investigations** are meant to engage you, the reader, in relating the topic to your own teaching, students, and classroom. They are activities which you can do alone or with colleagues, to reflect on teaching and learning and/or try out ideas in practice.

Each strand offers a point of view on the book's topic. The **Teachers' Voices** relate the points of view of various practitioners; the **Frameworks** establish the point of view of the professional community; and the **Investigations** invite you to develop your own point of view, through experience with reference to your setting. Together these strands should serve in making sense of the topic.

Assessment is a complex topic, the technical and sometimes political dimensions of which can often put teachers off. In this book, Kathleen Bailey approaches language assessment through the eyes and experiences of practitioners, thus firmly grounding her examination in actual classrooms. Teachers in diverse settings explore the issues the author raises, creating a unique counterpoint of theory and practice which presents a well-balanced, grounded case for assessment as part of teaching. Much of teachers' work is shaped by forces beyond their immediate direction; learning about language assessment counteracts that trend. Bailey believes that "assessment is an integral part of teaching and learning, but should be subordinate to both." Her book brings assessment back into the heart of language teaching, so that teachers can make sense of it and therefore direct it to support effective teaching and worthwhile learning in their classrooms.

This book, like all elements of the **TeacherSource** series, is intended to serve you in understanding your work as a language teacher. It may lead you to thinking about what you do in different ways and/or to taking specific actions in your teaching. Or it may do neither. But we intend, through the variety of points of view presented in this fashion, to offer you access to choices in teaching that you may not have thought of before and thus to help your teaching make more sense.

—Donald Freeman, Series Editor

Author's Preface

One day while my assistant, Paul Firth, and I were working on this manuscript, my colleague Leo van Lier stuck his head into my office and asked what we were doing.

"We're writing a book!" I glibly replied.

"Oh. What's it about?" Leo asked.

"Uh—" (I was hard-pressed to answer his apparently simple question.) "What's it about, Paul?" I asked.

"Well," Paul hesitated. "I guess you could say it's an experiential treatment of language assessment." That sounded better than anything I could have come up with, so I've stuck with Paul's idea ever since.

Indeed, my intent in writing this book has been to meet the challenge that Donald Freeman posed to all the authors in the **TeacherSource** series. He asked each of us to think about the following questions (and others) with regard to our chosen topics:

1. What do I think is centrally important to know about this topic?
   What do I think is critical to know about it?

2. How have I helped teachers-in-training to understand the topic?
   What kinds of activities or experiences have I organized to do so?

3. How has my own understanding of the topic changed or evolved?
   How have I learned this aspect of teaching? What have been the critical experiences or turning points in the development of my own understanding?

The answers to these questions are woven throughout the book, so you can see that—to the extent that I have been successful—Paul's characterization was appropriate. My own experiences and those of the teachers quoted here in the "Teachers' Voices" sections in each chapter serve to illustrate but also to motivate the ideas put forth in the "Frameworks" section. In the "Frameworks" I have not attempted to cover everything teachers should know about language assessment. Instead I have selected a few procedures and key concepts and explored them in light of various teachers' experiences, including my own.

The "Investigations" at the end of each chapter include both "Tasks," involving the concepts presented, and "Suggestions for Further Reading," in case you would like to pursue more in-depth study of the topic. These tasks and references are intended to help you, the reader, cross the bridge from the printed page to your own classroom. I hope the journey will be pleasant, entertaining, and informative.

Introduction: Twenty Questions

Do you remember the children's game called "Twenty Questions"? Language teachers often use it to get learners to practice yes/no question formation, because answers to the questions posed in the game are restricted to "yes" or "no."

I have laid out the introduction to this book in the format of "Twenty Questions." I tried to think of the questions that you, the reader, might have in beginning to read a book about language assessment. I have taken a few liberties with the strict yes/no answer format, and in each case I have elaborated on the one-word response to explain my thinking as I wrote this book.

Perhaps your first question is not a yes/no question. Perhaps you are asking yourself, "Why should I read this book at all?" After all, the topic may seem a bit dry—perhaps even downright boring! My graduate students at the Monterey Institute of International Studies are often horrified to learn that they are required to take a course in language assessment. For many of them, *test* is a four-letter word.

Here are some other questions that come to mind:

1. Is the alliterative subtitle of this book—"Dilemmas, Decisions, and Directions"—meant to be meaningful (as opposed to just "catchy")?

   Yes. I believe that our assessment responsibilities present us as teachers with numerous dilemmas, many of which center around our discomfort with evaluating the work of the learners we've been trying to help. I also believe that the main reason to do any sort of testing at all is to gain solid, meaningful information with which to make better decisions. And finally, I hope this book will suggest several positive directions to practicing or pre-service teachers—directions leading to improvement in our ability to carry out our assessment responsibilities.

2. Do I have to be taking a testing seminar or working with a group of other teachers to benefit from reading this book?

   No. There are several activities in the "Investigations" sections of the book that might be more profitable (and more fun!) if you could do them with classmates or with colleagues, but I have tried to keep in mind the needs of the individual teacher working alone. There are also some "Investigations" that you can do with students or with friends or family members. The important point is that you will sometimes want other people to share with you their insights when they attempt to do the assessment tasks you have read about or designed.

3. **Do I have to be teaching a language class to benefit from this book?**

No. There will be many activities you could do with your students if you are teaching a language class (or even tutoring individual language learners). However, I hope this book will be useful to nonlanguage teachers as well.

4. **Do I even have to be a practicing teacher to benefit from reading this book?**

No. It is my hope that the book will be useful to pre-service teachers as well. As I said above, many of the tasks can be done with friends or family members rather than with actual students. In addition, many of the ideas will ask you to recall your own experiences as a language learner and reflect on your memories of tests you have taken.

5. **Do I have to read languages other than English to benefit from reading this book?**

No. The entire text is written in English, although there are some comments and one example in Spanish. Of course, my hope is that these ideas will be helpful to teachers of any language.

6. **Will I learn about developing a test by reading this book?**

Yes, although there are many aspects of professional test development that will not be covered in this brief volume. I will concentrate on those aspects of test development that are typically under a teacher's control (e.g., developing classroom or program-based tests rather than commercially developed standardized tests).

7. **Will I learn anything about the major commercially published language tests by reading this book?**

Only a little. As suggested above, the topical focus in this book is squarely on tests that teachers create or help to create (e.g., in a team situation where a group of teachers writes a placement test for a program). We will discuss several concepts that are important in reviewing and evaluating commercially developed tests, and some will be used as examples, but we will not examine those measurement devices to any great extent.

8. **Will I learn about communicative language testing by reading this book?**

Yes. Communicative language testing, as the name suggests, is a movement that has followed naturally (but slowly) from the development of communicative language teaching. Our emerging understanding of communicative language use has necessitated radical shifts in the way we think about assessing learners' language abilities. We will review an important set of principles and constructs underpinning communicative language tests, with particular emphasis on measuring meaning.

9. Will I gain access to research and information about language testing by reading this book?

Yes. All the "Investigations" sections include references to books and accessible articles related to the topic of the chapter in which they appear. My intent here is to steer you, the interested reader, toward resources that will enable you to further your own understanding of the topics covered in the book.

10. Will reading this book give me new ideas about assessing my students' reading and listening skills?

Yes. We will explore some important concepts that underlie reading and listening comprehension. I believe that understanding these concepts will help us assess learners' comprehension more accurately and fairly. We will also examine a variety of techniques that can be used to assess reading comprehension in a classroom setting and promote language learning.

11. Will reading this book give me new ideas about assessing my students' speaking skills?

Yes. The appropriate assessment of speaking is a central concern for language teachers today. We will look carefully at role play as a procedure for eliciting and evaluating speech samples from learners.

12. Will reading this book give me new ideas about assessing my students' writing skills?

Yes. We will compare three historically important approaches to scoring students' writing and look at each approach in terms of the information it provides. We will also try to square the notion of writing assessment with the "process approach" to teaching writing.

13. Do I need to know about statistics to understand this book?

No. Some kinds of statistical analyses are extremely important in developing assessment instruments and in analyzing test results. But the statistics used in this book will be explained as they are cited, so I don't expect readers to start with background knowledge of mathematical procedures, except for averages, decimals, and percentages.

14. Do I have to know a lot of testing jargon to understand this book?

No. Every new technical concept used in this book is printed in boldface type, and is explained and exemplified at its first occurrence. The concepts are recycled in subsequent discussions, so that by the time you reach the end of the book you should feel completely conversant with the basic lexicon related to language assessment.

15. **Will I learn to write better grammar tests by reading this book?**

Perhaps, but probably not. I believe that grammar, one of the "levels" of language, is usually better assessed through its actual use in one or more of the four skills (reading, writing, speaking, and listening) rather than in isolation. For this reason, grammar tests will not be treated as a separate topic.

16. **Will I learn to write better vocabulary tests by reading this book?**

Probably not. Again, the separate testing of vocabulary does not seem as useful to me as the assessment of students' abilities to produce or interpret appropriate vocabulary in context to express or derive meaning.

17. **Will I learn to write better pronunciation tests by reading this book?**

No. The assessment of pronunciation per se is not treated in this book. This is not because I think pronunciation is unimportant. On the contrary, it is an extremely important issue, but one that falls outside my areas of expertise.

18. **Will I learn about writing multiple-choice tests by reading this book?**

Yes, but I hope to introduce a fair amount of caution and a degree of healthy skepticism regarding the value of multiple-choice items.

19. **Will I learn about "alternative" assessment procedures by reading this book?**

Yes. Throughout the book I will suggest alternative uses of traditional assessment mechanisms. But two chapters will also focus specifically on some procedures that have been labeled "alternative" assessment. These include portfolios, performance tests, and self-assessment procedures.

20. **Will reading this book help me be a better teacher?**

Yes, I hope so. The approach I take to assessment is that it is an integral part of teaching and learning, but should be subordinate to both. All the assessment procedures discussed in this book will be explicitly linked to teaching and learning, so I hope my discussions of testing will influence your thinking about teaching and learning. By promoting such insights, I hope to promote both better teaching and better assessment.

1

ASSESSMENT AS INFORMATION GATHERING

There is an old story about a poor farmer who decided one day that he would go to the market and sell a goose, a large basket of grain, and his ferocious watchdog. To get to the market, he had to cross a river in a very small rowboat. Unfortunately, the rowboat was only big enough to hold the farmer and one item of cargo. So in any one trip he could take either the basket of grain, the dog, or the goose with him, but he'd have to make several trips across the river before he could get his entire cargo to market. This tedious procedure also presented the farmer with an additional problem: If he took the grain on his first trip in the boat and left the dog and the goose behind, the dog would eat the goose. Likewise, if he took the dog and left the goose behind with the basket of grain, the goose would eat the grain. The poor farmer was very perplexed. He sat down beside the river and tried to decide what to do while the goose eyed the grain hungrily and the fierce dog watched the goose and licked his chops.

In this chapter we will explore some key concepts associated with language assessment. We will also lay the groundwork for the types of information you will encounter in this book and the format of the chapters to follow. I will begin with a teaching and assessment dilemma, and then in the "Frameworks" section I will offer a framework that will help us examine tests critically. Next, in the "Teachers' Voices" section, we will hear from the teacher whose situation begins this chapter.

Some years ago my friend Diane Williams, who was a novice teacher at the time, was offered a job in a local adult school program. Diane was completing her master's degree, and had not yet taken a language testing seminar, so she was not totally conversant with many of the procedures associated with language assessment. She came to me with something of a dilemma.

The dilemma was this. Diane had just been recruited to teach the second course in a series of English as a Second Language (ESL) courses offered by the local community college for the adult school population, but that was all she knew. No records had been kept from the earlier course. There were no test scores or grades, there was no predetermined curriculum, and the former teacher had left the area. In short, all Diane knew about the class was that the students would use book two in a particular textbook series.

This lack of information presented her with a problem. Could she assume that book two would be appropriate for all her students? Some students would probably try to enroll in her class without having taken the previous course.

Would they be ready for book two, or would they benefit more from book one? Given the population in the area, she knew it was likely that some of her students might even be illiterate not only in English but in their native languages as well, and that book two would certainly be inappropriate for them. Some of her students would be literate in their own language but perhaps not in English. Would book two be appropriate for them?

To complicate matters further, the coordinator of the program had told Diane that the course would be offered only if a sufficient number of students enrolled. The coordinator was unavailable to help Diane but had, nevertheless, given her a specific task and it was this task that presented the dilemma she came to see me about. She was supposed to find out about the students' language proficiency in the first class meeting, but she also needed to make them feel welcome so they would be encouraged to enroll and to return to class. Diane wanted to plan a lesson for the first class session that would allow her to assess the students' abilities without scaring them away. We talked for some time and came up with a set of activities that would provide her with information for decision-making purposes, but that also would start the class in a positive and academically viable manner.

What would you have done if you were Diane? What advice would you have given her?

In my experience, Diane's dilemma was very real and the situation she encountered is quite common. We teachers, especially those of us working with students who are not true beginners, often need information to help us make appropriate curricular decisions. The main purpose of language assessment, as I will treat the topic in this book, is to help us gain the information we need about our students' abilities and to do so in a manner that is appropriate, consistent, and conducive to learning. And because we are almost always faced with limited resources for developing, administering, and scoring tests, our assessment mechanisms must also be practical.

When we talk about a test being "appropriate," the issue is partly whether the test provides us with the information we need to gain about the students we serve. In designing a test, first we have to decide which skills, processes, or knowledge we want to assess. Then we need to figure out how to go about measuring those traits. If a test actually measures what it is intended to measure, we say it is a **valid** test.

It is also important that a test measure students' skills and knowledge consistently. Suppose Diane had decided to interview each of her students and rate their speech on a scale of one (barely intelligible) to five (sounds like a native speaker). It would have been very unfair to some students if Diane grew tired after she'd interviewed ten or twelve people, and became less (or more) forgiving in rating the remaining students' speech samples. If she became stricter (or more lenient) in her evaluations as the evening wore on, then in effect her ratings (i.e., the measurement of the students' speaking skills) would be inconsistent. But being inconsistent in rating the students' speech would be both unfair to the students themselves and problematic in terms of the resulting faulty information to be used in her decision-making. For these reasons and others, it is desirable to be consistent in assessing students' abilities. When a test or a rating system measures students' performances consistently it is said to be **reliabile.**

Another major concern is whether a test promotes effective language learning and teaching. The effect a test has on teaching and learning is known as **washback.** Washback can be either positive or negative. For example, if a test requires that students spell a number of unusual (or "low frequency") words and recite their definitions, then students facing this test are likely to spend their time memorizing the spelling and the definitions of such words. This would be an instance of negative washback in a course promoting communication skills, since these endeavors would probably not promote the learners' abilities to use the target language for their day-to-day communication needs.

And, of course, assessment consumes resources. Developing, revising, administering, and scoring tests all take time, money, and person-power. So assessment mechanisms must also be **practical.** If only ten or twelve students had shown up the first night of class, then Diane probably could have interviewed each one individually. But if forty or fifty students were present, Diane alone could not have interviewed them all individually in the time available. Under those time constraints, the one-on-one interview format would not be practical.

Unfortunately, there is often a trade-off, a dynamic tension, among the concerns for the four criteria by which tests are normally evaluated: validity, reliability, practicality and positive washback. Sometimes a test that is perceived as highly valid and as having positive washback may not be very practical. For example, the *Interagency Language Roundtable Oral Proficiency Interview (ILR OPI)* is a face-to-face oral interview used by U.S. government agencies to assess the speaking ability of federal employees. It takes 10 to 30 minutes to administer, depending on the candidate's oral proficiency. And normally, two interviewers work with each test candidate! Under most circumstances, this format would be prohibitively expensive. So we must seek more practical methods of assessing students' speaking abilities in reliable and valid ways that promote positive washback.

The issues of validity and practicality intersect with the questions "What are we testing?" and "How shall we test it?" In Diane's case, all she knew was that the course was intended to be an "all-skills class." But what does that mean? Most language teachers recognize that this phrase refers to listening, speaking, reading, and writing. Because the issue will become important later when we talk about test development and scoring, it may be helpful at this point to classify the four skills in terms of directionality and modality.

Directionality entails the direction of language used relative to the learner. Is the language learner receiving incoming language? If so, we refer to the **receptive skills** of listening or reading. On the other hand, if the learner himself is generating the language used, then we are talking about the **productive skills** of speaking and writing.

Modality refers to the channel of language use. Is it written or aural/oral? As you can see, given these concepts, we can construct a simple framework for classifying the four skills (Figure 1.1).

Figure 1.1: Directionality, Modality, and the Four Skills

		Directionality:	
		Receptive	Productive
Modality:	Aural/Oral	Listening	Speaking
	Written	Reading	Writing

It will be helpful to keep this framework in mind as you read this book because there are different problems and challenges associated with testing the receptive skills and the productive skills. There are also different issues involved when the learners are being assessed in the aural/oral mode as opposed to the written mode. In Diane's situation, for instance, one question that arose was whether she could interview each potential student individually. This issue is a concern because typically (though not always) we can only attend to one person's speech at a time.

In addition to our concerns about valid and reliable assessment of the four skills, there may be times when we will want to assess students' mastery of the hierarchical components of language. These components of language are listed on the vertical axis in Figure 1.2.

Figure 1.2: The Four Skills and the Hierarchical Components of Language

Hierarchical Components of Language	Listening	Speaking	Reading	Writing
Discourse				
Syntax				
Lexicon				
Morphology				
Phonology/Phonetics				

As you can see, in attempting any given test item, students might be completing mental work represented by just one box or by many boxes. In an interactive oral interview situation, for example, all the components in the Listening and Speaking columns would be invoked. If a student taking a test must read an article and then write an original essay arguing for or against the position taken in the article, then all the components in the Reading and Writing columns would be involved in performing the task. In Chapter 11 we will examine a test in which students participated in oral interviews based on newspaper articles they had read previously. This combination involves all the components in the Reading and Speaking columns.

This simple two-dimensional model only partially represents the complexity of language as it is used in communication. In fact, Oller (1979, 172–175) has collected several increasingly complex models that have evolved over time to depict what it means to assess second or foreign language skills. For now we will work with just these issues, realizing, however, that the oversimplification is intentional.

In summary, then, we have seen in this "Frameworks" section that there are four main criteria by which language tests have traditionally been evaluated. These are validity, reliability, practicality, and positive washback. Likewise, when we talk about the assessment and design of language tests, we need to be clear about which of the four skills and/or levels of language we are attempting to measure. These frameworks will emerge as repeated themes in this book as we consider different means of assessing students' second or foreign language skills.

We began this chapter with a description of Diane Williams's dilemma when she faced a new class with no information. Nearly fifteen years after that experience, I asked Diane to tell me what she would do now if she were presented with the same dilemma and the same timeline for preparing her initial lesson plan. I am happy to tell you that she answered my questions easily and with confidence. Here is a summary of our conversation:

Kathi: If you were to start a class now, under those circumstances again—where basically the coordinator had no information to give you, and there was a very short lead-time, and as far as you knew, it was going to be only you teaching, and you had no idea how many students there would be—what would you do that first night?

Diane: Well, I think I would negotiate more aggressively with the coordinator. At the time, I was probably intimidated by his position, and by just the fact that I was in a new situation, teaching a new course. It was a new place. If I were to do it today I would tell him that we're working at cross purposes here—that you can't say, "You will use this particular book," when I have absolutely no idea what the needs of the students are. So I think that I would negotiate with him and say, "I need to do a needs analysis, and at that point I can decide if book two is appropriate." If that negotiation proved to be unsuccessful, then I would pick and choose selectively from book two, based on a needs analysis that I did with my students. I think I would have to be very careful to help the students understand the needs analysis, so that even though I was asking information about what they wanted to do, they would be secure with me. Sometimes if students aren't used to that kind of setting, they think "Why am I here? Doesn't she have an idea of what she wants to teach me?" So it would be important to give them a framework for what I wanted to do, how I wanted to approach the class, but then to tell them that I would need information about them.

I was intrigued by this response. Diane's perception of the problem had shifted from "What am I going to do during the first class meeting?" to the more confident stance of a professional teacher finding out first what the students needed, even if it meant arguing with the coordinator. Next I asked Diane what information she would need about the students' actual language abilities, and how she'd go about getting it:

Kathi: You've talked a lot about needs assessment. But what would you want to know about the learners' language abilities, and how would you go about finding that out, in addition to, say, their functional needs for language use that a needs assessment would show you?

Diane: Right. I think I would look at what I want the outcome to be. What do they need to use the language for? I would approach it based on what they want to do with the language, and then I would—depending on the size of the class—maybe pull them aside and do a little informal oral inventory, an oral interview. I'd see if they were able to respond to simple factual questions, and if they were able to form simple factual questions. Could they converse about basic topics? I would probably give them a form to fill out. Could they respond to questions about their names? Their addresses? I might give them directions and see how well they could follow those directions, to get at their listening.

Kathi: Can you give me an example?

Diane: Well, let's say if I'm giving them a form to fill out, possibly they would fill out one section but not another. Or they could fill out one section before another. You know, there are different ways of giving them sequential instructions to see if they can respond correctly. And I think that would be the limit of what I'd do in terms of writing, especially if I had some suspicions that they were illiterate. Maybe I could make it a group task where they could come up with information, and the group could choose one recorder or something like that, if I had some suspicions that some people couldn't write.

Kathi: Why?

Diane: Well, because if some were illiterate, and if I required them to write the first day of class, they wouldn't come back. And they would be shamed, horribly.

Kathi: So the group possibility allows you to get the information but protect those people who can't write.

Diane: Yes. And then I think that it would become clear very rapidly who was illiterate and who wasn't—who was preliterate.

You may have noticed that Diane said "depending on the size of the class" when she talked about interviewing students. Donald Freeman (1996, 97–98) points out that experienced teachers are very sensitive to contextual factors when they make planning and teaching decisions:

[T]eaching is not simply an activity that bridges thought and action; it is usually intricately rooted in a particular context. This may be why, when asked about aspects of their work, teachers will often preface their responses with the disclaimer "It depends."

Freeman goes on to say that these "It depends" statements "offer evidence of the individual and subjective nature of what teachers think about their instructional work" (ibid.). He feels that these "It depends" understandings demand a view of teaching that stresses "knowing what to do," that is, an interpretivist view that combines, but is greater than, the perspectives of "teaching as doing" and "teaching as thinking." You will see this interpretivist view exemplified as the conversation with Diane continues:

Diane: So I think there are two purposes that I'd have in mind. One would be to find out as much information as I could about the students, and the second would be to make them want to come back—to create an environment in which they would feel like they have a chance of succeeding.

Kathi: You've specifically mentioned talking with the students—seeing if they could answer and form simple questions, and doing a kind of subtle listening procedure just to see if they could complete tasks as directed. And the form you'd give them would include having them write a little bit. Would you also assess their reading?

Diane: Well, I thought the form might get at that, but not necessarily. I think, again, it would depend on my sense of their level. I mean, there are all sorts of reading tasks you could do. In the same way that I did a pull-aside oral interview, I could pull them aside and do an informal reading inventory where they would read a couple of sentences aloud and then I could ask them a comprehension question and I would get at what sort of miscues they have. The traditional way you do it is to have them read one paragraph aloud and one silently so that you're getting at comprehension—silent reading comprehension—and then what kind of miscues they're making.[1] That depends on the size of the class and what I thought I could get done. If I thought that wasn't going to be feasible, then I really think I would approach it in terms of filling out the form with information about the class. Were they able to read the instructions? Were they able to respond to something like "How many years have you studied English?" or "When do you use English?"

Again, the "It depends" statements of an experienced teacher guide Diane's response. In the following comments you can see that Diane's priorities for the first class meeting go beyond issues of language assessment. They include environmental concerns (both physical and affective), as well as her awareness of the ongoing administrative constraints that are operative in this situation.

---

1. A reading miscue analysis involves comparing what we expect someone to say when reading aloud with what that person actually says. So for example, if the text says "cat's fur" and the child reads "cat fur," we may take this miscue as one source of possible evidence that the possessive "s" has not yet entered the child's interlanguage system, especially if the error is repeated in other phrases (e.g., if the child says "dog tail" for "dog's tail").

Kathi: Do you remember doing anything like a grammar test?

Diane: The first day? No.

Kathi: I don't think you did because I remember the situation being very much, "You'll have your job if there are enough students."

Diane: Right. Oh, it was very much that situation. There was a lot of pressure in that respect. And I think that's true of adult education a lot of the time.

Kathi: Yes, very typical.

Diane: So it was as important to me that it was a nice place to be as that I get information about the students. And most of them were, as I recall, military wives, a lot of Korean women, and some students from Latin American countries. They wanted to learn English, but they also wanted a community. They wanted a group of people they could belong to as well. So it became a social time, which I know is often the case. And as I recall, it was really kind of nice at the end. We all gave each other presents and I think that exemplified the fact that it was a community for them as much as it was a language learning experience.

To me it seems that Diane's situation, in beginning a class with very little information about the students, is—as she says—very common in adult school programs in the United States. The dilemma is probably not uncommon in other contexts. As language teachers, we are often faced with new classes in which we must use assessment devices to gather information, while at the same time we wish to establish a positive environment. The "Investigations" in this chapter were designed to help you think through your options, in case you find yourself facing a similar dilemma.

---

1 *Now that you have heard Diane's voice, let's return to the situation with which this chapter opened. Put yourself in Diane's place and think about what you would do if you were faced with her dilemma (the need to gather key information about the students in order to make good decisions, but to do so in the limited time available without scaring them away).*

Diane's original situation is summarized below.

■ Congratulations! You have just been hired as an ESL teacher in an evening program for adults. The class meets two nights a week for 2½ hours. You are looking forward to the experience.

■ However, there is one slight problem. It is Friday afternoon and the first class meeting is Monday night. The program coordinator has told you only that some of the students have completed book one, though with varying degrees of success. The course syllabus consists loosely of book two and whatever activities you can develop to help the students improve their general English skills (i.e., it is an all-skills class).

■ You would like to know more about the students—particularly about their abilities and proficiency in English. But the previous teacher has moved away and the program coordinator is out of town for a week. Since this is an ungraded program for adults, no records, test scores, or previous grades are available.

First, sketch out a lesson plan for the first class session. Allowing for a fifteen-minute break, plan to use the 2½ hour period to learn as much as you can about your students' English language skills. (This is your primary objective, since you want to develop a course syllabus before the second session on Wednesday.) Note that a second important objective is to get to know the students and make them feel welcome and at ease in your class.

---

2 *In Diane's case, she was the only teacher hired to teach in the program. She would be running an independent class. But many times, as professional language teachers, we find ourselves working within the context of a language program. The curriculum of such a program typically includes many different levels of instruction (beginners, high beginners, intermediates, upper-intermediates, and advanced learners), and may even include many different sections at each level. Under those circumstances, in addition to creating an effective means of assessment for our own classes, we must also coordinate and compromise with other teachers. The paragraphs below put Diane's dilemma into the context of a multicourse, multisection program.*

■ Surprise! You had just finished your lesson plan when the coordinator of the adult school program called to tell you that, given the large number of inquiries, it was likely that there would be not one but three or four sections of the book two ESL course meeting simultaneously. The coordinator wants all the teachers to agree on a common lesson plan to ensure uniformity across the sections. The coordinator feels this is especially important for the opening session since first impressions may influence enrollment (which *could* still influence your job).

■ Unfortunately, the other teachers are also new to the program, so they don't know any more than you do about the students. An added complication is that with the potentially larger number of students, the coordinator wants the teachers to try to find out if the students are really at the same level or if there should be different levels within the program. This decision must be reached quickly so that actual instruction can begin in earnest at the next class meeting (two days from now).

■ Keep in mind your original objectives as you meet with the other teachers. Your task is to:

1. share your individual lesson plan with the other teachers; and

2. choose together the best elements of each individual lesson plan and write a joint plan that everyone in the group can agree to follow.

You and the other teachers must be prepared to explain your lesson plan to the coordinator. In particular, you must address the question of multiple levels versus a single level with multiple sections. At the same time, you want to accomplish your own goals of learning about the students' English abilities and making the students comfortable in your class.

If you were really faced with one of these situations, whether as an individual teacher or as a member of a team, could you quickly pull together a lesson plan using assessment procedures that would yield the information about the students' abilities in all four skills—information you'd need to make effective decisions—without scaring away the students? And could you defend that plan to an administrator as using assessment procedures that were reliable, valid, and practical, and that would promote positive washback?

---

3 *See if your language students, working in pairs, can solve the farmer's problem with the goose, the grain, and the ferocious dog. (It will help if they draw a map.) The solution, which is given at the end of this chapter, illustrates that difficult dilemmas can be resolved with a bit of creative thinking.*

Suggested Readings

I have often thought that we teachers, when faced with language assessment responsibilities, are rather like the farmer. His predicament in trying to get the dog, the goose, and the grain across the river to market with only a tiny rowboat (meanwhile trying to keep the dog from eating the goose, and the goose from eating the grain) is rather like the apparently competing goals we face. For many teachers, evaluating students seems inherently contradictory to trying to help them. The competing goals we must achieve and the various audiences we must answer to (students, parents, sponsors, administrators, etc.) create dilemmas for us—many of which seem to hinge on our assessment procedures.

This book is intended to help you enhance your skills and increase your confidence in those areas of your professional teaching responsibilities that deal with assessing your students' skills and knowledge. The chapters that follow all present sections entitled "Teachers' Voices," "Frameworks," and "Investigations," that are designed to help you achieve that goal. And, where appropriate, I will suggest other avenues for exploration, in case you'd like to learn more.

For example, several chapters of Arthur Hughes's book, *Testing for Language Teachers* (1989), provide brief but accessible discussions of reliability, validity, practicality, and washback (which Hughes calls "backwash"). Andrew Cohen's book, *Assessing Language Ability in the Classroom* (1994), is also geared specifically for language teachers.

J. B. Heaton's *Writing English Language Tests* (1988) is aimed at helping teachers write their own tests. It includes a chapter devoted to each of the four skills, as well as vocabulary and grammar. It also starts with a useful chapter that examines reasons for testing.

Harold Madsen's text, *Techniques in Testing* (1983), contains a chapter on each of the four skills, as well as separate chapters on testing the "language subskills" (as he calls them) of vocabulary, grammar, and pronunciation. He gives examples of many different item formats.

A Guide to Language Testing, by Grant Henning (1987), includes excellent coverage on the topics of reliability and validity. We will return to material from Henning's book in later chapters.

Two important articles about washback have been written by Charles Alderson and Dianne Wall (1993) and Wall and Alderson (1993). The first breaks down the washback hypothesis into several useful components that are specifically related to teaching and learning in classrooms. The second reports on the institution of a new national English test in Sri Lanka and examines the effects of that test on language teaching. My own review of the washback literature (Bailey, 1996) was influenced by Wall and Alderson's work.

Fred Genesee and Jack Upshur have written a book entitled *Classroom-based Evaluation in Second Language Education* (1996). It opens with several scenarios (similar to Diane Williams' in this chapter) that contextualize assessment issues.

Charles Alderson, Caroline Clapham, and Dianne Wall coauthored *Language Test Construction and Evaluation* (1995). It addresses many of the issues raised in my conversation with Diane Williams from the perspective of professional language test developers.

Postscript

By the way, the poor old farmer was finally able to resolve his dilemma. He realized that if he took the goose across the river first, the dog wouldn't be tempted to eat the grain. So he ferried the goose across the river and left it there. Then he went back for the dog and ferried it across the river.

Now at this point you may be saying to yourself, "But wait a minute! When he goes back for the grain, the dog will eat the goose!" This is where some creative thinking comes into play.

The farmer deposited the dog on the far side of the river, picked up the goose, and put it in the little boat. Then he rowed back across the river to pick up the grain. When he got there, he left the goose alone on that side of the river and loaded the basket of grain in the little boat. He rowed the grain across the river and left it on the far side with the dog. Then he made one more trip across the river, rowing toward his home in the empty boat. He picked up the goose and rowed back across the river once again. At that point the farmer had all three—the dog, the goose, and the grain—on the right side of the river, and they all proceeded to the market.

2

ANALYZING TESTS: THE CASE OF DICTATION

In a scene from T. H. White's The Once and Future King, *(1939, 229–230) Merlyn the Magician is instructing the young King Arthur and his foster brother, Kay, about the racial history of the British Isles. After a long lecture, Arthur interrupts Merlyn.*

"So it comes to this," he said, "that we Normans have the Saxons for serfs, while the Saxons once had a sort of under-serfs, who were called the Gaels—the Old Ones. In that case I don't see why the Gaelic Confederation should want to fight against me—as a Norman king—when it was really the Saxons who hunted them, and when it was hundreds of years ago in any case."

Merlin responded, "You are under-rating the Gaelic memory, dear boy. They don't distinguish between you. The Normans are a Teuton race, like the Saxons, whom your father conquered. So far as the ancient Gaels are concerned, they just regard both your races as branches of the same alien people, who have driven them north and west."

Kay said definitely: "I can't stand any more history. After all, we are supposed to be grown up. If we go on, we shall be doing dictation."

Have you ever taken a dictation when you were studying a foreign language? Many people have less than fond memories of dictations, especially in French classes. It seems that the dreaded *dictée* is the particular bane of many students of French because French teachers often subtract points for missing accents and French spelling can be so difficult. (This is because French has a low **phoneme-grapheme correspondence:** the actual sounds apparently are not represented by the written symbols on a one-to-one basis.) However, dictation need not be a fearful experience.

I was fortunate to be able to teach English at the Chinese University of Hong Kong for one year. On the first day of every new term, I told the class that we would start with a dictation. Although these students were extremely polite, and even reserved by Western standards, at this announcement several rolled their eyes or glanced worriedly at one another and some even groaned. When I asked them why they had reacted negatively to the proposed dictation, they said that dictations are difficult, every little spelling error counts, teachers usually read too fast, and it is very hard to understand and write new words. Also, dictation scores had been extremely important in their secondary school tests. So I told my students that our dictation would be different: Spelling wouldn't count, I wouldn't correct their errors, and I wouldn't even collect their papers. The point of the dictation was for them to get accustomed to my voice and accent, and for them to make their own copy of the text—our class rules. I then followed the standard dictation procedure, but had the students compare the results with their classmates and then keep the papers. They were surprised at this procedure, as well as greatly relieved.

Generally speaking, a standard dictation goes like this. The teacher reads aloud a passage (or plays a tape recording). Usually the passage is only about one paragraph in length. The first time it is read, the students listen to get the main idea. Then the teacher reads the passage again, this time pausing to break the paragraph into sense groups, phrases, or clauses called **bursts**. The teacher pauses after each burst. During the pause, the students are expected to write down exactly what the teacher has just said. Then the teacher reads the passage once more, without pauses, for the students to check their work. In order to promote self-monitoring and careful editing skills, many teachers build in a minute for the students to review what they have written before this last reading. Does this procedure sound familiar?

In fact, dictation is really a family of teaching and assessment procedures. The procedures and variables that define the different types of dictation can be restructured to meet your own assessment goals, depending on what information you wish to gain for your decision making. In this chapter we will use dictation as an example to illustrate a system for analyzing tests.

Mari Wesche has provided a simple yet useful framework for examining tests. I always introduce her idea to the graduate students in my language assessment seminar because I have found that an understanding of this structure helps me to see options for creating alternatives in the ways I assess my language students' skills and knowledge. (I also use it—both here and in my seminar—as a very straightforward example of a *framework,* since some of those we study later will be much more complex.) According to Wesche (1983, 43), every test consists of four parts, and we will use this framework to analyze the standard dictation procedure.

STANDARD DICTATIONS AND WESCHE'S FRAMEWORK

The first component of any test is the **stimulus material.** This term refers to whatever linguistic or nonlinguistic information is presented to the learners to get them to demonstrate the skills or knowledge we want to assess. So in the standard dictation described above, for example, the stimulus material would be the text read aloud by the teacher.

The second component and the third go hand-in-hand. The second is the **task posed to the learner** and the third is the **learner's response.** The student's response is the observable manifestation that he or she can indeed do the mental task that has been set for him or her. The task itself, however, is often psycholinguistic in nature, and thus is not always observable. In our example of the standard dictation, the task posed to the learners would be to understand the text well enough to reproduce it. We cannot directly witness what happens in our students' minds as they go about the process of understanding. So in the case of a dictation, the students would demonstrate their understanding by writing the passage as they have heard it, word for word, with a certain level of morphological accuracy.

The fourth component of any test, according to Wesche, consists of the **scoring criteria**. In scoring a standard dictation, it's up to you, as the teacher, to decide what you are trying to assess (i.e., a validity issue) and what you want the students to attend to (i.e., a washback issue). For example, spelling errors may not be counted wrong these days if the learner's meaning is clear and the text the student has written shows that he or she has understood the morphemes. If a student writes "learnd" or even "lernd" for the word "learned," both would be counted as correct: The student has heard and reproduced the past-tense morpheme and the verb itself. Oller (1979, 278–282) has shown that spelling scores do not correlate with other scores on a battery of language tests. This should not be surprising, since many native speakers are not good spellers!

We can use Wesche's framework to help us analyze the components of various tests and also to help us generate options for alternative means of assessing our students' language skills. For instance, suppose we don't want to test our students' accuracy in reproducing what they've heard as much as their grasp of the key points in that text. In that case the stimulus material might be the same as in a standard dictation, but the task posed to the learner would be to understand and reproduce the main points rather than the exact words. The learner's response, as in a standard dictation, would be to write. But the scoring criteria would be based on the number of bits of information the learner wrote rather than on the morphological accuracy of his reproduced text. (In fact, this procedure is sometimes called the **dictocomp**. We will consider it more fully in Chapter 10.)

The relative ease or difficulty of any test will be affected by these components. Think about a dictation you have given or a dictation you have taken as a language learner. Which features of the stimulus material and the task posed to the learners would make a dictation easy or difficult? Probably at least some of the following factors spring to mind:

1. The speed and clarity with which the text is read;

2. The complexity of, and the learners' familiarity with, the syntactic structures in the passage;

3. The learners' familiarity with the vocabulary, their familiarity with the topic in general, and their familiarity with the structure of the discourse genre; and

4. The lengths of the "bursts" and of the pauses between bursts.

Keeping these variables in mind, as teachers we can select more difficult texts or easier texts as the stimulus material for the dictations we create. We can also vary the length of the bursts, the speed of delivery, and the length of pauses as we read the stimulus material.

For example, let us consider just the issue of pause length. How long should the teacher pause between the bursts during the second reading? I have come across three "rules of thumb" in response to this question:

1. The examiner should "subvocalize the spelling of each sequence of verbal material twice during the pause while the examinees are writing it" (Oller, 1979, 274).

2. The examiner should repeat the entire burst silently to himself four or five times while the students are writing.

3. The examiner should count the number of letters in the bursts, divide by two, and follow each burst with a pause of that many seconds. So a burst containing 22 letters would be followed by a pause of eleven seconds, and so on (Lin, 1982, 116).

Of course, if you are delivering the dictation stimulus material live (instead of making a tape recording to be used in a test), you can simply watch the students and see when they have finished writing. As Oller points out, "The purpose of the test is decidedly not to assess the speed with which the examinees can write" (1979, 274). However, having students write under time pressure may indeed be a legitimate goal if you are trying to help them develop lecture note-taking skills or in taking timed exams. The key point here is that you must keep your assessment goals in mind as you decide how to vary the dictation procedure.

Here are two variations on the standard dictation procedure that have interesting implications for washback. They are each related to the difficulty factors listed above, and each involves manipulating the stimulus material in a standard dictation in order to achieve different goals. The first is called a "partial dictation" and the second is called a "graduated dictation."

PARTIAL DICTATIONS

As its name suggests, giving a **partial dictation** involves altering the stimulus material presented to the learners. As in a standard dictation, the teacher reads a passage aloud. What is different, however, is that instead of writing on a blank page, the learner is presented with a sheet of paper on which some parts of the text have already been reproduced. The task posed to the learners is to understand the text that's read aloud, but the learners' response is to copy into the blanks on the page those parts of the text that have been omitted from the printed version, rather than to write the entire text. For this reason a partial dictation may be less intimidating, particularly to lower-proficiency learners, than a standard dictation. (The partial dictation is sometimes referred to as a "listening cloze procedure," for reasons that will become clear in Chapter 5, when we look at cloze tests.)

In creating a partial dictation you must first decide what you are trying to assess. You may choose to delete single words, phrases, clauses, or entire sentences. The choice rests largely on the purpose of the assessment.

Given their tight focus on the deleted items, partial dictations can be useful as diagnostic tests. A diagnostic test, as the name suggests, is one that attempts to diagnose, or identify, a learner's strengths and weaknesses, typically so that an efficient and appropriate course of instruction can be presented. (There's no point expending lots of time, energy, and resources trying to teach language learners what they already know!) If I were trying to assess my students' grasp of function words, for instance, I might use as the stimulus material a text in which many of the function words and perhaps also some of the words surrounding them had been deleted.

Suppose I was considering doing a lesson or a unit on understanding numbers in spoken English. I could first choose or write a text rich in numeric references. Here's an example:

> *(The scene occurs in the passenger cabin of a commercial airliner. The plane is arriving late and is about to land at its destination. A voice is heard over the plane's public address system.)*
>
> Ladies and gentlemen, this is the first flight attendant again. I do have some connecting gate information for those of you making connections to other flights here in Chicago. At this time we have been informed about the following flights:
>
> Flight **seven-oh-six** to St. Louis will depart from gate **seventy-three** at **nine-thirty** P.M.
>
> Flight **ten-forty-five** to San Francisco will depart at **nine-fifty** P.M. from gate **seventeen.**
>
> Flight **four-forty** to Philadelphia will depart at **nine-thirty-five** P.M. from gate **sixty.**
>
> And flight **sixteen-oh-three** to Denver will depart from gate **nineteen** at **ten-fifteen** P.M.
>
> Please be sure to check the television monitors when you enter the terminal building, since gate assignments may change.

I could then provide the students with a written version of the text from which only the numbers set in **boldface** type above had been deleted. The written sheet and the entire text read aloud to the students would constitute the stimulus material. The task posed to the learners would be for them to focus their listening on the missing numbers. The learners' response would be to write the actual numbers they hear (not the words representing those numbers) in the appropriate blanks. The scoring criteria would typically be *correct* or *incorrect,* but you could also decide to give partial credit for a partially correct answer. So, for example, if a student wrote "9:15" where the stimulus material had said "9:50," you would decide how many points to award for that answer. If some of my students made this error (confusing *fifteen* for *fifty*), I could use this information to help with my future lesson planning—an illustration of the diagnostic potential of a partial dictation.

Partial dictations can also be used profitably as achievement tests (or as part of an achievement test), in order to assess what your students have learned after a lesson or a unit of instruction. An **achievement test** is intended to assess what students have learned relative to the curriculum they have studied. Thus, achievement tests are written to reflect the content and the objectives of a particular syllabus. Achievement tests are contrasted in this regard with **proficiency tests,** which are intended to be syllabus-free. So, for instance, a valid French proficiency test would assess students' competence whether they had studied

French in a university in Australia or had worked as *au pairs* in Paris. (We will return to this issue in Chapter 3 when we examine several purposes for testing.)

The point here is that a partial dictation is a variation on the standard dictation which allows you, the teacher, to help the learners focus their listening on some portions of the text you read aloud, rather than on the entire text. The written parts of the text reproduced on the test sheet can be made longer or shorter, depending on how much visual linguistic support you want to give the learners as they listen to the incoming message. In terms of Wesche's framework, a partial dictation differs from a standard dictation in that (1) the stimulus material has been altered, and (2) the task posed to the learners is more specific.

GRADUATED DICTATIONS

A **graduated dictation** is one in which the bursts at the beginning of the text are rather short. Successive bursts gradually increase in length until they become quite challenging. So in terms of Wesche's framework, it is only the stimulus material that has been altered from the familiar format of the standard dictation.

An example of a text for a graduated dictation was developed by Nien-Hsuan Jennifer Lin (1982, 127–128). It is based on a passage from an ESL reading book, entitled *American Topics*, by Robert Lugton (1978). In Table 2.1 the bursts of Lin's graduated dictation are listed, along with the number of words in each item. You will see that the length of the items increases from 2 to 19 words in the subsequent bursts of the stimulus material:

Table 2.1: Item Length (in words)

Item	Length
1. Wild animals	2
2. used to wander	3
3. over the country	3
4. in uncounted numbers.	3
5. Today these animal populations	4
6. have decreased to a great extent.	6
7. Some animals have disappeared altogether,	5
8. destroyed by the advance of human civilization.	7
9. The same story can be told in the African continent,	10
10. once covered with big game such as elephant, buffalo, and antelope.	11
11. In Central and South America, where animals once were thought safe, they are now threatened.	15
12. In the last three centuries, over two hundred species of mammals, birds, and reptiles have become extinct.	17
13. Our wild animals are being swept from the land, the birds from the air, the fish from the sea.	19

The graduated dictation format provides an interesting way to demonstrate why dictation works as a means of assessing comprehension. As Oller notes (1979, 273) in discussing dictation in general:

> Breaks should be spaced far enough apart to challenge the limits of the short term memory of the learners and to force a deeper level of processing than mere phonetic echoing. The amount of material that can easily be held in short term memory without really understanding its meaning will vary from learner to learner somewhat according to the proficiency level of the learners. More proficient examinees will be able to handle longer sequences with the same ease that less proficient examinees handle shorter ones. Probably sequences much less than seven words in length should be avoided. In some cases sequences in excess of twenty words in length may be desirable.

In other words, learners will be able to reproduce in writing what they hear and understand (rather than just hear), because it is our comprehension of messages that allows us to store them in our memory long enough to deal with them. It is this emphasis on meaning that makes the dictation assessment family much more than a routine copying process.

At this point let us consider in more detail the washback concept, introduced in Chapter 1. You will recall that washback is the effect of testing on teaching and learning. There are many things that teachers can do to enhance the potential for positive washback in our assessment activities. Even with a testing procedure as traditional as dictation, there are many directions a teacher can take to connect the assessment device to learning. For example, the simple step of allowing some extra time for students to review what they've written before the final reading of the stimulus material will help them to identify the gaps in the reproduced text. The learners can then focus their listening during the final reading on those areas in which they are lacking information.

Another variation for making the task more communicative and for promoting students' awareness in a nonassessment context is to have students exchange papers and compare their own work with their partner's dictation. One student may have gotten something another was unable to catch. In pair-work they can fill in the missing bits together, negotiating their understanding as they do so. In this sense, dictation can be used as a teaching/learning activity instead of (or in addition to) an assessment device. The next section of this chapter describes a very interesting application of standard dictation in a college-level writing class. The process exemplifies a clear emphasis on washback that the teacher developed by adding extra tasks after the standard dictation had been done.

Teachers' Voices

My friend Melinda Erickson teaches in the writing program at the University of California at Berkeley. Melinda uses dictations in her writing classes, which is surprising, because dictation is typically perceived as a very traditional test of listening skills. How could it be useful in a college-level composition course? In reading the following material, you will see that Melinda has expanded on the tasks posed to the learners, and on what is expected in each learner's response, to use Wesche's terminology.

Table 2.2 outlines Melinda's procedure for using dictation in her writing class. Double Xs in either the teacher's column or the student's column indicate a waiting period for that party while the other party does something.

Table 2.2: Melinda Erickson's Use of the Dictation Procedure[2]

Phase of Activity	Teacher's Actions	Student's Actions
Dictation:	1. read	1. listen
	2. read with pauses	2. write
	3. read	3. fill in missing words
	4. XX	4. proofread
Correction:	1. XX	1. trade paper with classmate
	2. XX	2. sign
	3. provide original text as model	3. compare, underlining differences
	4. XX	4. return paper to classmate
	5. collect papers	5. XX
Discussion:	1. elicit vocabulary	1. identify new words
	2. elicit grammar/ punctuation	2. identify grammar/ punctuation
	3. guide discussion on content	3. participate in discussion on content
Analysis:	1. grade/record	
	2. analyze class set	
	3. prepare follow-up	
	4. return papers	
		1. interpret underlined words
		2. identify error types
		3. chart frequency of errors
		4. analyze data over time
		5. correct paper

Melinda's students took several brief dictations during the term and compiled them to observe any patterns of error types and to chart their own progress over time. Each dictation involved a peer correction component as well as a discussion of both form and content. Each dictation experience provided information to both the teacher and the learners, a combination that should promote the likelihood of positive washback.

Melinda lists several advantages when she talks about her use of the dictation procedure. These include the following:

1. Having a dictation as a regular (e.g., weekly) starting routine gets the students to class on time and gets them settled down.

---

2. I am grateful to Melinda Erickson for letting me reproduce this table and other information from her 1990 CATESOL Conference presentation.

2. The dictation texts selected through the term provide the students with varied examples of style, punctuation, vocabulary, grammatical structure, and so on.

3. Over the course of the academic term, the students compile a collection of their dictations, and thus can follow their own progress.

4. The students themselves perceive the procedure as helping them to become more confident about writing under pressure (e.g., when taking in-class exams or lecture notes).

In fact, here are some of Melinda's students' specific reactions to the use of dictation in their writing class:

Student Comments:

"I skipped at least five words in early dictations. Well, sometimes, Ms. Erickson read too fast so I couldn't catch up with her. Also I missed words because I was too concerned about spelling. Maybe it is because of pressure; I sometimes could not write words that are easy or familiar to me."

"It was a little awkward in the beginning. Regardless of my feelings, I took a dictation almost every meeting and jotted down my mistakes. I think that errors in spelling and punctuation result from my careless manner and they can be reduced if I pay more attention when proofreading."

"I made some mistakes more frequently than others. By finding out the kinds of mistakes I made, I could work on these areas more carefully and over time, the amount of errors lessened."

"This type of exercise helps us to know more about ourselves as writers."

To summarize, then, dictation is really a family of related procedures that can be systematically altered (by manipulating the stimulus material, the task posed, the learners' response, and/or the scoring criteria) to meet different assessment purposes. Although it is an old procedure, it has many creative potential applications, as illustrated by Melinda Erickson's use of dictation in her writing classes.

Investigations

1 *Think of a test with which you are familiar. What types of stimulus material are presented to the learners as they take this test? What are the tasks posed? By what responses do the students demonstrate their ability to do the tasks? Finally, what are the criteria you use when you score the test? It might help you analyze the test if you fill in the blanks below with brief comments:*

Name of Test _____

Stimulus Material _____

Task Posed _____

Learner's Response _____

Scoring Criteria _____

If you are dissatisfied with this test, what part(s) of it do you find to be problematic? Could the problem area(s) be changed?

2 *These questions can also be posed in a comparison of two or more tests.*

	Test 1	Test 2
Stimulus Material		
Task Posed		
Learner's Response		
Scoring Criteria		

Think of two tests that both purport to be measures of language proficiency, or of grammar, or of reading—whatever construct you are interested in assessing. How do these tests compare using Wesche's framework?

3 *Here is an experiment you can try to see how dictations work. I often use the Spanish paragraph reprinted below as the text for a dictation in my language assessment seminar because someone always believes (or has heard) that dictation is nothing more than a test of spelling and memory. But it's really true that we retain better in memory that which we understand, and trying to do a dictation in a foreign language often demonstrates this concept experientially and convincingly.*

I use a dictation in Spanish for the following reasons:

1. Spanish spelling is relatively straightforward: The language has a high phoneme-grapheme correspondence.

2. It uses the same alphabet system as English, so since I work in an English-medium program, my students can't say they don't know the written system.

3. I am fairly comfortable reading Spanish aloud (though I have also asked students who know Spanish to read the passage aloud for their classmates).

4. My classes usually comprise a number of people who are good at Spanish (including a few native speakers), some who have studied Spanish and achieved varying proficiency levels, and some who know no Spanish whatsoever.

This typical range of proficiency levels allows us to conduct an informal experiment, which you can replicate if you wish. I ask my students to rate their own Spanish on a scale of zero (no functional knowledge of Spanish whatsoever) to five (at virtually a fluent level of understanding). Then we do a standard dictation with the passage. Next we divide into groups according to the students' self-ratings (the zeroes and ones together, the twos and threes, and the fours and fives) to compare our results. Invariably (if people have been accurate in their self-assessments), the three different groups are markedly different in the amount of information they have been able to write, with those who identified themselves as more proficient speakers of Spanish capturing much more of the text than the less proficient learners. Sometimes the less proficient learners are only able to write the names of the countries that are mentioned. Here is the passage (Johnson, 1949, 3):

> *(1) Para comprender la América Española, (2) es preciso recordar que su cultura (3) ya era vieja en algunas partes (4) —México, Guatemala, Ecuador, Perú, y Bolivia— (5) cuando llegó Cristóbal Colón. (6) La personalidad de dichas regiones (7) ha sido determinada, (8) y todavía lo es, (9) por su legado indígena. (10) En las repúblicas hispanoamericanas, (11) exceptuándose el Uruguay y la Argentina, (12) cuyas poblaciones son predominantemente blanca, (13) abundan millones de personas (14) de sangre mezclada. (15) El español no tenía prejuicios de raza.*

The numbers in parentheses indicate how I divide the text for a standard dictation. You could also use this text (or one like it) to create a graduated dictation, following Jennifer Lin's model. There should be a correspondence between the students' self-rating of their Spanish proficiency and their ability to correctly write the increasingly long bursts of the Spanish text. If you try this procedure, it would be worthwhile to save the resulting data, because we will return to Lin's graduated dictation in Chapter 9 when we discuss item analysis procedures. At that point you might wish to compare the results of your graduated dictation with hers.

Suggested Readings

In this chapter I have tried to show that by changing the stimulus materials, the task posed, the learners' responses, and/or the scoring criteria, teachers can vary the standard dictation to suit their purposes. If you are interested in reading more about the dictation family, John Oller's (1979) chapter on "Dictation and Closely Related Auditory Tasks," although somewhat dated, provides an interesting review of the research on dictation. Oller gives clear examples of how to score dictations as well as a cogent explanation of the underlying theory.

Charles Stansfield has written a fascinating history of dictation in foreign language teaching and testing. In fact, his opening lines (1985, 121) hearken back to the Arthurian scene with which we began this chapter:

> Dictation is one of the oldest techniques known for testing progress in the learning of a foreign language. Until the end of the Middle Ages, it was used to transmit course content from master (teacher) to pupil in the first language classroom. It was also the usual way of publishing a book in the medieval *scriptorium*, a room in a monastery where a master commonly dictated to a group of scribes. From these origins, which represent a kind of prehistory of dictation, it passed into the second language classroom as certain groups began the study of modern foreign languages in the sixteenth century.

Dictation is particularly interesting as an assessment procedure because, depending on how you set the scoring criteria, it can be either very narrowly focused on linguistic competence or more broadly focused on the communication of meaning—communicative competence being a more up-to-date conception of language. Indeed, we will see that many of the language assessment problems we face today are (in part) the result of using earlier models of language to try to measure students' skills and knowledge when our entire conception of language has changed. (This topic will be taken up again in Chapter 10, when we consider communicative language testing.)

Paul Davis and Mario Rinvolucri have written an entire book, *Dictation: New Methods, New Possibilities* (1988). They open with the following observation:

> Sometimes, when introducing teacher training techniques in teacher training workshops, we have asked "How many of you do dictation in your classes?" At first only a few hands go up. There is inhibition in the air—can one admit to doing something as reprehensible and old-fashioned as dictation in what is meant to be a progressive, 'communicative' workshop? What might colleagues think? But if we repeat the question more hands go up. It normally turns out that in any average group of European teachers more than half *do* use dictation either regularly or from time to time in their teaching. And with good reason (1).

Davis and Rinvolucri then go on to describe "a new methodology for an age-old exercise."

Ruth Wajnryb's *Grammar Dictations* (1990) has numerous creative ideas for using variations on the dictation procedure in language classrooms.

Finally, as you can see from my repeated use of her four-part framework, I found Mari Wesche's (1983) article to be very helpful. We will return to it often throughout this book, especially when we investigate communicative language testing in Chapter 10. However, as we get further into language assessment issues we will see that there are many other ways to analyze language tests. One of the most thorough is found in Lyle Bachman's book, *Fundamental Considerations in Language Testing* (1990, 119).

3

CONFLICTING PURPOSES
OF ASSESSMENT

*At a national symposium on issues related to Limited English
Proficient (LEP) students in the United States, Russell L. French
made the following observations (1992, 252–253):*

> **There is obviously a need to assess what LEP students really
> know and are able to do.** *At issue in any assessment are its validity
> and reliability. In their simplest form, these concepts represent two
> questions: "How do I know that what I am measuring is what
> I really wanted to measure? (validity) How do I know that I am
> measuring consistently (reliability)?" Those issues are no less
> important to classroom assessments developed by teachers than
> they are to standardized tests. . . .*
>
> **There appears to be a need to reinforce a student's native
> language, not destroy it.** *Several recent articles and papers on the
> instruction of LEP students report that the LEP student's self-con-
> cept, family relationships, and academic achievement suffer when
> instruction attempts to make him/her monolingual in English rather
> than bilingual or multi-lingual. Common sense also should tell us
> that we need an increasing number of persons proficient in two or
> more languages in our society to meet the increasing demands for
> international interaction. Why should we deplete or destroy some
> of our best resources?*
>
> *If, then, we attempt to reinforce a student's native language in
> our instruction, we cannot do less in our assessments. Evaluation
> which allows only for the use of the English language sends a
> message quite contradictory to that being portrayed through
> instruction, and the "louder" message will be that sent through
> assessment. Whether we like it or not, assessment drives
> curriculum, or, more specifically, assessment drives students' per-
> ceptions of what is important in the curriculum. Further, assess-
> ment procedures inconsistent with instructional procedures also
> create an invalid test.*

Many teachers have found themselves faced with the dilemma described above.
This chapter begins with the voice of one such teacher. Her dilemma is how to
help a child whose weaknesses are revealed but whose strengths are not tapped
by the kinds of exams typically used in the school system. I think you may find
this story to be sadly familiar.

Like many teachers, Ellie Mason wears several hats, even though she is a new teacher in her school. Officially she has three titles. She is the reading resource specialist, the bilingual resource coordinator, and the English language development teacher for a small school district in an agricultural area of central California. These titles mean that she works with about one hundred children in kindergarten through sixth grade (ages five to thirteen) every week. All of the English language development students speak Spanish as their first language. Although Ellie's program is officially considered a bilingual education program, she says first-language maintenance is apparently not seen as a primary goal. Instead, the school's emphasis is on getting the Hispanic children to make the transition to English as quickly as possible so that they can be "mainstreamed" (i.e., moved into regular English-medium subject matter classes with native speakers).

Ellie's responsibilities include meeting with parents and the children's regular classroom teachers, attending meetings with district and county officials, observing and helping in classes, teaching reading skills and English language development lessons, serving on committees that track children's progress, assessing the children's strengths and weaknesses, administering tests, and interpreting standardized test scores. Although a great deal of coordination with other teachers and school officials is involved in her job, Ellie makes the following comment about working with the children:

> **Ellie:** Once they come to me, I'm free to do my own thing. My program is a "push in, pull out" program. I'm supposed to be working with the rest of the staff [about twenty other teachers], going into their classrooms and doing English language development work there, or doing reading development with individuals, or sometimes taking the children into my classroom. But most of the teachers don't really want me to go into their classrooms. They have this mentality about bilingual education. They feel I should take the Hispanic kids out of their classrooms, get them to learn English, and then to bring them back in—which isn't really my philosophy. I'd much rather go into the classroom and work with the children there, with the other kids—even working in peer groups.

When Ellie talks about her "push in, pull out" program it means that she will either work inside the child's regular classroom, serving as a bilingual assistant to the teacher, or that she will pull the child out of the classroom and independently design an entire set of activities to promote that student's reading and/or English development.

I asked Ellie about the assessment of reading in her school, since the development of literacy skills in elementary school students is typically seen as the key to their future academic success.

> **Ellie:** The approach of many teachers to reading is very phonics-based. That isn't really my approach. I do a little phonics, but I'm really focused on whole language. I do a little bit of both, but my

teaching and my methodology don't necessarily coincide with what the students are doing in the regular classes. So my testing doesn't coincide with what they're learning. But there are certain tests that are in place that I have to use.

Kathi: What are those tests like?

Ellie: The reading tests are isolated reading passages that the students read aloud, word-by-word. Then you count the miscues. It's called a reading miscue analysis. You write down how many they got right and that's how you decide, according to the school, which grade level they're reading at. And it's one little passage! Since that's not my approach to reading—my approach is more experiential—they're not being tested on what I'm teaching them. They might be being tested on what their other teachers are teaching them, but I don't get into the classrooms enough to know. And this is what we're using to determine their grade level for reading! This is what we're telling their parents. This is what we're writing in their cumulative records. And I'm not sure if it's testing what they're learning. I'm not sure if it's right. So I'm really concerned with the way that the testing takes place at my school.

I asked Ellie to tell me about a student who has puzzled or interested her—someone she may have been concerned about. Without any hesitation whatsoever, she told me about a nine-year-old third-grade girl whom we will call "Maria."

Maria's family has been in the United States for over three years. Her parents are migrant farm workers, so they don't get much interaction with native speakers of English, except in their contacts with the school. Ellie reported that from the first day she started working at the school Maria took to her, because Ellie spoke Spanish with the child when no one else would.

Here is a summary of the conversation Ellie and I had as she told me about Maria. Notice the frequency of the word *yet* in the excerpts that follow as Ellie talks about this child.

Ellie: Maria took the *SABE* [*Spanish Assessment of Basic Education*] test in Spanish and did really well. She's definitely very proficient in her first language. But in English she hasn't developed yet. Her brother, Carlos, who is two years older than Maria, is doing well. He's progressing perfectly well at his level. He's where he's supposed to be. But Maria's records show that she has just not developed. In the last three years she has not developed at all in English. She speaks very few words in English. Most of what she does say is translated from Spanish to English. From what I can see from spending time with her, she just doesn't speak English. She just hasn't developed yet. From the point where I first met her, she doesn't appear to be progressing very quickly in English.

Three years with no demonstrable progress seemed like a long time to me, so I asked Ellie if there was any evidence that Maria might be learning disabled. She responded quickly and with conviction:

> **Ellie:** Maria has no learning disabilities. She's very articulate in Spanish. It's just that in English, she's got this big block.

> **Kathi:** What do you think is going on with her? What's the source of the block?

> **Ellie:** I think it might be an affective thing. She doesn't fit in very well with the other students. She doesn't feel comfortable. Like I said, when I first arrived, she found out that I speak Spanish, and she's by my side all the time. She's just bubbly when she's with me. I observed her in her mainstream class—and there's just nothing. There's just a big blank on her face. Her teacher has told me she's very concerned about Maria. She thinks that Maria needs to go through a "Child Case Study Team," where they analyze the child with a microscope to find out what's wrong. I don't see Maria as having a learning challenge at all. I just see her as being really kind of freaked out about the fact that she's in this new environment and no one's been there for her.

At this point I urged Ellie to make sure she's on the "Child Case Study Team" if one is formed to review Maria's case. Ellie assured me that she will be on the team and then she talked about Maria's performance on the subject matter achievement test that's given in Spanish.

> **Ellie:** As an example of this testing thing, when I gave her the *SABE* test, she did fine. She did very well. She's definitely at grade level. She reads very well in Spanish. I think her mom works with her at home in Spanish. She's fine in Spanish but the rest of the school thinks she's got kind of a problem because she doesn't quite fit in. She's not mainstreamed yet. She doesn't have any friends, and she hasn't done well at all on the *California Achievement Test.*

(The *California Achievement Test* is a multisubject standardized subject matter examination in English that is administered statewide at the end of every school year. At Ellie's school the results of this exam are used to determine which children need reading help, in hiring more special education teachers, and as an exit mechanism for the secondary school students. The *SABE* is used as the Spanish equivalent of the *California Achievement Test.*)

Given that the student's performance on the Spanish achievement test is normal, I was curious about her lack of production and interaction in English after three years of exposure. I wondered if Maria was simply undergoing an exceptionally long silent period.

> **Kathi:** Does it look like a silent period to you? I mean, do you think she's processing the incoming language?

Ellie: Possibly. She might be processing or she might just feel so anxious about the language because sometimes she's the subject of critique. She's the one in her class who doesn't speak English and she's been thrown into this situation. I just think she bottles up and feels nervous, because when she's with me alone, she produces a little bit more English.

Kathi: Give me an example of something she can say.

Ellie: One day she made me a watercolor picture. She's in an after-school program and they had a big bouquet of flowers, and they were learning to paint with water colors. She brought in her painting and she said, "Miss Mason, Miss Mason! Look, look, look! I draw a picture! I draw you a picture!" And she always says, "See you later!" She knows some stuff.

Some children (perhaps especially those in an immersion situation like Maria's) seem to acquire formulaic expressions before they begin to process the morphemes and individual lexical items in the target language. Since Ellie had said, "She always says, 'See you later!'" I wondered if Maria was acquiring English chunks.

Kathi: "See you later" sounds like a learned chunk. Does she have any other chunks or set expressions that she says, like "I dunno"?

Ellie: Yeah. She says, "I dunno." Let's see. She says "See you later!," "I dunno," and "How are you?" I don't know of anything else, other than "Hi, Miss Mason!" Oh, she says, "What is that?" She always asks, "What is that?"

Kathi: Will she answer the question, "What is that?" if you ask her?

Ellie: No. It depends. If she's alone with me, yes. She can read a little bit in English as well. She knows most of the sounds. She has all the phonics down, so that she can read. She's not very confident yet, but if she's alone with me, she can. If I say, "What is that in the picture?" when we're reading a book, she'll tell me what it is. Usually she answers in Spanish though. But she's very intelligent and she's able to draw conclusions from a number of things. She has higher levels of intelligence. She's smart. She's really a smart kid in Spanish. It's just that she hasn't yet developed in English.

Ellie's "It depends" response above is reminiscent of Diane Williams's couching her decisions in the situational variables faced by her individual students in the adult school class discussed in Chapter 1.

I asked Ellie to give me an example of why she thinks Maria is so smart. Her attitude struck me as a curiously strong conviction, given that the rest of the school seems to think Maria is learning disabled. Here is Ellie's response, which clearly illustrates Maria's analytic ability.

Ellie: Okay. We were reading a story about Peter Rabbit. And there had been another story about a boy named Peter, which we had read about three weeks before. So when we were talking about Peter Rabbit, Maria said in Spanish, "Didn't we read another story about Peter, and both Peters like to go out at night and play, and both Peters liked to do this . . ." and so on. They were totally different stories, but she was the one who came up with the idea. She was using her background knowledge, and doing things that I haven't seen a lot of third-graders do.

Maria's spontaneous comparison of the two different characters named Peter, in two entirely separate stories which she had read at different times, shows that she understood the two stories. She also *retained* the content of the first at least long enough to compare it to the content of the second.

The emerging picture of Maria that Ellie had provided thus far suggested an enigmatic child of many contrasts: bright, analytic, and creative in one context, and passive, with "just a big blank on her face" in another. I was curious about the tenuous spark inside this child, so I asked what she likes to do. And, of course Ellie, being an observant teacher, had a ready answer to my question.

Ellie: She likes to come to my classroom [the Reading Resource Room]. She likes to stay inside. She loves to draw. She doesn't like to be outside at all. She likes to be inside the classroom. She likes to do what the adults do. She really likes to hang out in the office and see what the secretary is doing. And she likes playing with the kindergartners. There are a lot of migrant kindergartners so she's always helping them out, teaching them about the school. She's a really sweet, sweet girl. She doesn't like to play outside with the rest of the kids.

Kathi: Would she want to play with you outside?

Ellie: Yes.

Kathi: So it's the kids—it's not being outside that she doesn't like.

Ellie: Right. She *loves* her culture. Most of the kids at school have the attitude, "No! We don't want to have anything to do with the Reading Resource Room, because it means we speak Spanish, and nobody wants us to speak Spanish, so let's not speak it!" So it's kind of a chore for them to have to come there, because they don't like it. But Maria loves it. She always wants to speak Spanish. She always wants to sing Spanish songs. She always runs to the Spanish books. She just really loves her culture, which is interesting because her brother is completely the opposite. He can't stand it when anyone speaks to him in Spanish.

So now what do we do? If we are professional teachers concerned with language assessment, what can we do about Maria? We have an apparently bright, eager child who doesn't speak much English (for whatever reasons) after three years at this English-medium school. Ellie is convinced she's capable; others are convinced she's not.

I asked Ellie to imagine that I was the newly appointed assessment psychologist for her school district, and that although I was a measurement specialist, I knew nothing about linguistics, bilingual education, or working with linguistic minority children. In setting up this scenario, I also said that in reviewing the children's school records, I had decided that Maria was probably severely learning disabled because she hadn't made any progress at all in three years. I suggested that she should be transferred to a remedial program for retarded children. (There is an audible gasp from Ellie on the tape recording of our conversation as I make this harsh but purely hypothetical pronouncement.)

I then posed an assessment problem for Ellie. I asked her how she could substantiate her conviction that Maria is indeed a smart child and support that claim to the district's imaginary measurement specialist.

> **Kathi:** Suppose I asked you to conduct a thorough assessment of Maria's English and her Spanish. What would you do? What kind of evidence could you muster that would be convincing to someone like me? I mean "me" in the role of the assessment psychologist.

> **Ellie:** I'm not sure exactly which test I would give her. We have some tests that would show—it would have to be a standardized test or some sort of "real" test in order to satisfy the district's needs, because they are very focused on what the tests say. So I might do something like the *Quick Start in English*. Have you heard of it? It's interesting. It gets at all the different skills and it seems pretty interactive. So I might do that with her. It has some pictures to test her English language development, where the child describes the pictures.

Ellie explained that the *Quick Start in English* test (1983) would be "acceptable for those guys" (i.e., the school district officials) and "somewhat acceptable" for her. We talked about the possibility of using the *Bilingual Syntax Measure* (1975), but then rejected that idea because the scoring criteria on the *BSM* would reveal Maria's weaknesses without noting her strengths. Ellie then moved away from a narrow concept of standardized testing and considered producing documentary evidence instead.

> **Ellie:** I would videotape Maria for a week if I could, ideally, so that she'd feel comfortable with the videotape, and so that they could see that she's not mentally retarded. Before even doing any testing, I would explain to them the notion of bilingual education and that students are at different levels. And I would explain that students'

anxiety levels have a great deal to do with how much they're going to produce. I would also explain the silent period—that maybe three years might not be enough for her, given that she loves her culture so much and she's so attached to her family and she's so attached to the Spanish language.

Here Ellie, like Diane Williams in Chapter 1, describes how she would challenge the authority structure in the school district on behalf of the child by explaining to the ill-informed measurement specialist certain basic facts about language acquisition and linguistic minority children. She continues her train of thought about how to document Maria's strengths:

Ellie: I might just give her a picture prompt and have her talk about that. I'd have her do some reading. I'd get at all the different skills. I'd try to do some writing, because she's okay in writing too.

Kathi: What can she do in writing?

Ellie: She can choose a book—we did this the last week of school so that I could get an idea about her skills. We have a big library. She chose *Rosie's Walk,* a book in English. She went through it and she didn't get the entire meaning, but I asked them to read the book or use the pictures and try to get as much of the meaning from the context as they could, and write a little story. I told them, "Write about whatever you feel like writing. It doesn't even have to be about the book. It could be about whatever the book reminds you of, and then draw me a picture of your story." So she chose the book and she used most of the pictures and a lot of the words. She didn't read it word-by-word, but she got some of the meaning from it and she wrote a small story about Rosie and how Rosie was feeling, and then she drew a picture about it. So she got the meaning from Rosie. . . . And then they had to do mini-presentations about their pictures, and she did that in Spanish.

So we know that Maria is able to read simple books in English and derive meaning from them with some help from the pictures. Afterward she could convey her ideas in Spanish. Ellie's main concern seems to be Maria's continued limited oral production of English.

Ellie: There's no asking her to speak English if she doesn't want to, because she just bottles up, and she just doesn't say anything. . . . With most of the other students I can say, "Okay, this is an English only activity. We have our time for Spanish, but this is English only," and they're fine with it. But if you say, "English only" with Maria, she won't even do it. If you say, "Just do it!" she'll do it. But in terms of assessment I would probably give her a choice of a book. Maybe I'd choose different books at different grade levels.

Kathi: So you'd have her either read a book and summarize it or react to it in some way, whether it's with a connection of some kind, or telling the story of what it made her think of and then drawing a picture.

Ellie: Yes, and then maybe she could give a presentation about that book. Or I might ask her to just tell me about herself. I would probably construct a more detailed test, based on what I've been teaching her over the past couple of months, so that we could note her progress. I would not give her some sort of an isolated reading test, and I would not give her an isolated listening test at all.

So far, Ellie had described activities for getting Maria to read, write, and speak. I was curious (given her last comment about "an isolated listening test") as to how she could document Maria's aural comprehension. I asked Ellie if Maria could follow simple commands and directions in English. Ellie asserted that she could, and gave the following example.

Ellie: We just organized my whole classroom, and she was the one who helped me. We basically played "Concentration" with my whole library. We put all of the books on the floor and we just walked around and put them on top of each other, because I had so many books that were in such disorder. So I said, "Maria, take this book and put it over there. Take that book—"

Kathi: In English?

Ellie: Yes. And she did it with no problem. So she follows basic commands. Her comprehension is good if she's not all nervous about it.

As Ellie continued to describe Maria's accomplishments and abilities, her voice took on more force. Each *italicized* word in the following excerpts received strong primary stress in Ellie's speech. Again, her description provides evidence of Maria's analytic and organizational skills.

Kathi: So you could videotape something like that interaction with you and the books, and that would be pretty convincing evidence that she is intelligent and she is processing English.

Ellie. Yes. And you know, the game of "Concentration," in and of itself, is a thinking game. And that's what we were doing with those books. She organized my whole library for me. All I did was make a list of the books I had, but she was the one who created the categories. She decided that these books are holiday books. You know, Thanksgiving, Christmas, Cinco de Mayo. *She* created that section for me. *She* did my library for me. She's *fine* with her intelligence, and I don't think the rest of the school understands that.

She created the holidays category in English and then she created a Spanish books category—just books in Spanish. Also Peter books because we have a hundred different "Peter-the-Everything" books.

We laughed at the idea of Peter-the-Everything books. It makes perfect sense to a teacher like Ellie that books about characters named Peter would constitute a category in the mind of a third-grade child. Ellie continued:

Ellie: She did a marine animals section, because we had books about sharks, and we had the Monterey Bay Aquarium and the Elkhorn Slough—so she created that section for me. She was the one who did *all* of this. She created a fairy tale section, with Mother Goose and all that. She was even supervising kindergartners. You know, she was saying, "You're gonna do this" and "You're gonna do that."

Kathi: Was she telling the little kids that in Spanish or in English?

Ellie: In Spanish, but you know, she was really able to supervise some kindergartners, and it worked out well.

Given Ellie's description of Maria, it doesn't sound to me as if she has a learning disability. I don't know why Maria isn't speaking English yet, though many factors were suggested in our discussion. It is clear that she is bright and capable, based on the tasks that Ellie described her doing. But none of Maria's strengths will be captured by her scores on the *California Achievement Test* or the reading miscue an .' .sis used by this school. It's up to Ellie to document and publicize those strengths at the same time she supports Maria's first language maintenance and furthers her English language development.

If there were some magical mechanism that would allow an author to make a wish (or two) in the process of writing a book, then it would be at this point that I'd make two wishes. The first would be the impossible wish that for every Maria there'd be an Ellie. Language students everywhere need well-informed teachers who are knowledgeable about assessment and who can explain language acquisition to less knowledgeable colleagues. My second wish—even more impossible than the first—is that Ellie and other teachers like her would continue to fight for children's language rights without becoming discouraged and burnt out by the massive systemic ignorance and blind reliance on standardized test scores that typify our schools.

We will turn now from a focus on the elementary school context and consider a problem in a university's language assessment program. I will use this context to introduce some concepts that are important to understand in any school system that uses external assessment devices, internally developed tests, or a combination thereof. In this chapter, again, the conflicting purposes of testing are revealed.

Many years ago J. D. Brown and I were teachers in the ESL Program at the University of California at Los Angeles (UCLA). This was a very large program that served hundreds of students at a time, the great majority of whom were taking courses in university degree programs. They attended English classes primarily because they were required to do so by the university. At the beginning of every term, students entering the university would be tested with the *English as a Second Language Placement Exam* (the *ESLPE*). So in our classes we would typically have some students who had been placed in a particular level by virtue of their scores on the *ESLPE*, as well as some who had moved through the system into that level by virtue of having successfully completed the course at the prior level.

J. D., being an alert and caring teacher as well as a budding researcher, noticed that there seemed to be some differences in ability between those students who entered his classes via the placement exam (the placed students) and those who progressed through the levels of the courses in the program (the system students). So he conducted an investigation in which he compared the performances of the placed and system students in the upper-intermediate ESL course on three measures: their end-of-course grades, their scores on the departmental final examination, and their scores on a fifty-item cloze test. Sure enough, the students who had been placed directly into the upper-intermediate course on the basis of their *ESLPE* test scores significantly outperformed on all three measures the students who had come through the system. In terms of classroom interaction, this meant that students in any given class might have very different abilities in the target language.

A situation in which students in a single language class have widely different proficiency levels can be very frustrating to students and teachers alike (although there are some benefits in working with students in multilevel classrooms and some creative teachers have devised useful techniques for dealing with this situation). The following letter to the editor appeared in a college newspaper. It succinctly expresses a student's frustration, which had arisen in part from methodological concerns, but also from problems in language assessment—specifically in (1) defining placement and exit criteria, and (2) determining students' entry-level and exit-level proficiency.

> Dear Editor:
>
> I can only cite my personal experiences as an undergraduate in giving reasons for my dissatisfaction with the language program. I began to study my second language at the school's summer language program, yet I now find myself ill-prepared for the upper-level courses in which I am enrolled.
>
> By completing the intermediate courses, I should have attained sufficient proficiency to comprehend and participate in the advanced classes. This is not the situation. I am forced to spend extraordinary amounts of time preparing for class. Yet other students in these classes—who have studied the language elsewhere—say that these courses are below their abilities.

In other words, this letter voices the same concern, from the student's point of view, as J. D. Brown had about the apparent differences in proficiency between the placed and system students in his upper-intermediate ESL classes.

Norm-referenced and Criterion-referenced Testing

In discussing his findings, J. D. pointed out a very interesting problem with the interface of our coursework, the *ESLPE,* and the final examination (1981, 116):

> The differences in proficiency found in this study seem to indicate a mismatch between the norm-referenced placement test (the *ESLPE*) and the amount being learned in the courses. In other words, students in lower-level courses do not appear to be learning enough in those courses to make up the number of points which separate levels on the *ESLPE,* and might not be placed in the next level if they had to take that test again.

In contrast to the norm-referenced *ESLPE,* the final examination had been cooperatively written by the teachers as a criterion-referenced achievement test. It was intended specifically to assess the students' mastery of the main objectives in our upper intermediate ESL course—so it was a test of the students' skill in academic reading, note-taking during lectures, and composition.

At this point we must distinguish between norm-referenced and criterion-referenced tests. These are extremely important concepts and the central distinction between them is one reason why students and teachers often feel so negative about large-scale standardized tests.

The terms norm-referenced and criterion-referenced have to do with how test scores are interpreted. **Norm-referenced tests** are those associated with the familiar bell-shaped curve, which is referred to in the phrase "grading on a curve." In this philosophy, grades or scores are based on a comparison of the test-takers to one another. So, for example, suppose I were taking a 100-point test that alone would determine whether I would be accepted into a prestigious university. I might be excited to learn that I had received a score of 95 percent (i.e., 95 out of 100 answers were correct). But if acceptance into the university were based on a norm-referenced decision that only the top 10 percent of the students would be accepted, then this score alone will not tell me whether I'll be accepted. If 10 percent or more of the students who sat for the exam scored 96 percent or better on the test, then in comparison with those students, I would not be admitted to the university.

Let's take a different exaggerated outcome to clarify the concept of norm-referencing. Suppose my test results were that I had only gotten 75 points out of the possible 100 points on the test. While I would certainly be disappointed with my own performance, would this result automatically mean that I would not be accepted to the university? Not necessarily, in a strictly norm-referenced context. Again the decision would depend on the performances of the other test-takers. So if by chance getting 75 percent of the items correct turned out to be the high score (either because it was an exceptionally difficult test or because my competitors were not well prepared for the test and scored even lower than 75 percent), then I would be admitted to the university.

Norm-referenced tests often utilize score reports that are interpreted in terms of percentiles. *Percentiles* are not the same as *percentages* or *percents*. A **percentile** is a particular place in a distribution of many scores on a norm-referenced test. So if your score report tells you that you scored at the ninety-sixth percentile, this means only that you scored better than 96 percent of the people who took the test. However, the percentile figure itself doesn't tell you what your actual score was (i.e., being at the ninety-sixth percentile doesn't necessarily mean that you got 96 percent of the items right, and vice versa).

In order to keep this explanation short and focused I have over simplified the discussion of norm-referenced testing. The missing piece of the puzzle is what's referred to as the norming group. When a standardized test is developed, it is administered to a number of people carefully selected to be representative of the types of people who will eventually take the test. The performance of a sufficiently large norming group is subsequently used as a standard against which the performance of future test-takers is compared. Test scores can be interpreted in a norm-referenced manner without establishing a norming group, but in the large commercial test publishing procedures, the use of a norming group is quite common.

Norm-referencing is a common approach to score interpretation in situations in which there are large numbers of test-takers (e.g., the *TOEFL*), and/or in situations in which the test scores will be used to screen in or out a certain number of people (e.g., where spaces in a prestigious program are limited, or where only a small number of people are to be certified as being of the highest caliber in a particular skill).

As teachers we need to ask ourselves if norm-referenced testing is always appropriate in terms of the information we need about our students. I think you'll find that the answer is no. So what is the alternative? Let's consider criterion-referenced testing.

If norm-referenced testing means that a score is interpreted against other test-takers' scores, then what does criterion-referenced testing mean? You have probably discerned that in **criterion-referenced testing,** a given score is interpreted relative to a pre-set goal or objective (the criterion), rather than to the performances of other test-takers.

The clearest example of a criterion-referenced test for my students is the California driver's license test. This exam involves both a paper-and-pencil test about traffic laws and a behind-the-wheel test of driving skill. The passing score level has been set by the California Department of Motor Vehicles, based on professional judgments about the knowledge and skill needed to be a safe driver. If a new student moves to California from another state or country he or she must pass this test in order to drive legally in California. If his or her score falls *below* the criterion level, he or she will not be granted a driver's license, even if he or she had the highest score of anyone tested that day. (None of the test-takers scoring lower than this student would be granted driving licenses either!) Likewise, if the student's score is *at or above* the criterion level, he or she *will* be granted a driver's license, even if his or her score was the lowest score posted that day. His or her performance is judged against the criterion—not against the performances of the other test-takers.

For many years, language testing (especially in the United States) has been strongly influenced (some would even say dominated) by the norm-referenced approach to score interpretation. In my opinion, however, norm-referenced tests are often *not* appropriate for classroom use. It's a question of the purpose of assessment. Are we trying to find out how students compare to other students or do we want to know whether students have (or lack) mastery over a certain body of knowledge or skills that are described in a set of objectives? (The latter is often the case in placement, diagnostic, and achievement testing, or in situations in which the total number of test-takers selected or rejected is irrelevant.) If the latter is the case, then criterion-referenced score interpretation is probably more appropriate than norm-referenced score interpretation.

Let's apply these concepts to Ellie's situation with Maria. The *California Achievement Test* is a norm-referenced test. Maria's score will be reported as a percentile (i.e., a representation of her place compared to many other students). In contrast, the kinds of tasks Ellie talks about having Maria do on videotape were designed to show what criteria the student *does* meet—what she can do on her own, without reference to the performances of other children. So norm-referenced and criterion-referenced score interpretation represents one of several contrasts that characterize some of the oppositions found in language assessment.

PURPOSES OF LANGUAGE ASSESSMENT

Another problem teachers face is that there are many reasons to conduct formal language assessment procedures. Some of these reasons are so common that they have specific names. In this section we will discuss eight particular purposes for conducting language assessments and learn the labels associated with those purposes. My hope is that this knowledge will make you a more informed consumer of commercially produced tests and will also prepare you to develop your own in-house tests. In addition, I hope it will enable you to be a better advocate for students like Maria.

One purpose of testing that may not directly affect you or your students (and will not be treated further in this book), is to determine a learner's potential talent or capacity for learning languages. This capacity is referred to as an **aptitude** for language learning, so tests designed to assess this construct are called **aptitude tests.** Aptitude tests do not test one's skill in a particular language—rather they are intended to assess a person's ability to learn *any* language. There are many arguments about what constitutes language learning aptitude that are too detailed to cover here. I recommend the collection edited by Parry and Stansfield (1990), if you would like to learn more.

A kind of language test that is especially related to contexts like Maria's is known as a **language dominance test**. Usually such procedures involve assessing potentially bilingual children in both languages they have been exposed to, in order to see which is the stronger (dominant) language for purposes of instruction. In Maria's case, given what Ellie said, the child would be identified as "Spanish dominant." Her brother, Carlos, might still be designated "Spanish dominant," but according to Ellie's description, he would also do well on the English portion of the test.

Another important purpose in language assessment is to determine someone's proficiency in a language. The problem here is how to define the construct of proficiency—a question that linguists and language teachers have considered for some time. Definitions of proficiency generally involve the concept of overall language use in a variety of circumstances involving all four skills and all levels of language. As you can imagine, the difficulty in designing a **proficiency test** is in selecting stimulus materials and tasks that will allow us to elicit an appropriate sample of behavior from the candidate so as to evaluate such a broad construct fairly.

One key factor in proficiency testing is that it doesn't matter how a language learner became proficient. You may have studied Spanish in college or spent a year as an exchange student in Buenos Aires, or you may have worked for several summers with native speakers of Spanish in a landscaping business. You may have been raised bilingually, or perhaps one of your grandparents spoke Spanish in your home when you were a small child. In proficiency testing, the way you learned the language is supposed to be irrelevant. In other words, proficiency tests are not meant to be tied to any particular curriculum.

Now, of course, if you learned Spanish in college, the grammar, vocabulary, and discourse structures included in your Spanish knowledge may be quite different from what you would know and be able to do in Spanish if you had spent a year in Argentina while a teenager. The problem in designing (or selecting) a proficiency test, then, is to determine what domains must be sampled in order to determine whether the language learner is indeed proficient.

Sometimes proficiency (or other) tests are used to make specific decisions. One perhaps familiar example is the use of the *TOEFL* (*Test of English as a Foreign Language*) as an admissions test for universities. An **admissions test** is intended to provide information about whether a candidate is likely to succeed in a particular program (these tests are sometimes referred to as **screening tests**). Such decisions are sometimes based on a shared history of previous candidates at various *TOEFL* score levels doing well or not doing well in the program. For instance, when our TESOL master's program was first started, 550 was chosen as the required *TOEFL* score for admission, partly because other well-established programs at the school required 550, and partly because some other TESOL master's programs required 550. However, within about two years we realized that given the amount of reading and writing required in our program, students with scores around 550 were floundering. So we raised the *TOEFL* requirement to 600, which has proven to be a more realistic cut-off point.

Once a student has been admitted to a program—especially to a large program—he or she may be faced with a placement test. (Sometimes scores on a proficiency test or an admissions test are used for placement purposes, but often a separate assessment procedure that is based on the specific local program is involved.) A **placement test,** as the name suggests, is intended to define a student's language skills relative to the levels of a particular program he or she is about to enter. So, for instance, in the earlier example of J. D. Brown's research on the system students and the placed students in our ESL classes at UCLA, the placement examination was the *ESLPE*. It was designed to elicit information that would assign students to one of five levels in the program or exempt them from further ESL instruction.

Since the purpose of a placement test is to assign students to particular levels of a program, then it makes sense that the content of the test should be related to the curricula of those levels. But here we return to the notion of criterion-referenced versus norm-referenced score interpretation. Some programs use a norm-referenced test (such as the *TOEFL* or the *ESLPE*) for placement and simply divide the students into instructional levels according to preset score levels.

Other programs use placement tests that are criterion-referenced, with the objectives measured on the tests derived from the objectives addressed in the various levels of the curriculum.

Once a student has been placed in a particular level of a program, the teachers in the program may use **diagnostic tests** to more closely identify their students' particular strengths and weaknesses. Diagnostic tests are very closely related to the syllabuses of the specific classes so that the teachers can decide precisely how to gear the instruction to be most appropriate for the students in that class. Diagnostic measures are also used in learning centers or self-access study programs to help the students themselves decide where to focus their attention.

During the course of instruction, teachers may want to determine how well their students are doing with the material that has been covered. Tests or quizzes that are used as part of an ongoing assessment procedure during the course of instruction are referred to as **progress tests.** It should be apparent that progress tests must be very closely tied to the course content.

Finally, at the end of a particular course of instruction, an assessment is sometimes required to determine how well the learners have mastered the skills or knowledge presented in the course. A test designed to provide this information is referred to as an **achievement test.** Like progress tests and diagnostic tests, achievement tests are ideally based on the objectives of the course. However, as is sometimes the case with placement tests, some programs use proficiency tests such as the Institutional *TOEFL* to try to assess each student's achievement. The Institutional *TOEFL* is an in-house version of the *TOEFL*, which is administered and scored by faculty members of the particular institution using it. Like the International *TOEFL*, it is a norm-referenced standardized test of English proficiency.

The following diagram, which was developed by my colleagues Peter Shaw and Jean Turner, depicts the linear relationship among these various sorts of tests, and their relationship to various phases of curriculum development (Turner, 1995):

Figure 3.1: Curriculum and Test Development as Complementary Activities

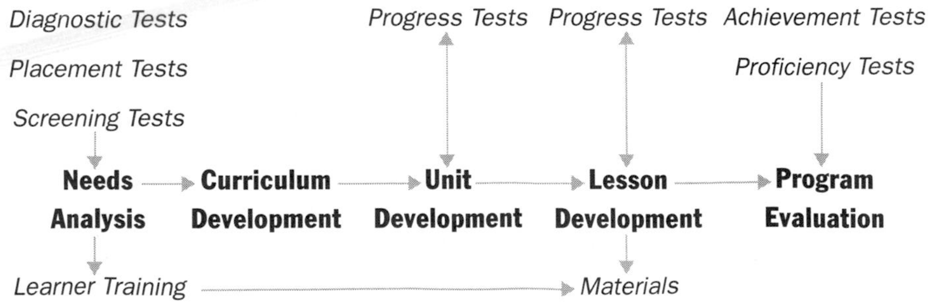

Clearly language tests can be written for many different assessment purposes. It is important for us to have a clear understanding of the various possible assessment purposes so that tests and their resulting scores are not misused or misinterpreted in ways that negatively affect language programs and learners' lives. The tasks in the following "Investigations" section were devised to provide practical experience with these issues.

1 *We have briefly identified several different purposes (at the macro level) for language assessment. The assessment mechanisms designed to address these various purposes include proficiency tests, admissions tests, aptitude tests, placement tests, diagnostic tests, progress tests, dominance tests, and achievement tests. It might be helpful if we pull the ideas about different types of tests together with a brief review in the form of a fill-in quiz:*

Directions: In each box, under "Type of Test," write
the name of one type of test selected from the list below.

Admissions tests	Proficiency tests
Placement tests	Diagnostic tests
Progress tests	Achievement tests
Aptitude tests	Dominance tests

Type of Test	Purpose of Test
	Assess second language learners' (2LLs') general ability to learn a language (any language) prior to actual instruction in the language.
	Are used for screening purposes, to make gross decisions (such as *in* or *out*) regarding 2LLs' ability to undertake a program of study.
	Assign 2LLs to appropriate levels of instruction within a particular program; such tests are related to course objectives.
	Identify 2LLs' particular existing strengths and weaknesses in order to help teachers tailor instruction to fit 2LLs' needs.
	Are used during a course of study to provide information about 2LLs' relative mastery of or difficulty with portions of the curriculum.
	Assess 2LLs' accomplishments relative to a particular curriculum, usually at the end of a course of study.
	Assess 2LLs' ability in the target language independent of any particular curriculum; provide a general assessment of all prior learning and/or acquisition.
	Assess 2LLs' relative strengths in two languages to see which is the stronger language.

2 *If you were the coordinator of the program described in the student's letter to the editor printed on page 34, what steps would you take to deal with the issues raised by the student? What sorts of language assessment measures could be used in this situation? (Focus on the interface between the intermediate and advanced classes.)*

Think of a language assessment situation with which you are familiar. What is the relationship of testing to curricular decisions? What is the ideal role of testing in providing feedback to individual students? (It may help if you try to answer these questions in chronological terms, as students enter and progress through a program. Refer to Figure 3.1 if you wish.)

---

3 *Imagine yourself in Ellie Mason's situation. What would you do to convince a measurement specialist that a linguistic minority child was not learning disabled?*

It may be helpful to think about two contrasting sets of information that you could produce in such a situation. There are standardized test scores (such as Maria's scores on the *California Achievement Test* and the *SABE*) and there is documentation of Maria's performance on various classroom tasks that demonstrate her comprehension and production of English (e.g., Ellie's videotape of Maria organizing the library). Note that standardized tests yield quantitative data that are amenable to many statistical manipulations and are recognized (and often revered) as "hard data." Videotapes, on the other hand, yield qualitative data, which may not always be as convincing to measurement specialists schooled in traditional psychometric principles and procedures. Nevertheless, any principal, district psychologist, parent, or teacher who thoughtfully viewed a video of Maria creating Ellie's book categories would be hard pressed to label her as mentally retarded.

I have often found over the years that one of the greatest challenges in my role as a language teacher is to explain test results—both the information they provide and their limitations—to people in positions of power over students: admissions officers, deans, employers, professors. To me, this responsibility is one of the main reasons we language teachers need to be well informed and totally confident about assessment procedures.

---

4 *Ellie's description of Maria's library organization skills and helpfulness with the kindergarten children struck a familiar chord for me. It reminded me of a descriptive vignette from a study by Carrasco (1981, 168) that was reprinted in Leo van Lier's book,* The Classroom and the Language Learner *(1988, 35). It is a summary of a videotaped interaction involving a child called "Lupita," whom the teacher had thought was not particularly capable. The description clearly shows that Lupita is a bright child with numerous academic and social skills.*

Rereading that vignette made me think about Ellie's description of Maria's capabilities and a possible task for this chapter. Imagine yourself in Ellie's situation, preparing for a meeting of the "Child Case Study Team" assigned to investigate Maria's progress (or lack thereof)—and knowing that the other members of the team believe Maria is learning disabled. The district psychologist has asked you to write a one-page statement about Maria's progress, based on verifiable evidence, to be distributed to the other team members as the basis of a discussion about Maria.

> Imagine yourself in Ellie's situation and write a one-page description of Maria's strengths and weaknesses, based on the information Ellie provided.

> Or, more importantly,

> Think of a student you have known well whose test scores did not reveal his or her strengths. How would you describe the student's capabilities (in one page or so) in such a way as to convey those strengths to someone who believes strongly in the unilateral veracity of standardized test scores?

Suggested Readings

A particularly appropriate book for teachers who work with children is *Assessment and ESL* by Barbara Law and Mary Eckes (1995). The authors call it a "handbook for K-12 teachers." I have found it entertaining and informative, with ideas clearly grounded in the authors' years of classroom experience.

Jaeger's *Statistics: A Spectator Sport* (1990) contains an excellent discussion of percentiles. If you have ever had difficulty explaining this construct to students, parents, or other teachers, I recommend Jaeger's examples and explanation as a starting place.

Grant Henning starts his book, *A Guide to Language Testing: Development, Evaluation, Research* (1987), with a chapter about the purposes and types of language assessment. It includes the issues raised in this chapter as well as others covered in Chapter 9.

J. D. Brown's *Testing in Language Programs* (1996), provides a useful chart (p. 9) that compares different purposes of testing and the types of information sought with the criterion-referenced versus norm-referenced framework.

Lyle Bachman's book, *Fundamental Considerations in Language Testing* (1990), provides very solid information about criterion-referenced and norm-referenced approaches to score interpretation. J. D. Brown (1995) and Dale Griffee (1995) have also written helpful articles on this topic.

Lyle Bachman and Adrian Palmer have coauthored a book called *Language Testing in Practice* (1996). It includes excellent coverage of language test development issues, as well as descriptions of many test development projects.

Language Aptitude Reconsidered, edited by Thomas Parry and Charles Stansfield (1990), is an anthology of research on the construct of aptitude.

Brian Lynch and Fred Davidson (1994) have written an excellent article about the development of criterion-referenced language tests.

4

THE ROLE OF BACKGROUND KNOWLEDGE IN THE ASSESSMENT OF RECEPTIVE SKILLS

We walked down the path to the well-house attracted by the fragrance of the honeysuckle with which it was covered. Someone was drawing water and my teacher placed my hand under the spout. As the cool stream gushed over one hand she spelled into the other the word water, *first slowly, then rapidly. I stood still, my whole attention fixed upon the motions of her fingers. Suddenly I felt a misty consciousness as of something forgotten—a thrill of returning thought; and somehow the mystery of language was revealed to me. I knew then that "w-a-t-e-r" meant the wonderful cool something that was flowing over my hand. That living word awakened my soul, gave it light, hope, joy, set it free! There were barriers still, it is true, but barriers that could in time be swept away (Keller, 1902, 36).*

I once team taught a content course on learning styles and strategies to a group of mixed-level ESL students in California. One of the students in the class was a young Asian woman whom we will call "Paa." She had been orphaned as a child and her schooling had been interrupted at a very early age when she was forced into a life of selling flowers on street corners to earn her keep. Paa had enrolled in our Intensive ESL Program, where she hoped to learn enough English to attend a junior college. Her progress in academic English was very slow, however, and her teachers sometimes got frustrated because she seemed to be inattentive in class, to need constant extra help in doing activities, and even to disrupt lessons by not following the instructions.

One day in the learning styles and strategies class, the students were to complete a grid activity individually and then compare their results in pairs. I explained the activity carefully and everyone got to work except Paa, who looked at her neighbors' papers but didn't start doing the task. She called me to her desk and asked me to explain what she was supposed to do. I was very puzzled at her request because I had tried to explain the task clearly and several students whose listening proficiency was lower than Paa's had gotten right to work. Fortunately, my team teacher was able to work with the other students as needed. So I sat down next to Paa's desk and explained the task again, carefully monitoring my speech to pitch it precisely to her level. She gave me positive back-channeling (nodding, smiling, and saying "yes") throughout this brief explanation and looked as though she understood completely. When I finished, I asked her if she understood what I had said. Paa answered, "Yes. But what should I do?"

At that point I was more puzzled than ever. I was sure she had been attending to our one-on-one instructions session, and I was reasonably sure that the vocabulary and structures I had used were well within her grasp. To sort out where the confusion lay, I asked Paa to tell me what she *did* understand, step-by-step. To my surprise she was able to repeat my verbal instructions very clearly —almost word for word. I congratulated her, praised her for listening so closely, and encouraged her to get started on the task. Paa smiled and thanked me and asked, "But what should I do?"

I was dumbfounded. No wonder her teachers were getting frustrated. But clearly Paa was trying. She had understood and recalled everything I'd said. What was the problem? I looked around the room and saw that my team-teaching partner had the class well in hand. Most of the other students had finished their individual tasks and were comparing their grids with others. But Paa's paper remained blank, the apparently understood task as yet not started. I decided to work part of the task with Paa, to shift modalities and see if another approach would work. The result, of course, was that I learned a profound lesson.

As every language teacher knows, the framework of a grid is a powerful stimulus for thought and conversation because the cells in the grid represent the conceptual intersection of whatever variable is represented by the horizontal axis with the variable represented by the vertical axis, as in Figure 4.1.

Figure 4.1: Illustration of the Grid Concept

Variable 1

Variable 2 (label at left of middle row)

The grid format can be used to practice many academic concepts. To practice math, for instance, variables 1 and 2 can represent numbers and the students' task can be to multiply the number on the horizontal axis by the number on the vertical axis and write the product in the cell. Or in a world geography "fact hunt" (like a treasure hunt) the horizontal axis of the grid can display a list of countries and the vertical axis can stipulate facts to be determined about each country (capital, population, main exports, etc.). The students then fill in the cells in the grid by looking up the information about the various countries in an encyclopedia or by interviewing their classmates about their home countries, if they are in a multilingual ESL class. These are tasks that every fourth-grader can do.

Just then I realized that Paa is not every fourth-grader. In fact, it's doubtful that she ever attended fourth grade. Suddenly the light dawned on *my* misunderstanding. I turned the paper over and on the upper half of the page I drew only the vertical lines of the grid. Together Paa and I labeled the columns. Then I folded the page in half and hid what we had just done. We then drew only the horizontal lines of the grid, and Paa labeled the rows. I then unfolded the page so that Paa could see the disassembled grid teased apart into its two components as we had drawn them—the vertical axis separated from the horizontal axis.

Then I had Paa put one hand on the vertically oriented picture (with her fingers pointing to the top of the page) and the other hand on the horizontally oriented sketch (with her fingers pointing to the side). Then, demonstrating with my own hands, I asked her to keep her hands pointed in the same directions but to lay one on top of the other.

Finally I turned the page over so that we were again looking at the original grid. I had Paa lay her overlapping hands on top of the grid and pointed out to her that the grid was really our two drawings superimposed: The vertical and the horizontal axes created the cells in the grid just as her overlapping fingers made windows in the lattice created by her hands.

When Paa seemed to grasp the notion of overlap, I took her two index fingers and drew down one of the columns with her right hand and across one of the rows with her left, until both fingers were located in the cell defined by that row and that column. We looked at the labels for the two columns and I asked her what to write in the cell. She didn't know, and a hurt, almost panicky look came into her eyes. I told her the answer and traced her two fingers back to the respective labels in the margins of the rows and columns. At that point she suddenly saw the relationship between the row and column labels and the concept I had written in the cell. She eagerly moved her index fingers to two other headings and traced them down and across to another cell, where she filled in the right answer. Paa continued to work on the task independently and eventually joined her classmates in the discussion of their grids.

Here's the lesson I learned: Paa had understood my English, and she had certainly been paying attention. What she had not understood was the formal framework of a two-dimensional grid—how two intersecting concepts create new concepts represented by and recorded in the individual cells of the grid. It was the framework she didn't understand and its connection to the writing and speaking activity the class was doing. Switching to a kinesthetic and visual explanation, using our hands to draw and model the grid, served Paa's learning style and conceptual development better than relying on the more abstract, academic visual and aural channels alone.

Paa's moment of awareness, when she came to understand how a grid depicts concepts, was perhaps not as dramatic as Helen Keller's powerful realization that finger spelling could represent ideas in the world. But for me, the moment had the force of revelation: Paa understood the English of my instructions but she didn't know how a grid works. That's why I believe that the information presented in the "Frameworks" section of this chapter is vital for us, both as teachers and as testers.

Suppose I said I was going to introduce the framework used in this chapter by telling you a Polish joke. What would you think? You might be somewhat surprised—even potentially offended. This reaction would be based on your background knowledge, and that background knowledge would take two forms.

First of all, you would probably expect such a joke to contain information that portrays Polish people as foolish. Second, you might expect the joke to begin with something like the standard phrase, "How many Polish people does it take to . . . ?" (Or you might even expect some defamatory label to represent the Polish people.) Given your expectations about the contents and the structure of Polish jokes, you would probably feel that it is inappropriate for a language teacher like me, someone who claims to be cross-culturally sensitive, to include a Polish joke in a book for other language teachers.

I make these comments to illustrate a point about background knowledge. The kinds of background knowledge that led you to predict what information my Polish joke would contain (for instance, putdowns of Polish people) are called **content schemata**. The kinds of background knowledge that led you to anticipate the structure of my Polish joke (for instance, the predicted opening line, "How many Polish people does it take . . . ?") are called **formal schemata**. Both content schemata and formal schemata are working in our minds as we interpret incoming information, either in our native language or in other languages.

I'm happy to tell you that in this case, your expectations are wrong. Indeed, the Polish joke I am going to tell you is not a joke about Polish people. Rather it is a joke *from Poland*. It was told to me (many times) during the summer of 1984 by my students in Poznan, Poland, who were future teachers of English. I will use this joke to illustrate how background knowledge influences our interpretation of incoming messages. Please pay attention to your own internal processing as you read the joke, which is printed in italics but interspersed by my comments in regular type:

> *Two strangers began to talk one hot August day as they stood by*
> *the open window of a train traveling from Warsaw to Krakow.*
> *And as the miles slipped by, they began to discuss cars.*

If you were familiar with train travel in Poland you would know that these men are standing because there are (or at least in 1984, there were) no reserved seats. Not having been lucky enough to get a seat during the boarding scramble, these two men are forced to stand, all the way from Warsaw to Krakow—a journey of many hours. Thus if you were familiar with train travel in Poland, your content schemata would provide you with the necessary information to interpret the scant details provided in the opening lines of the joke.

> *Eventually one man said to the other, "If you could buy any car in*
> *the world, what kind of car would you buy?"*

At this point, if you were familiar with social and economic factors of daily life in Poland in 1984, you would know that the average person typically did not own a car. At the same time, your formal schemata—your knowledge of the conversational structure in jokes—would lead you to predict that the second man would answer the first man's question with the name of a car. And sure enough, he does:

"Hmm . . . . What an interesting question. I suppose," he hesitated.
"Yes, I suppose I would buy a Warszawa."

Now if you were familiar with Polish vehicles, your content schemata would be telling you that a Warszawa (pronounced "var-SHA-va") was a state-manufactured car, produced in factories owned by the Polish government, and not a particularly reliable or prestigious vehicle. Your formal schemata about jokes in general are probably leading you to predict that the first man will respond with an expression of surprise at this response, as indeed he does:

"A Warszawa! No, no, no! I mean if you had lots of money
and you could buy any car you wanted. A Porsche, perhaps a
Jaguar, even a Rolls—anything in the whole world. What kind
of car would you buy?"

Once again, your formal schemata should lead you to expect that the second man will respond with the name of a car. But your content schemata may be making you suspicious. What sort of car will the second man say? The joke continues:

"Oh well, under those circumstances, hmm, let me see," said the
second man. "Under those circumstances, I would probably buy a
Warszawa."

Now your formal schemata are probably suggesting to you that the first man will repeat his question, perhaps with further elaboration. Your formal schemata are also probably telling you that the second man will respond one more time before we get to the punch line, because jokes in this tradition often build to a climax with a series of three events or people (the farmer's three daughters; the rabbi, the priest, and the minister; the Englishman, the Scotsman, and the Irishman; and so on).

"A Warszawa!!" gasped the first man getting annoyed. "No, no,
no! I mean if you had LOTS of money—U.S. dollars, British
pounds sterling, even Japanese yen! If you had lots of money and
could buy ANY car in the whole world, THEN what car would
you buy?"

So now your formal schemata are telling you that the second man will respond one more time with the name of a car. And your content schemata, perhaps modified a bit by your experience of the joke so far, may be leading you to predict that he will name a Warszawa one more time.

"Ohh . . . . Well, yes! I see! Hmm . . . . Under those
circumstances," the second man paused, "Well, under THOSE
circumstances, I would certainly buy a Warszawa."

Now, of course, your formal schemata, in terms of the structure of the joke, are telling you it's time for the punch line. And if you know anything about the effect of the political climate on social life in Poland in the mid-1980s, the punch line will not surprise you very much.

"A Warszawa! Why?" exclaimed the first man, very exasperated by
now. *"You certainly don't know much about cars, do you?"*

"On the contrary, Comrade," responded the second man. *"I know
a great deal about cars. But I know nothing at all about you."*

Your formal schemata should now be telling you that the joke has ended: We
have the resolution to the tension that built up in the repeated question-and-
answer sequence. And your content schemata should be telling you that the second man refused to engage in a meaningful conversation with the first man, for
fear that he might be an informant. To admit to wanting a non-Polish-made car,
particularly a luxury car, in 1984 would be to admit disloyalty to the State.

Does this joke seem funny to you? In the Poland of 1984, with Soviet troops
on the street corners, when people rode the buses in silence, the future English
teachers who were my students found this joke very amusing indeed. I recently
told this joke to a group of teachers (by way of illustrating content schemata
and formal schemata). The six Americans and the Colombian in the group
groaned collectively at the punch line, but the Russian laughed long and heartily.

What does this set of frameworks have to do with teaching and testing? Let's
return to the story I related about Paa at the beginning of this chapter. What I
learned by working with her individually was that Paa lacked the formal
schemata for using a grid. She *wasn't* being obtuse; she *was* paying attention;
and she *had* understood the English of the instructions. She just didn't know
how grids worked.

I believe that language learners often lack either the formal schemata or the
content schemata (or both) to successfully complete a task, whether that task is
used for teaching or for assessment. When nonnative speakers read or listen to
a text in the target language, they may use formal schemata and/or content
schemata from their first language and culture. The inappropriate application of
mismatched schemata may lead to incorrect interpretations of the message. In a
language-testing situation, the use of inappropriate schemata may cause the students to miss some items—not because of their proficiency in the target language, but because of their lack of familiarity with the culture or the assessment
procedures.

In face-to-face interactions, the use of inappropriate schemata can lead to
communication breakdowns. Here is an example. I visited a language teaching
organization in Italy some years ago. I didn't know it at the time but there was
a cigarette strike in progress—no cigarettes were available, except those smug-
gled into the country and sold on the black market at exorbitant prices.

One day I was leaving the U.S. Embassy in Rome with my friend Dee Parker,
who worked there. Dee was momentarily detained, but she told me to go ahead
and get the taxi that was parked at the curb. The driver was leaning against the
car smoking a cigarette. As I got into the taxi the driver asked me a question in
Italian—a language I don't speak. I only understood a tiny part of what he said,
something about "okay" and "smoking." My California-based content schemata led me to believe that he had asked me if I minded that he smoked while he
drove. I responded with my best fakin'-it Italian accent and said, "No proble-
ma." At that moment Dee came out of the Embassy and got into the taxi. The

driver spoke to her in rapid Italian, to which she responded vehemently in her own very fluent Italian, "No! Absolutamente no!" She then turned to me incredulously and said, "Kathi, did you tell him we'd buy him cigarettes at the Embassy store? It's illegal!"

Needless to say, I was very surprised. My inappropriate schemata use had led me to completely misinterpret the taxi driver's question.

This anecdote illustrates two more important concepts about background knowledge and language assessment: top-down processing and bottom-up processing. **Top-down processing** refers to using the big picture, the contextual features, to help interpret incoming language. (Since I was about to enter a small enclosed space with him, it was only right that the driver would request my permission for him to continue smoking.) **Bottom-up processing** refers to focusing on small components of the language (individual sounds, morphemes, or words) to interpret the message. (My reliance on the only two words I understood, "okay" and the Italian word for smoking, is an example of bottom-up processing.)

For efficient readers and listeners, top-down and bottom-up processing work simultaneously. In recent years much interesting research, in both first and second language contexts, has been motivated by schema theory. However, very little research has been conducted about the roles of formal and content schemata in assessment situations. I hope you will be aware of these issues as you design assessment tasks for your students.

The "Investigations" section of this chapter is designed to give you firsthand experience with the role of schemata in language assessment. While the example of Paa and the grid deals with the role of formal schemata, the task below focuses on content schemata.

---

1 *Printed below is a story, followed by ten multiple-choice recall items. Read the story once. Then without turning back to look at the text, answer each question by circling the letter that represents the best answer. Please* do not *refer to the story as you answer the ten questions—try to work from memory alone. Again, be aware of your mental processing, both as you read the text and as you respond to the test items that follow.*

> She had eagerly awaited and—yes—even dreaded this moment for months. She knew the mental preparation had not been enough. The necessary physical actions were not yet automatic.
>
> They drove through the pre-dawn darkness in silence, 'til a pungent smell assaulted her senses. Her hands began to shake and sweat, despite the chill, as she followed him along the path and they clambered out onto the ledge.
>
> "There," he said, pointing to the void below. "Are you ready?"

She swallowed and nodded, then watched, enthralled, as he removed the equipment from its casing and assembled the slender tube. She knew full well that—for all its balance and craftsmanship—this was indeed an instrument of death.

He handed her a tapered metal object. The cylinder fit neatly in the palm of her hand. She hefted its weight and knew its purpose in the deadly pursuit.

Next came the stage of preparation that she herself had never done. He squinted into the darkness and judged the distance, and then began, methodically, to tie the knots. She marveled at the strength in the slender filament as he tightened the ends. She flinched, in spite of herself, when he pulled a knife. "You don't want any loose ends," he explained.

"He knows I'm nervous," she thought. "I must be calm and learn all I can."

When all was ready, he showed her how to judge the distance and take aim. She knew the proper handling of the mechanism was crucial and she deliberately squeezed her index finger against the grip. Her first attempt fell short and her second was wide of the mark. She checked her grip again, aligned the metal loops and aimed once more, the effort and the thrust wrenching her shoulder and her arms.

Again and again, she heard the whizzing sound of small objects speeding past her head. Twice the stinging metal pierced her flesh, but she ignored the pain. She marveled at his patience and his calm. He was an old hand, accustomed to waiting, and he was not bothered by the incessant roaring noise or the frequent, shrill cries piercing the half-light.

After what seemed like hours of concentrated effort, she suddenly heard a snap and a hiss behind her. She turned to see him watching her with appraising eyes.

"Here, take it," he said. "I think you're probably ready." Was she? The metal was cold and her tired hand shook a bit as she took the canister from his outstretched hands. Her stomach churned at the thought, but she had come this far: She would do this too.

Reading Comprehension Test

The ten multiple choice items below are based on the story you read. Circle the letter of your choice for each item. If you are not sure, make a good guess. Don't leave any items blank.

1. What was the pungent smell that assaulted the woman's senses?
   A. The smell of gunpowder and dying animals
   B. The salty smell of the ocean and seaweed
   C. The smell of gunpowder and burning buildings
   D. The smell of smoke from a raging forest fire

2. What did she see when she climbed out on the ledge and looked down below her?
   A. Herds of animals grazing quietly in the dawn
   B. A few unsuspecting people in the streets below
   C. Prisoners milling about in a prison yard
   D. Waves breaking on the rocky shore below

3. What was the piece of equipment he removed from the casing and then assembled?
   A. A rifle with a telescopic sight
   B. The metal framework for a hangglider
   C. A fishing pole
   D. A cross-bow

4. What was the cylindrical metal object he handed her?
   A. A bullet
   B. A weight
   C. An arrowhead
   D. A dog whistle

5. What was the man doing when he was tying knots?
   A. Preparing a rope ladder for an assault
   B. Preparing a net for catching animals
   C. Preparing some fishing tackle
   D. Preparing a hangman's noose

6. Why did the man say "You don't want any loose ends"?
   A. In this situation, there should be no witnesses
   B. Loose ends could trip the person descending the ladder
   C. Loose ends could cause a snag in the fishing line
   D. Loose ends would make the net less effective

7. What was the woman doing that hurt her shoulder and her arms?
   A. Firing a hunting rifle
   B. Casting with a fishing pole
   C. Firing a powerful bazooka
   D. Shooting with a cross-bow

8. What was the source of the "incessant roaring noise"?
   A. Herds of large animals running by
   B. The crashing of the surf on the rocks
   C. Bombs exploding and buildings collapsing
   D. Airplanes zooming by just overhead

9. What was the source of the "frequent shrill cries"?
   A. People screaming for help
   B. Small animals trapped in a net
   C. Sea gulls flying nearby
   D. Animals that had been wounded

10. What was the metal canister the man handed the woman, the thought of which made her stomach churn?
    A. A hand grenade
    B. A can of tuna
    C. A can of gun oil
    D. A can of beer

What exactly was this story about? Perhaps as you read the story you found yourself posing and then discarding hypotheses about its plot. As you can see from trying to answer the questions, selecting the best option among the four depends to a large extent on your assumptions about the topic of the story line. These assumptions are based, in part, on the information provided as the story unfolds, but in part on the content schemata you bring with you to the reading.

I recently read this story aloud to a group of eight teachers in a language assessment seminar. But before I read it, I manipulated the teachers' expectations about the story content. Two teachers were told there was no title for this story. Two others were told the title was "Her First Safari." Two others were told it was "A Young Terrorist's First Mission." And the last two were given the title "Her First Fishing Trip." This information was given to my test-takers in writing at the top of the answer sheet: They did not know there were three different titles to the story.

After listening to the story once, the teachers were given the ten multiple-choice items as a listening comprehension test. They were told to choose the best answer and to guess if they weren't sure. When they were finished, I had the pairs of people who had been given the same titles compare their responses to the test. Some interesting results occurred:

1. The two people who had been given no title had many different answers.

2. The two people who thought the story was about a safari had the same answers on nine out of ten items.

3. The two people who believed the story was about a fishing trip had the same answers to nine of the ten questions.

4. The two people who had been told the story was about a young terrorist's first mission did not have similar answers, but that was because one of them decided the story was really about a fishing trip. And, in fact, his chosen answers closely matched those of the pair who had been told the story was about a fishing trip.

Furthermore, people who have been given any one of the three titles typically report that understanding the story was easy and that recalling it later would be easy. In contrast, people who are given no title usually report the story as difficult to understand and predict that it would be difficult to recall later.

In fact, this story was actually written after my first fishing trip. (This explains why option D, "a can of beer," is the correct answer to item 10: Fishermen in California often drink beer, even early in the morning.) I tried to write it so that it could describe a safari as well. When I had some friends read it, they pointed out that it could also be about a terrorist attack.

2 *The point is, our content and formal schemata help us to process incoming information by leading us to predict what we are about to encounter when we listen or read. And as long as our expectations are met, we continue to interpret incoming information in terms of our working hypotheses about the topic. Supplying a title (provided it's noticed and remembered) can serve as a **schema activator**—something that triggers the use of your existing schemata. If you believe the story is about a safari, for instance, then your content schemata regarding safaris are likely to be activated, and you will interpret the incoming information through the filter of that assumption.*

A schema activator is one kind of stimulus material (whether verbal or non-verbal) that gives the listener or reader (or test-taker, in our case) some idea in advance as to what the topic and/or genre of the incoming text may be. A schema activator is also called an **advance organizer** because it helps the listener/reader prepare to pose and test hypotheses about the nature of the incoming text. So, for example, in Chapter 2, when we looked at examples of partial dictation, the following scene-setting comment served as a schema activator for the listeners:

> (The scene occurs in the passenger cabin of a commercial airliner. The plane is arriving late and is about to land at its destination. A voice is heard over the plane's public address system.)

The information that "a voice is heard over the plane's public address system" prepares the listeners for an announcement, thus activating the appropriate formal schemata. And the information that the plane is arriving late and is about to land prepares the listeners for a likely topic of the announcement (further confirmed by the flight attendant's opening remarks), thus activating the appropriate content schemata.

Using the concept of advance organizers as tools to try to activate appropriate content and formal schemata, examine the stimulus material of a reading test or a listening test with which you are familiar. Are the necessary schemata for interpreting the material made explicit to the test-taker? Look for advance organizers such as the following:

1. the presence of an informative and appropriate title;

2. an illustration (chart, graph, or picture) that clearly depicts the content of the text; and/or

3. an explicit label that identifies the genre of the text (something like "You will hear a conversation" or "The following article appeared in a newspaper" or "These are the opening paragraphs of a famous essay").

If there are no explicit schemata activators, try to determine what information students could use that *is* available in the text in order to generate appropriate hypotheses.

3 *You can try this experiment with your friends. Use the story about the fishing trip as the stimulus material in either a reading test or a listening test format. Reproduce the multiple-choice questions, but at the top of the page, write one of the following:*

1. This story has no title. Think of a good title for the story.

2. The title of this story is "Her First Safari."

3. The title of this story is "A Young Terrorist's First Mission."

4. The title of this story is "Her First Fishing Trip."

I suggest you write the title in bold print and circle or underline it with a bright color (e.g., with a red felt tip pen). Provide your test-takers, whether they are friends or actual students, with the title (or lack thereof) *before* they hear or read the story. (In other words, the title should function as an advance organizer.) Then give them the multiple-choice comprehension questions after they read or listen to the story. When they are done, have them compare answers. I think you will find that the content schemata triggered by the advance organizer of the title will definitely influence how your test-takers respond to these ten items.

Suggested Readings

Patricia Johnson (1981, 1982) has written two interesting and easily accessible articles about background knowledge and reading comprehension. Pat Carrell and Joan Eisterhold (1983) have also written a useful article about schema theory and reading comprehension. In fact, Pat Carrell's work (see, e.g., Carrell, 1984) has prompted many investigations. These include Cathy Roller and Alex Matambo's (1992) investigation of proficient bilingual secondary school readers in Zimbabwe.

Some years ago, Jack Richards (1983) wrote a landmark article about listening comprehension that incorporated the ideas of top-down and bottom-up processing. His taxonomy of the micro-skills involved in some listening comprehension tasks should be useful to test designers.

For teachers working in a foreign language context, some chapters of Alice Omaggio's book, *Teaching Language in Context* (1986), present very clear information about the implications of these ideas for foreign language pedagogy. (See Chapter 4 in particular.)

5

A Cloze-knit Family

*When my friend Mark Dale was six years old, he became
tremendously interested in reading. Once he got the idea
that letters represented sounds and printed words represented ideas,
he was fascinated by the reading puzzles that surrounded him.
Not only books, but also signs, directions on packages, television
advertisements, labels on canned goods, and many other elements in
his environment offered him opportunities to exercise his developing
reading skills.*

*One morning as we were returning a videotape to the video
store before it opened, Mark hopped out of the car to drop the
tape through the slot in the door—something he had done many
times. But now that he was becoming a reader, he saw a sign on
the door that he had never noticed before. It said*

IGHT DRO

*because some of the letters had fallen off the door. Mark tried to
sound out the letters and then turned to me and asked "Kathi,
what does it say?"*

"You can read it, Mark," I answered.

*"But it's not any words I know. It says, 'ight dro'! What's 'ight
dro'?" he responded.*

*"Okay, you did a good job of figuring out those words, and
you're right—they're not really words. Would it help if I told you
two letters are missing? I think they fell off the door."*

Mark looked again. "I can't figure it out!" he complained.

*"Okay. Look where the sign is. It's a label for something. Can
you tell by looking at the door where the sign is what it might be
labeling? That might give you a clue about the missing letters."*

*He looked again, squinting his eyes and pursing his lips in con-
centration. "Night Drop!" he exclaimed triumphantly. (Notice that
his six-year-old content schemata about what sort of message might
be printed near a slot on a video store door had helped him to
decode this puzzle.)*

This chapter begins with a story I'll tell you, so the first Teacher's Voice we will
hear is mine. At the time of the event I was in the role of observer rather than
the official role of teacher. But I feel that there is much to be gained by watching learners learn when they are not being taught. I have used this story many

times (complete with overhead projector transparencies) to illustrate to my graduate students the amazing power of the mind to generate closure—to fill in missing parts of incoming messages, based on partial information. This ability forms the basis of several item formats that are useful in language assessment.

Teachers'
Voices

A few days after the "IGHT DRO" incident, Mark and I were driving home to the Carmel Valley, following a very dirty truck. This time the puzzle was even trickier, because mud had splashed over most of the sign on the back of the truck. Fortunately, since we followed the truck for several miles, Mark was eventually able to figure out the meaning of the half-hidden letters. Here's what he could see:

VALLEY PLASTERING

Can you figure out what the sign said? Try to be aware of your mental processing as you reconstruct the possible words these partial letters might represent. For most people to whom I've shown this reading puzzle, the process goes something like this (and indeed this was the reasoning that Mark used):

1. The reader realizes by the visible spacing of the letters that there are probably two words here.

2. It looks as if there are sixteen letters.

3. The second word appears to end in -ING.

4. The letter before the -ING looks like an R. The combination of one straight leg and one slanted leg seems to eliminate most other possible letters.

5. It looks as if there are two As, one in the first word and one in the second.

6. The first word seems to begin with a V.

At this point for Mark, the puzzle became somewhat frustrating. He had already figured out seven of the letters:

V A L L E Y   L A S E R I N G
(1) (2) (3) (4) (5) (6)   (7)   (8)   (9) (10) (11) (12) (13) (14) (15) (16)

But he got stuck on the numerous letters that could be represented by a single vertical post at the bottom (spaces 6, 7, and 11, above). He was also puzzled by the letters that had a horizontal bar across the bottom (spaces 3, 4, 5, 8, and 12, above). I tried to get him to focus on this latter group first.

"Okay, Mark," I said. "What are the letters in the alphabet that have a horizontal bar across the bottom like that?"

"B?" he asked.

"Well, the bottom of a B is kind of curved on the side. Those letters look pretty straight across the bottom to me," I answered.

"E?" he responded, obviously reciting the alphabet mentally.

"Yes, that's a good choice. Do you think they're all Es?"

"Can you have three Es together?" he asked, scrutinizing the back of the truck.

"Hmm. Maybe not. Is there any other letter that has a horizontal bar on the bottom like that?"

A moment of thought resulted in an exuberant shout: "L! L looks like that!"

"Okay, so some of these could be Ls and some could be Es," I coaxed. But Mark was way ahead of me.

"The first word is V-A-L-L-E- —uh, what's the next letter?"

"Hmm. Yeah, now we have several letters left where all we can see is a single post at the bottom. What letters stand on one leg like that?"

A few moments of thought yielded F, I, P, T, and Y. Mark noticed too that some of the posts were in the center of the individual letter's space (probably I, T, or Y) and some were slightly to the left of center (probably F or P).

"VALLEY!" he shouted. "It's for Carmel Valley!" (Again, his content schemata had served him well in providing a context and narrowing the range of possibilities.)

"Yeah, I think you're right. Now what do we have left?" I asked him. At this point he had discovered the following pieces of the puzzle:

VALLEY ⌐ ⌐ A ⌐ ⌐ ⌐ RING
(1) (2) (3) (4) (5) (6)   (7)   (8)   (9) (10) (11) (12) (13)(14) (15) (16)

Based on his previous logic about the horizontal bars on the bottom of the Ls and Es, Mark decided that slots (8) and (12) could be filled with Ls (perhaps based on his success with the double Ls in *valley*). But then he realized it would be hard to say *-LRING*. So he substituted E in slot 12 and came up with -*ERING*:

VALLEY ⌐ LA ⌐ ⌐ ERING
(1) (2) (3) (4) (5) (6)   (7)   (8)   (9) (10) (11) (12) (13)(14) (15) (16)

At that point he was stuck and rapidly tiring of the game. "Kathi, just tell me what it says. I know you know," he complained, slouching in his seat, realizing that what for him had been a reading puzzle had become a teaching puzzle for me.

"Well, I'm not one hundred percent sure, but I *think* I know. Let's look at one more clue and then if you want, I'll tell you my guess," I said.

"Okay, what's the clue?" he asked.

"Well, there's one letter in the second word that has a round bottom. We haven't figured out what that might be yet," I answered.

Mark sat up straight and peered at the muddy truck. He began to tick off the options on his fingers as he recited the alphabet aloud: "B, C, D—no, not D—it doesn't look like that," he reasoned. "It could be a G—no, it's not the same as the G at the end." He continued, "A J maybe. Or an O. Os are shaped like that at the bottom."

Out of the corner of my eye, I could see him trying to process the second word with an O in slot (10).

"It could be an S or a U," he suggested.

"What about a Q?" I asked him

"No, Kathi. It can't be a Q," he said with the patient but slightly exasperated tone of someone explaining the obvious. "There's no tail, and besides it doesn't have a U after it. See?" he gestured to the truck.

Mark surprised me then by not giving up. The driver of the truck put on his turn signal, indicating that our paths were about to part. Mark scrunched up his face, squinting and wriggling his nose in the utmost of six-year-old concentration.

"Plastering!" he shouted triumphantly. "Valley Plastering!" he squealed, clapping his hands in satisfaction with his puzzle-solving skills. "It's Valley Plastering, isn't it?"

"That's what I think," I responded. "You did a good job of sticking with the puzzle."

"Yeah, but, Kathi, there's just one thing," he said, solemn again. "What exactly is *plastering*?"

This question surprised me, but it illustrates an important point. Even though Mark didn't know exactly what *plastering* meant, his formal schemata, in terms of the possible spelling of words in English, had given him a plausible shape for a word. His developing competence as an emerging reader of English had allowed him, through the psycholinguistic processes that generate closure, to guess at the shapes of words that were largely obliterated.

This chapter reviews several different test formats that all revolve around the amazing capacity of the mind to provide missing linguistic information on the basis of partial data. These test formats include fill-in items, cloze tests, and C-tests.

Tests that involve filling in blanks of various kinds work in some interesting ways in language assessment, because of what John Oller (1979) has called the **pragmatic expectancy grammar.** This is the portion of our internalized language competence that enables us to predict likely sequences of incoming language, whether we are reading or listening. So for example, if you hear someone say, "The cat ate the _____," but the last word is muffled, what word would you be likely to fill in? What do you think a cat might have eaten?

When I ask my students to complete the sentence, "The cat ate the _____," the most frequently supplied answers are rat, mouse, cheese, cat food, fish, and pizza. For some reason people often say *rat* first, perhaps because it rhymes with *cat*. You will notice that all of these items are things that are edible by cats, although some are more likely than others. You will also notice that each of these items is a noun.

Indeed, our experience with English grammar tells us that a noun is needed to fill this slot. We know we need a noun because the phrase begins with the definite article *the* and also that because of the verb *ate* (which is transitive in this case), we need a direct object. (Of course, various modifiers could precede the obligatory head noun. So we could have noun phrases like, "the terrified, writhing mouse" or "the pepperoni, black olive, and cheese pizza," but eventually a head noun would be necessary.) Furthermore, our experience of the world, and with cats in particular, tells us what things are likely to be eaten by cats.

At least two kinds of mental competence are invoked in filling in this blank. One is our **syntagmatic competence;** it tells us what part of speech is needed. (The word *syntagmatic* comes from *syntax*—having to do with the rules of word order.) The second is our **paradigmatic competence,** which tells us the semantic features required of the missing item. So in this case our syntagmatic competence tells us we need a noun, and our paradigmatic competence tells us that the noun must represent things that are edible by cats. Although my students sometimes humorously suggest "the cat ate the dog," they never fill in the blank with words like *freedom* or *very* or *alternate* or *go*. In fact, when they suggest that the cat ate the dog, the humor in this remark is based on manipulating our paradigmatic competence: We know that cats don't typically eat dogs and that's what makes the comment funny.

The use of syntagmatic and paradigmatic competence underlies many familiar language testing formats. These include fill-in items, cloze passages, and C-tests. An example of each of these formats is given below.

"FILL-IN" ITEMS

1. A fill-in item typically consists of only one _____.

2. Syntagmatic competence involves rules of _____ _____ order.

3. Paradigmatic competence involves _____ sets.

A traditional fill-in item typically consists of one sentence with one blank. The limited context provided by the sentence allows the test developer to focus the item on the one thing she wishes to assess. However, this **discrete-point approach** to designing language test items has been criticized because typically language is not used in such isolated bits. Normally, language is used in longer stretches and in context. (We will explore the concept of discrete-point testing in more detail in Chapter 6.)

One of the appeals of discrete-point testing is that items can be written that have one and only one correct answer. However, we need to carefully **pretest** such items (i.e., try them out with native speakers, proficient nonnative speakers, and/or with students like those whom we actually plan to test before the items are deployed in a real test, the results of which will be used for decision-making purposes). Even these three simple fill-in items are not as straightforward as they may seem. Would you mark the following responses as correct or incorrect?

Name: *Juan*

1. A fill-in item typically consists of only one *blank*.

2. Syntagmatic competence involves rules of *word* order.

3. Paradigmatic competence involves *semantic* sets.

Name: <u>Anna</u>

1. A fill-in item typically consists of only one <u>sentence</u>.

2. Syntagmatic competence involves rules of <u>syntactic</u> order.

3. Paradigmatic competence involves <u>lexical</u> sets.

To me, Juan's and Anna's responses seem equally correct. It is important, in creating open-ended fill-in items, to pretest the items before using them in an actual test. Pretesting language test items enables you to generate a key of possible correct answers, and it will also help you "debug" the items by identifying any ambiguities or problems they might contain.

CLOZE TESTS

In contrast to fill-in items, cloze passages consist of texts longer than a sentence—usually at least a paragraph in length. Here is an example of a cloze passage that talks about cloze passages. See if you can fill in each blank with one and only one word. A contraction counts as one word. (The intended answers are given in the "Investigations" section of this chapter.)

> Cloze tests consist of texts of at least one paragraph in length (usually longer). The first sentence is left intact, _____ thereafter every "nth" word is systematically _____ (every fifth, seventh, or ninth word), _____ the students' task is to write _____ appropriate and grammatical word in each _____. The ability to do so depends _____ the learners' syntagmatic competence and paradigmatic _____, as well as their discourse competence. _____ are usually thirty to fifty blanks _____ each cloze passage.
>
> Although originally devised _____ a test of first language reading _____, the cloze test is thought to _____ the general proficiency (in the written _____) of second language learners. The two _____ common scoring procedures are the "exact _____ method" and the "acceptable word method." _____ the latter is more generous to _____ (it yields higher scores), the two _____ systems yield similar rankings among the _____ of the test-takers.

Cloze tests have been widely used in language assessment, particularly for the assessment of reading skills and overall proficiency. But there are many potential pitfalls associated with their use and development, and teachers who use cloze tests must be aware of several issues.

One such issue is how to score learners' responses to cloze tests. If you are using a cloze passage as a teaching/learning device instead of as an assessment mechanism, then the question may be irrelevant. But if the cloze passage is to be scored, then we must determine the scoring criteria. There are two main ways to approach the scoring of a cloze test (although other methods have been devised; see Brown [1980]).

The first is called the **exact word method.** As the name suggests, with this scoring procedure the test-takers get credit for a correct answer if and only if the word they write in any given blank is the exact word that was deleted from the original text in that space. This approach to scoring a cloze test is very quick (and therefore practical). It is also highly reliable: A simple key based on the original text is provided by the test developer and the scorers do not deviate from the answers on that key, so there is no need for thought or discussion about possible correct answers (which would slow down the scoring process and might introduce variability into the answers accepted by the judges). If you use the exact word method it is even possible to create multiple-choice cloze passages, which have the advantage of being machine scorable.

However, the exact word method may seem too rigid, in the sense that it doesn't reward creativity on the part of the test-taker. I was once a member of a team of teachers who were scoring the ESL placement test at a large university. The teachers themselves all completed the cloze passage prior to scoring the students' tests. The passage was based on a text about how pearls are formed. One of the words that had been deleted was *nacre*. Do you know what *nacre* is? According to the dictionary it is the substance that creates mother-of-pearl. The other teachers and I certainly did not know this word, so as you can imagine, the scoring team thought it was unfair to require the ESL students to supply a missing word that none of the teachers (all well-educated, adult, native speakers of English) could supply, and a serious argument followed with the test designer about whether this item was fair.

The second major approach to scoring cloze passages is called the **acceptable word method.** In this procedure, any response that (a) is grammatically correct, and (b) makes good sense in the context is given full credit as an acceptable answer. The acceptable word method may promote positive washback, since it could encourage learners to use their pragmatic expectancy grammars creatively. However, it may slow down the scoring process, especially if you are evaluating a very large batch of cloze passages. It could also dampen the scoring reliability of the cloze test if different scorers don't communicate or can't agree about the acceptability of some of the words supplied by the test-takers.

In addition to choosing a scoring method, it is important to select or write a text of appropriate difficulty. If a text is too difficult for the test-takers to read easily without blanks, imagine how difficult it would be once the blanks are inserted! In fact, John Oller has suggested using cloze passages to predict students' frustration level with reading materials. Oller (1979, 353), citing Anderson (1971), states that when using the exact word method to score a cloze passage, a score of 53 percent or higher can be called the "independent level of reading." That is, the learner could have read the original text independently without much difficulty. A score falling between 44 percent and 53 percent can be considered the "instructional level," where the learner could benefit from guidance and supported practice with this text. A score lower than 44 percent indicates that the passage is probably at the "frustrational level" and would therefore be too difficult. As Oller points out, Anderson's work provided guidelines for native speakers attempting cloze passages, so you may find that these percentages need to be adjusted for nonnative readers.

The difficulty level of a cloze passage is determined by many variables. These include:

1. the length of the text as a whole;

2. the amount of time the learners are allowed to complete the task;

3. the learners' familiarity with the vocabulary and the syntactic structures in the passage;

4. the length and complexity of the sentences in the text;

5. the learners' familiarity with the topic and with the discourse genre of the text (note that this item embodies the concepts of *content schemata* and *formal schemata*); and

6. the frequency with which the blanks are spaced (every fifth word versus every ninth word, for instance).

All of these factors come into play in developing a suitable cloze passage for your students.

Once you have selected or written an appropriate passage, the next decision is how to create the blanks. In test construction jargon, the process of deleting words to create a cloze test is known as **mutilation.** (I'm not making this up.) Basically there are two widely used ways to mutilate a text. The first is known as **rational deletion,** in which the test developer deletes words on the basis of some rational decision. (This process is sometimes referred to as "selected deletion.") So, for example, if I wished to test my students' knowledge of verb tenses, I might delete only verbs. The second method is known as **fixed ratio deletion** or **nth word deletion,** which means that, regardless of its part of speech or the semantic load it bears within the text, every nth word is omitted (every fifth word or every seventh word or every ninth word, etc.) and a blank line is inserted in its place. The problem with the word *nacre* described above came about as a result of using strictly random nth word deletion to create the cloze passage.

Lyle Bachman did some interesting research on cloze tests, in which he compared two cloze passages developed from the same original text. One used a fixed ratio deletion pattern (every eleventh word) and the other used a rational deletion pattern. The tests were scored by the acceptable word method. He found that although the two resulting tests were equal in terms of reliability and validity, "the fixed ratio test was significantly more difficult" (1985, 535) for the students who took it.

Bachman addressed an interesting problem related to the validity of cloze tests. He wanted to figure out exactly what it is that they measure. Here's how he categorized the various kinds of language processing it requires to fill in any given blank in a cloze passage:

Type 1: information located within the clause;

Type 2: information spread across clauses but within a single sentence;

Type 3: information distributed across sentences but within the text; and

Type 4: extra-textual information.

Bachman found that using the eleventh word fixed ratio deletion pattern created a cloze passage in which Type 1 and Type 4 blanks predominated (37 percent and 53 percent, respectively). This finding called into question whether cloze tests actually measure discourse level processing (as represented by Type 2 and particularly Type 3, above). He is careful to point out, however, that more research (with more cloze passages based on different texts) is needed in this area.

Given Bachman's concern, what are our alternatives? Researchers working in Europe have experimented with a test format based on the principle of closure that involves deleting parts of words instead of entire words. This format is known as the C-test. An example is given below. (The key is printed in the "Investigations" section of this chapter.)

C-TESTS

A C-test is a type of language test in which the students read a brief paragraph in the target language. The first two sentences are left intact. There_ _ _ _ _, every ot_ _ _ word i_ printed int_ _ _, but f_ _ each alte_ _ _ _ _ word, on_ _ the fi_ _ _ half o_ the wo_ _ is wri_ _ _ _, and t_ _ second ha_ _ is indi_ _ _ _ _ by a bl_ _ _ space repres_ _ _ _ _ _ each let_ _ _. T_ _ students' abi_ _ _ _ to fi_ _ in t_ _ blank spa_ _ _ is tho_ _ _ _ to b_ a mea_ _ _ _ of th_ _ _ language profi_ _ _ _ _ _.

As you can see, the individual letters of every other word have been replaced by blanks. This approach to text mutilation is referred to as "the rule of two." That is, starting with the second sentence of the text, the second half of every second word is deleted (Klein-Braley and Raatz, 1984, 136). In words having an odd number of letters, there are more blanks given than letters (e.g., *thought* is represented as tho_ _ _ _), but you could alter this pattern to meet your students' needs.

M y friend Tim Hacker gained experience with C-tests when he taught future English teachers for the Peace Corps in Sri Lanka. Here is his comment about the context in which he used C-tests:

Teachers'
Voices

> In the mid-80s the Sri Lankan Ministry of Education authorized new curricula for English language instruction. Exams for these new curricula were designed by experts from the British Council. They wanted instruments that would assess proficiency rather than achievement, and they wanted them to be "cutting edge." So they included C-tests, which were brand new at the time.

My students' reaction to C-tests was the same as to all of the proficiency tests: They hated them. They were used to studying specific content in order to prepare for a test on that content, which they could no longer do. They were angry, frustrated, and fearful of not passing the course—on which their future livelihood as teachers was staked.

Tim used passages in which the cultural content would be familiar to his students, even though the text was written in English. Printed below is a C-test that Tim developed to use with his Sri Lankan students, which is based on a text by Keuneman, a native speaker of Sri Lankan English (1983, 158). The diagonal lines indicate that a word consisting of only one letter is needed. (Apostrophes do not take up a space.)

A short distance before the highway enters Kegalle, a road
leads north toward Pinawella. Here a government supported
elephant orphanage is located on the banks of the Maha Oya.
Some fif_ _ _ _ elephants, mo_ _ of th_ _ babies le_ _ than
/_ / year o_ _ , are rai_ _ _ to matu_ _ _ _ after hav_ _ _ been
fo_ _ _ abandoned o_ injured i_ the coun_ _ _ _ jungles.
Th_ _ are tra_ _ _ _ to wo_ _ and event_ _ _ _ _ are so_ _
to comp_ _ _ _ _ or tem_ _ _ _. It is most interesting to visit
at feeding or bathing time.

(The key to this C-test is printed in the "Investigations" section of this chapter.)

Since the learners' response in a C-test only involves supplying the missing half of every other word, you may think this procedure is quite mechanical in nature. However, based on his experience in Sri Lanka, Tim felt that C-tests make excellent *teaching* devices because they provoke creative reasoning among the students:

When students are asked to complete C-tests as pair or group work, it creates an amazingly communicative activity, with focus on language itself as content. I can clearly remember exchanges between students such as, "No, that's not enough letters; we need an adverb [as opposed to an adjective] here."

While Tim was completing his master's degree in TESOL, he reviewed some of the research that had been conducted on C-tests. He noted that the proponents of C-tests believe that an adult educated native speaker should attain a perfect score on *any* given C-test. Tim raised an important concern, however:

Isn't some control in selection over content or the appearance of proper nouns necessary for this to be true? Also, while the feasibility of exact word scoring is greatly improved over that for the cloze procedure, there are occasions when more than one response is appropriate for a given deletion in a C-test.

Indeed, the traditional scoring method for C-tests is very precise. If a letter is wrong, or if the test-taker writes more or fewer letters than are called for, the item is marked as incorrect.

Here is another example of a C-test that Tim developed from another text about Sri Lanka (also from Keuneman, 1983, 288). See if you can fill in the missing letters. As before, each small blank line indicates that a single letter must be supplied in that space. As you respond to Tim's C-test, try to be aware of your own mental work: By what psycholinguistic processes do you make decisions about what the missing letters should be? I think you will find that (unless you are familiar with Sri Lankan culture) the cultural content makes this text quite challenging.

> An architectural feature that is basically a mass of fine sculpture is the Sinhalese staircase. It includes an intricately decorated flight of steps flanked by ornate balustrades with a frontal stand formed by a pair of guardstones.

> (1) The elabo_ _ _ _ moonstone a_ its ba_ _ is i_ itself /_ / distinctive ele_ _ _ _ of anc_ _ _ _ sculpture i_ the isl_ _ _ . (2) These se_ _ -circular sto_ _ _ acquired increa_ _ _ _ _ _ complex ba_ _ _ of decor_ _ _ _ _ over t_ _ years. (3) Th_ _ range fr_ _ the abst_ _ _ _ —tongues o_ fire a_ _ bands o_ creeper vi_ _ _ _—to symb_ _ _ _ interpretations o_ the fo_ _ perils o_ life. (4) T_ _ latter con _ _ _ _ of t_ _ elephant, /_ / symbol o_ birth; t_ _ bull, indic_ _ _ _ _ of de_ _ _ ; the li_ _ representing dis_ _ _ _; and t_ _ horse, /_ / symbol o_ death. (5) So_ _ also ha_ _ a ba_ _ of ge_ _ _, which repre_ _ _ _ _ the disti_ _ _ _ _ _ between go_ _ and ev_ _ . (6) At t_ _ heart o_ many moons_ _ _ _ _ is /_ / lotus pe_ _ _ . (7) Buddhists reg_ _ _ the lo_ _ _ as /_ / sacred flo_ _ _ , and i_ the moon_ _ _ _ _ it repre_ _ _ _ _ the cen_ _ _ crowning se_ _ of suc_ _ _ _.

> The total effect, then, of mounting the stairs begins with the devotee at the lotus, his back to the world, preparing to ascend to the shrine of wisdom and insight.

Notice how your own background knowledge (or lack thereof) may influence your ability to complete this C-test. (The intended answers are printed in the "Investigations" section of this chapter.) I myself find this passage very difficult to complete with confidence. I have used it often over the years, with Tim's permission, to illustrate to my graduate students—native and nonnative speakers alike—how much our content schemata influence our ability to process texts.

I do find C-tests to be useful on several levels, however, both as teaching and testing devices in English, because so many of the grammatical morphemes load at the end of words in English (e.g., plurals, tense markers, aspect markers, etc.). In addition, C-tests seem to force discourse-level processing. For instance, you may have decided, in completing the C-test above, that the second sentence begins with "These semi-circular *stones* acquired . . ." because you realized that the topic and grammatical subject of the preceding sentence was *moonstones*. Likewise, many people initially complete the fourth sentence by writing "The latter consist of the elephant, a symbol of birth; the bull, indicative of *death*, . . ." (perhaps by association with *birth* in the previous phrase). But then a little further in the same sentence we come to the phrase, "and the horse, a symbol of *death*." At this point we realize it would be unlikely that both the bull and the horse would be symbols of death, given the listing structure of the paragraph (and this insight is motivated in part by our formal schemata). It is a given that the horse symbolizes death, since the word *death* is printed in its entirety in that clause. So here we are forced to reconsider our options for filling the blanks in the clause, "the bull, indicative of de _ _ _." Tim comments:

> This is what caught my eye too, way back when! My students
> needed the decay/death distinction pointed out to them.

Tim felt that since C-tests were on the exams his students would face, it was important to familiarize them with the format (another example of washback in action):

> So every week we did C-tests in class, and we'd have a practice exam
> every Saturday afternoon, too. By the time of the final exam, the
> students were very comfortable with the technique and felt confident
> about their performance. I don't believe we ever were told their spe-
> cific scores, but they all passed and went on to become teachers.

> Familiarity with the C-test procedure helped them a lot. This, I
> think, is not what the developers of C-tests would have anticipated;
> they expected that proficiency alone, not familiarity, would deter-
> mine success!

Tim found that one way to manipulate the difficulty of C-tests for his stu-dents was to alter the stimulus material as follows:

> Once the C-test procedure is established, I like to crank up the dif-
> ficulty by providing one continuous blank for each deletion—that
> way, the students must decide how many letters to provide. At first
> students may need the support of specific numbers of letters to sup-
> ply (e.g. "Popeye li_ _ _ spinach"), to help them see that we must
> have an "-s" or a "-d" at the end of the verb. Eventually, however,
> they should be able to do this themselves.

Tim has some words of advice for teachers who may not have used the C-test format before:

> Usually, the exact word is the only acceptable word in C-tests. But
> teachers and testers should not assume that's *always* the case. They
> should read each student's responses carefully to make sure that
> "erroneous" responses are not in fact "acceptable" ones.

> And teachers should check and double-check their work to make
> sure they have followed the rule of two and provided the right
> number of blanks. Developing a C-test passage so that it's correct is
> much harder than anyone who hasn't done it can imagine!

Tim points out, however, that once you have developed some C-tests, they are easy to administer and score, so in that regard, they meet the criterion of practicality. For Tim, though, the main value of C-tests is their use in promot-ing consciousness-raising and metalinguistic awareness among his students (Hacker, 1991).

I teach English composition mostly now, but I continue to teach ESL classes in the summers, and an occasional section of composition for international students. In these I still use C-tests as a teaching—not as a testing—technique. Done in pairs or groups of three, they are remarkably communicative and metalinguistic activities.

To summarize then, fill-in items, cloze passages, and C-tests all use the mind's capacity to restore incomplete texts, based on our pragmatic expectancy grammar. If you try using any of these formats with your students, it is important to pretest the items thoroughly, to develop the stimulus material carefully, to analyze the resulting items so you are sure about what you are measuring, and to select the scoring criteria that are appropriate for the teaching and learning context.

---

1 *Here are the intended keys to the cloze test and the first C-test printed in this chapter. It may be interesting for you to compare your own answers with the keys, and with the answers supplied by your colleagues or classmates:*

Investigations

Cloze tests consist of texts of at least one paragraph in length (usually longer). The first sentence is left intact, *but* thereafter every "nth" word is systematically *deleted* (every fifth, seventh, or ninth word), *and* the students' task is to write *an* appropriate and grammatical word in each *blank*. The ability to do so depends *on* the learners' syntagmatic competence and paradigmatic *competence*, as well as their discourse competence. *There* are usually thirty to fifty blanks *in* each cloze passage.

Although originally devised *as* a test of first language reading *ability*, the cloze test is thought to *assess* the general proficiency (in the written *mode*) of second language learners. The two *most* common scoring procedures are the "exact *word* method" and the "acceptable word method." *Although* the latter is more generous to *learners* (it yields higher scores), the two *scoring* systems yield similar rankings among the *scores* of the test-takers.

With the cloze passage it is highly likely that you wrote words other than those intended in at least some of the blanks. Some blanks will have many alternatives, while others will have very few. See if you can generate a definitive and complete list of acceptable words to be used to score this cloze passage using the acceptable word scoring method. On the cloze test, how would your score differ if your responses were evaluated with the acceptable word scoring method, as opposed to the exact word scoring method?

A C-test is a type of language test in which the students read a brief paragraph in the target language. The first two sentences are left intact. There*after*, every ot*her* word i*s* printed int*act*, but *for* each alter*nate* word, on*ly* the fi*rst* half o*f* the wo*rd* is wri*tten*, and th*e* second half is indicated by a blank space representing each letter. The students' ability to fill in the blank spaces is thought to be a measure of their language proficiency.

As Tim Hacker pointed out, usually the exact word is the only acceptable word in a C-test. Did you find any possible alternatives in completing this C-test?

---

2 *On the C-tests based on elements of Sri Lankan culture, were the items you found to be difficult the same ones your colleagues or classmates considered challenging? You may find it interesting to introspect with your colleagues about the source(s) of the difficulty you experienced. Here are the keys to these two C-tests:*

> A short distance before the highway enters Kegalle, a road leads north toward Pinawella. Here a government supported elephant orphanage is located on the banks of the Maha Oya. Some fifteen elephants, most of them babies less than / a / year old, are raised to maturity after having been found abandoned or injured in the country's jungles. They are trained to work and eventually are sold to companies or temples. It is most interesting to visit at feeding or bathing time.

For many people who have not lived or traveled in areas of the world where there are elephants, it is difficult to complete the words "companies" and "temples." I personally find the C-test about the Sinhalese staircase quite difficult, in part because it doesn't match my existing content schemata. Compare your answers to the following key, which is based on the original (Keuneman, 1983, 288).

> An architectural feature that is basically a mass of fine sculpture is the Sinhalese staircase. It includes an intricately decorated flight of steps flanked by ornate balustrades with a frontal stand formed by a pair of guardstones.
>
> (1) The elaborate moonstone at its base is in itself / a / distinctive element of ancient sculpture in the island. (2) These semi-circular stones acquired increasingly complex bands of decoration over the years. (3) They range from the abstract—tongues of fire and bands of creeper vines—to symbolic interpretations of the four perils of life. (4) The latter consist of the elephant, / a / symbol of birth; the bull, indicative of decay; the lion representing disease; and the horse, / a / symbol of death. (5) Some also have a band of geese, which represents the distinction between good and evil. (6) At the heart of many moonstones is / a / lotus petal. (7) Buddhists regard the lotus as / a / sacred flower, and in the moonstone it represents the center crowning seat of success.

The total effect, then, of mounting the stairs begins with the devotee at the lotus, his back to the world, preparing to ascend to the shrine of wisdom and insight.

We saw above the two C-tests developed by Tim Hacker for and about the Sri Lankan context. Most people who take these tests find the passage about the baby elephants to be easier than the one about the Sinhalese staircase. Do you agree?

Try completing these C-tests yourself, or better yet, have a friend take them for you. Ask him to introspect out loud while you record the verbalizations of his thought processes. If you were to transcribe what your friend said as he filled in the missing letters of the C-test, the resulting transcript would be called a **think-aloud protocol.** (A protocol is something written down—in this case, your friend's thoughts as he completes the C-test task.) Think-aloud protocols provide data on what is going on in the minds of learners, including test-takers. Andrew Cohen (1984) conducted an interesting study along these lines. He used verbal self-report data from university students in Israel to get information about their reactions to various item types and about their test-taking strategies.

For more information about think-aloud protocols, see David Nunan's book, *Understanding Language Classrooms: A Guide for Teacher-initiated Action* (1989). Pages 62–70 are directly related to this topic, and pages 91–92 give an example.

---

3 *You can create a cloze passage, following the procedures described in the "Frameworks" section above. Use either n^th word or rational word deletion. Try to get some language learners to take your cloze test. Or ask some of your friends if they would take it for you. (For the purposes of pretesting, they should be native speakers of, or proficient in, the language of the cloze test.)*

When you have gotten responses from four or five people, score the cloze passages using first the exact-word scoring method and then the acceptable word scoring method. To do this you must generate a list of acceptable words for each blank in the cloze passage. Some blanks will have one and only one permissible word which is grammatical and makes sense in the context. Other blanks (typically those where nouns, verbs, adjectives, and some adverbs have been deleted) may have numerous acceptable words. It is possible that the people who complete the cloze passage for you may come up with plausible responses that you yourself didn't think of in compiling your list of possible alternatives. These need to be added to the list of acceptable words.

---

4 *After you have finished scoring your cloze passage with both the exact word and the acceptable word scoring methods, assign each test-taker an identification number (where "S" stands for student or subject). Tally your results in the following format:*

Student identification number	Exact word score	Acceptable word score
S1		
S2		
S3		
S4		
etc.		

I think you will find in every case that the acceptable word score is higher than the exact word score for that same student (unless the person gets a perfect score). But is the rank ordering the same? That is, if you list the students from best to worst in terms of their cloze test scores, is the order of the list the same for both the exact word and the acceptable word scoring methods? For example, if you have six people take the cloze passage, you might find that your data look something like this:

	Exact word score	Acceptable word score
Highest Score	S1	S6
	S6	S3
	S5	S1
	S2	S4
	S3	S5
Lowest Score	S4	S2

These data (both the actual scores and your rank ordered list) will be useful for an investigative task in Chapter 8, when we study the correlation family.

---

5 *Think about these two different scoring methods in terms of the four traditional criteria for evaluating tests: reliability, validity, practicality, and positive washback. How do the two scoring procedures compare? Enter a plus (+), a check (√), or a minus (–) in the boxes in the chart below to reflect your thinking. A plus indicates that the scoring method rates high on that criterion; a check indicates a moderate performance on that criterion; a minus indicates that the scoring method falls short (or even exerts a negative influence) in terms of that criterion.*

	Exact word scoring method	Acceptable word scoring method
Reliability		
Validity		
Practicality		
Positive washback		

In thinking about these two scoring methods, I evaluated them as follows:

	Exact word scoring method	Acceptable word scoring method
Reliability	+	√
Validity	?	?
Practicality	+	√ / −
Positive washback	√ / −	+

Do you see why I assigned these values? To me it seems that the exact word scoring method may be considered superior to the acceptable word scoring method in terms of reliability and practicality because there is only one correct answer per blank. This fact should eliminate judgment calls on the part of the scorers and cut down on the time needed to mark the cloze tests. However, I believe the acceptable word scoring method is superior to the exact word procedure in terms of washback because it should promote creativity and risk-taking among the language learners. J. D. Brown puts this point even more strongly (1980, 316):

> Perhaps the best reason of all for taking the trouble to use the AC [acceptable word] method is that it appears much fairer than the EX [exact word] method to the students themselves. There is something inherently repugnant about counting an answer wrong, which is actually correct, simply because the author of the original passage did not choose to use that word; yet, precisely that often happens when the EX method is used.

For me the issue of the cloze format's validity is still an open question that depends on many factors, including the scoring method. Clearly the cloze procedure is in large part a measure of reading skills because the stimulus material is presented to the learners receptively and in the written mode. But depending on which words have been deleted, it may be a test of grammar, of vocabulary, of discourse-level processing, or of general proficiency. If you use cloze tests, it is up to you as the teacher/test developer to decide what you wish to assess, how the passage will be mutilated, and how the learner's responses will be scored.

6 *Here's another idea that might be an interesting investigation. Try using the same text as the basis for both a cloze passage and a C-test. If you can get a group of students (or friends) to help you, have half of them take the C-test first while half of them complete the cloze passage. Some time after you have collected their responses to the first test they take (whichever it may be), give each person the form of the test he or she has not yet taken. Thus the design of your test distribution will look like this:*

	Group 1	Group 2
First task	C-test	Cloze passage
Second task	Cloze passage	C-test

It would be ideal if there could be a time lapse of several days between the first and second tasks, since the two test formats are based on the same text. If test-takers repeat a test or take two very similar tests within a short period of time, the results on the second test may be influenced by what's known as the **practice effect.** That is, the experience of taking the first test may have provided the learners with practice that boosted their scores on the second test. Their language proficiency has probably not improved, but due to practice, their ability to take this test (or this kind of test) will have been enhanced. By altering the ordering of administration (as in the box above) we guard against this possibility to a certain extent. Using this design is called **counterbalancing for an ordering effect.**

After you have scored the two tests, compare each person's answers on the cloze test with his or her answers on the C-test. Do the two procedures yield similar scores? Do they seem to be measuring the same thing? (If you do try out this task, save your data. They will also be useful when we get to Chapter 8, about correlation.)

Finally, ask some of your test-takers to describe the experience of taking these two types of tests. Did the mental processes involved seem to be the same or different? Did they prefer the C-test over the cloze passage, or vice versa? Again, it would be interesting to develop think-aloud protocols as part of the contrast.

Suggested Readings

I recommend the research articles I referred to in this chapter. Lyle Bachman's (1985) paper about fixed ratio versus the rational deletion approach to creating cloze passages raises important questions about what cloze passages measure. John Jonz (1990) conducted an interesting follow-up study that built upon Bachman's research. Hughes (1989) offers examples of both C-tests and cloze passages. And J. D. Brown's (1980) comparison of four different methods for scoring cloze passages is a very readable analysis with clear practical implications for deciding on scoring criteria.

One question that is sometimes raised is how C-tests would work with languages that are not written from left to right, or with students whose first language uses a written ordering other than left to right. Christopher Cleary (1988) conducted an interesting study with native speakers of Arabic, in which he used left-hand deletions instead of right-hand deletions.

There is now available a bibliography of research on C-tests (Grotjahn, 1996). A review of the research literature up to the early 1980s is found in Klein-Braley and Raatz (1984).

Lyle Bachman's book, *Fundamental Considerations in Language Testing* (1990), includes a very interesting summary of the research on the relationship between language test performance and various cognitive styles (275–276). One of the most frequently studied cognitive styles is field independence: "the extent to which a person perceives part of a field as discrete from the surrounding field as a whole, rather than embedded, or . . . the extent to which a person perceives analytically" (Witkin, Moore, Goodenough, and Cox, 1977, 7). A number of studies have found that performance on cloze tests is related to field independence. One way to interpret this finding is to raise the concern that learners who are not field independent may be at a disadvantage in taking cloze tests.

Roberta Abraham and Carole Chapelle (1992) conducted a study in which they investigated the relationship between the type of words deleted in cloze tests and the difficulty of each item. (The notion of item difficulty will make more sense after you read Chapter 9.)

Susie Llewelyn (1990) did an interesting study of the language used by her adult ESL students in Australia as they tried to complete cloze passages in a groupwork format. Her article includes the cloze passages she used, as well as a very clear analysis of her students' negotiations as they tried to fill in the blanks.

6

ANOTHER DILEMMA: CONTRASTING PAIRS OF CONCEPTS

I wish I could create a written test which shows how well my pupils can use their English and not just how well they have learned grammar and vocabulary. I really dislike objective-style tests like multiple-choice ones, because they are not creative enough. I'd rather give my pupils a test where they can use their English. If I do that, however, I'm left with the problem of marking them objectively and justifying the marks I give to my pupils' parents and my colleagues. Is there a way to test students which is both creative and safe? ("Alma's Letter," from Kenny and Tsai, 1993, 16–17.)

Questions of which skills to assess and how to test students' skills invariably lead us to a number of apparent contradictions in assessment. One major concern for teachers (like Alma) who must design classroom assessment procedures is whether they should test students' knowledge of components of language, or their abilities to use the language in context. Another is what kind of items to write, and a third is how to score the students' performances.

In the Frameworks section of this chapter we will examine three contrasting pairs of concepts that are important in the design and evaluation of language tests. These are (1) direct and indirect testing, (2) discrete-point and integrative testing, and (3) objective and subjective scoring. (These pairs of concepts can best be viewed as the ends of continua, rather than as separate and distinct categories.) In the Teacher's Voice section we will see how one teacher investigated these issues in order to improve the assessment procedures at her school.

The part of Alma's letter quoted above aptly summarizes one of the dilemmas facing language teachers and test designers. The problem of whether to assess grammar, vocabulary and other enabling skills, or to assess students' ability to use the language itself, is captured in the contrast between direct testing and indirect testing. Some people think of these concepts as a dichotomy; others see them as a continuum. But what do the terms mean?

DIRECT AND INDIRECT TESTS

Direct tests are those in which the learner's response involves actually doing the skill being assessed. The concept of direct testing is more commonly associated with the productive skills than with the receptive skills because in assessing the productive skills there is an observable output (the students' speech or writing samples) that we can hear or see. So, for instance, in a direct test of speaking, the language learner would actually speak in the target language to communicate his or her ideas. A direct test of writing would involve the test-taker in some original composing task.

It may seem odd to you that there might be a use for anything other than direct tests, but in some circumstances, for various reasons, people have chosen to assess the hypothesized components, or enabling skills, underlying the macro skills. (For example, trying to assess the enabling skills is not uncommon in diagnostic testing, since a tight focus on the components of language is thought to provide teachers with the information needed to plan instruction.) When we devise procedures designed to tap into the enabling skills underpinning the macro skills, the resulting assessment devices are said to be **indirect tests** of the skill in question. For instance, if we believe that knowledge of the grammatical structures of a particular language contributes to the ability to write in that language, then we might use a grammar test as an indirect test of writing. (The "Structure and Written Expression" section of the *Test of English as a Foreign Language* [*TOEFL*] is an example.) Likewise, because pronunciation is thought to be a component of speaking, phonemic distinction tasks are sometimes interpreted as very indirect tests of speaking ability.

Of course, you can see that there are problems with these assumptions. Someone who is good at selecting the correct response on multiple-choice grammar items might not be an effective writer. Someone who could correctly distinguish between *ship* and *sheep* on a phonemic distinction test might not be able to carry on a conversation effectively. This is a question of validity: Can a very indirect test really provide valid assessment of the skill it is intended to measure?

Another problem with indirect tests is that they may result in negative washback. For instance, if learners spend time studying bits of decontextualized grammar in preparation for an indirect test of writing, they may spend less time actually writing in the target language.

DISCRETE-POINT AND INTEGRATIVE TESTING

So why do people use indirect measures at all? Well, it's partly because many indirect tests are discrete-point in focus, and for many years discrete-point testing was thought to be the fairest, most objective, and most precise way to evaluate language skills. In **discrete-point testing,** each item on a test is intended to measure one and only one linguistic element. So, for example, the phonemic distinction test mentioned above would be considered discrete-point in nature. Let's analyze the item using Wesche's (1983) framework, which was introduced in Chapter 2:

1. **Stimulus material:** The test-taker hears a single word, *ship,* spoken aloud. His test booklet contains a picture of a ship and a picture of a sheep.

2. **Task posed to the learner:** The test-taker must discriminate between the phonemes /I/ and /i/ and associate the sound she hears with the correct picture.

3. **Learner's response:** The test-taker must circle or check the picture representing the word he heard (i.e., the word that contains the specific phoneme produced in the aural stimulus material).

4. **Scoring criteria:** The test-taker's response to the item is marked either correct or incorrect on the basis of a preestablished key set by the test designer.

The item above is very clearly a discrete-point item, but there are problems with it. For instance, because there are only two answer options (as represented by the two pictures), the test-taker has a 50 percent chance of getting the item right just by guessing, whether or not she can perceive the difference between /I/ and /i/, and whether or not she associates the meaning of the spoken word with the concept conveyed by either of the two pictures.

Suppose we want to change this to a four-option multiple-choice item, in order to decrease students' chances of guessing the answers. In that case we could change the visual stimulus material from pictures to printed words. The test-taker would still hear the aural stimulus material, the word *ship* spoken aloud. But now the learner's response would be to circle or check the correct answer from among the four options listed below:

    a. chip   b. ship   c. cheap   d. sheep

So now the test-taker only has a 25 percent chance of guessing the correct answer, but what has become of our "pure" discrete-point item? Notice that it has been altered in two ways:

1. Now, in addition to the aural discrimination task, the test-taker must also read in the target language (although only four words) to complete this item successfully. Thus, we may be assessing his reading skill as well as his aural discrimination.

2. In terms of the written options, we have now introduced the /š/ versus /č/ distinction in addition to the /I/ versus /i/ distinction. In other words, instead of testing the learner's ability to distinguish between two phonemes, we are now asking him to distinguish among the possible combinations of two pairs of phonemes.

By now it should be apparent that it is very difficult to write a pure discrete-point item—that is, an item that measures one and only one linguistic element. In fact, the concept of discrete-point testing can be located at one end of a continuum. Its conceptual opposite is referred to as integrative testing. As the term suggests, **integrative testing** involves one or more levels of language (phonology, morphology, lexicon, syntax, or discourse) and/or one or more skills (reading, writing, speaking, and listening). So, to return to our example of the dictation family described in Chapter 2, you can see that dictation is a classic example of an integrative test. Why? Think about the things a learner must do when taking a dictation. Here is a (partial) list of the mental tasks involved:

1. process the meaning of individual words and structures in the auditory mode;

2. distinguish between contrasting phonemes;

3. listen to the entire text and to the bursts;

4. discern the meaning and structure of the overall text;

5. retain the bursts in active memory long enough to write them verbatim;

6. write what is retained (depending on the scoring criteria, this might also include responsibilities for spelling correctly and adding punctuation); and

7. read the rewritten text in order to self-check.

In other words, many psycholinguistic processes are involved in the attempt to complete a standard dictation or other integrative test. (In terms of Figure 1.2 in Chapter 1, several different hierarchical components and/or macroskills are involved in integrative tests.)

OBJECTIVE AND SUBJECTIVE SCORING

There are some advantages to discrete-point testing. Because discrete-point items are typically written to have one clearly correct answer, they can be easily scored using an established answer key. Many of them are written in a multiple-choice format, which is machine scorable. Either way, the preset scoring criterion is *right* or *wrong,* so no judgment is involved on the part of the scorer. (Note, however, that considerable judgment was probably involved on the part of the test developer!) This makes discrete-point tests appear to be very practical to administer and score, and you will recall that practicality is one of the four traditional criteria used for evaluating tests.

And because the scoring of discrete-point multiple-choice tests is objective, it would appear that such tests are reliable. This is true, up to a point. Indeed, **objectively scored** tests, by eliminating the subjectivity involved in rater judgments, reduce the possibility of unreliability of the sort introduced via the scoring process. In other words, with an objectively scored test it is unlikely that the raters will be inconsistent (although it is certainly possible for scorers to make mistakes even if they are using a perfect key). There are, however, other issues related to reliability that are not addressed simply by using an objectively scorable format.

Another reason why people seem to cling to the objective scoring appeal of discrete-point testing is that, historically, there has been some concern that integrative tests would result in subjective and/or unreliable scoring. Formerly, this was especially the case with direct tests of speaking and writing, which were **subjectively scored** (i.e., by raters making value judgments about the texts produced by the test-takers). Indeed, this is the dilemma that was captured in Alma's letter, quoted at the beginning of this chapter, when she talked about the problem of marking direct tests objectively and justifying the marks afterward. These days, however, written level descriptors and highly codified procedures of rater training have been developed to insure reliability in rating the learners' responses in direct tests of writing and speaking. (We will return to this issue in Chapters 11 and 12.)

To summarize, this section has introduced three contrasting pairs of concepts:

1. indirect versus direct tests;

2. discrete-point versus integrative testing; and

3. objective versus subjective scoring.

It is important to keep these constructs separate in our minds, even though there are likely groupings among them. For example, it is common for indirect tests to consist of discrete-point items that are objectively scored. Likewise, direct tests are typically integrative in format and often involve subjective scoring. But neither of these situations is universally the case, and understanding the differences among these three pairs of constructs can help teachers, both as consumers of language test information and as developers and interpreters of our own assessment procedures, to get better results for our efforts.

The "Teacher's Voice" section below shows how one teacher tried to investigate the relationship between an indirect and a direct test (using discrete-point and integrative formats, respectively), comparing subjective and objective scoring methods. The section includes the teacher's own comments and her original test of writing, as well as my interpretations and additional explanations throughout the section.

Christine Houba, an English teacher who had worked at a language school in Japan, was curious about the components of her school's placement test. The only writing section of the existing placement test involved an editing task. In an editing task, test-takers must identify the portion of a text that contains an error. The stimulus material in an editing task may be presented at the sentence level or at the discourse level, as exemplified by items (1) and (2), respectively.

1. When Jonathan finished studying, <u>he decided</u> to relax <u>for a while</u> by
A   B

    <u>listen to music</u> <u>as he cleaned</u> his apartment.
C   D

2. The first thing she noticed was <u>that the morning was crisp and cool</u>.
A

    Mai-ling stretched and sniffed the air with delight upon hearing
    <u>her mother worked</u> in the kitchen. She <u>had long awaited</u> this special
B   C

    day, and finally <u>it had come</u>.
D

Regardless of whether the stimulus material is sentential or discoursal in length and type, the task posed to the learner in a multiple-choice editing task is to read the sentence or passage and decide which of the underlined portions of the text (typically labeled A, B, C, or D) is incorrect. The learner's response then is usually to circle the letter of his or her choice or mark the appropriate blank on an answer sheet. The scoring criteria, *correct* versus *incorrect* in this case, are determined in advance (via both judgment and pretesting) by the teacher or the test developer.

The assumption underlying an editing task as an indirect test of writing is that if a learner can correctly identify errors in the stimulus material, he or she can detect and correct errors in his or her own writing. This is an interesting hypothesis and one that bears investigation. It is by no means a well-established fact.

Christine decided to investigate this problem, so she created a two-part test that included both a direct test of writing and an editing task made up of twelve sentences that embodied errors typically made by her Japanese students of English. Here is what she wrote to frame her investigation (Houba, 1996, 1):

> In his discussion on testing writing, Hughes (1989, 75) writes, "Even professional testing institutions are unable to construct indirect tests which measure writing accurately." If this is true, then what is it that indirect tests of writing, such as editing tasks, actually measure? What is the relationship between what indirect tests measure and what direct tests measure? Is there any relationship at all? In an attempt to investigate this issue, I constructed a two-part test, with an editing section and an essay writing section. The resulting scores were correlated to show what kind of relationship exists between the two tests.

We will study correlation in some detail in Chapter 8. At this point, suffice it to say that Christine used a statistical procedure that allowed her to systematically investigate a classic problem in language assessment: the relationship between two different ways of measuring the same construct. Christine's question parallels Alma's in a way: To what extent can we use the scores on an indirect test, such as an editing task, to evaluate students' abilities to use a macroskill, such as writing? The following is Christine's description of her test. (Page numbers from her paper are given in the parentheses after each quotation.)

> On the editing task, students were asked to circle the letter of the underlined portion of each sentence that contained a grammatical error. On the essay test, students were asked to use the lines provided (about one page) to write an essay in response to one of the three prompts.

> The test was created for students at an English school in Japan. Students at the school are adults, primarily working people and university students. The test was administered, for pilot testing purposes, by a faculty member on the school premises. Sixteen students sat for the test, which was given in a single administration.

> The editing task consists of twelve items, each worth one point. Students were given ten minutes to complete this portion of the test. The editing section was scored objectively (pp. 2–3).

Although this description is clear, you may understand Christine's investigation better if you examine (and even take) her editing task. It is reprinted below, beneath the instructions to the students:

For each sentence in this section, there is one underlined portion that is grammatically incorrect. Draw a circle around the incorrect portion, making sure that you only circle one underlined portion per sentence.

Example: Keiko probably prefers skiing <u>than</u> hiking, <u>but</u> she
                                   A   B

<u>came hiking</u> with us <u>anyway</u>.   ◯
   C   B

The correct sentence would be, "Keiko probably prefers skiing to hiking, but she came with us anyway." This is why a circle has been drawn around part A.

You will have 10 minutes to complete this part of the test.

Now begin (p. 23).

After reading these instructions as they were read aloud, the students received a printed page containing the following twelve items (pp. 23–25):

1. She <u>used to marry</u> a rich man, but they <u>got divorced</u> about five
            A   B
   years <u>ago</u>, and now she's <u>engaged to</u> a bus driver
       C   D

2. Some famous people will admit that they <u>are</u> a serious disease such as
                                              A
   AIDS <u>or</u> Alzheimers', but <u>others</u> probably want to keep <u>it</u> a secret.
      B   C   D

3. <u>If you just</u> think about your <u>past problems</u>, you will be
     A   B
   <u>a negative person</u> and you won't be able to enjoy <u>rest of life</u>.
        C   D

4. <u>At that time</u>, <u>most of French</u> in North America were hunters and
     A   B
   trappers, so they moved <u>from place to place</u> <u>in search of</u> animals.
                       C   D

5. Sherlock Holmes is <u>a detective who</u> is only interested in <u>the facts</u>, and
                        A   B
   works hard <u>for finding</u> a clue, like footprints <u>on the stairs</u>.
         C   D

6. The thing <u>that</u> he <u>had not understood</u> was that being a good friend
             A   B
   <u>is</u> not always <u>same as</u> saying nice things.
   C   D

7. They <u>were scheduled to</u> take a trip to <u>the Philippines</u> last January,
          A   B
   but he <u>met an accident</u> <u>in December</u>.
          C   D

8. In order to join <u>the</u> Entrepreneur Association, you have to be
               A
   <u>the inventor</u> of <u>the new business</u>, and be <u>successful at it</u>.

           B   C   D

9. "Fiction" means stories that <u>people creates</u>, and there is <u>a limit to</u>
                                 A   B
   <u>human imagination</u>, so truth is always <u>stranger than</u> fiction.
       C   D

10. He wants to have as much fun <u>as he can</u> while he's still a student,
                                     A
   because <u>after he graduates</u> he will have to spend <u>most of</u> his time
                     B   C
   <u>to work</u>.
     D

11. <u>One of the investor</u> predicts <u>a rise</u> at the end of the first term, after
            A   B
   <u>an improvement in</u> <u>the supply and demand</u> relationship.
          C   D

12. <u>Upon hearing</u> the report that the famous actor <u>was died</u>, fans
      A   B
   <u>the world over</u> were overwhelmed <u>with sadness</u>.
       C   D

As you can see, the stimulus material in Christine's editing task involves sentence-length items, each containing one grammar error, but with four possible locations of the error suggested to the learner. (You may feel inclined to criticize Christine's use of decontextualized sentences as part of the stimulus material in her editing task, and indeed, the thrust nowadays is toward more contextualized discourse-length samples of language in both the stimulus material and the learners' responses. Please keep in mind, however, that Christine's intent was to investigate the relationship between the student performances on a direct test of writing and the sort of editing task that was included on the placement exam at her school i.e., one in which the stimulus material consisted of decontextualized sentences). The task posed to the learner is to correctly identify the location of the error. (The test-takers do not have to correct the error or explain what was wrong.) The learner's response is to circle the letter indicating the location of the error, and the scoring criteria are right or wrong, based on a preestablished key. (Christine had some native-speaking friends complete the editing task to help her devise the key.) Table 6.1 is the key, in case you would like to check your answers against the intended correct responses.

Table 6.1: Key for Christine Houba's Editing Task

1. A	5. C	9. A
2. A	6. D	10. D
3. D	7. C	11. A
4. B	8. C	12. B

Christine goes on to describe the essay portion of her test. The "*TWE* guidelines" she refers to are those of the *Test of Written English* (a standardized direct test of writing that uses a six-point holistic scoring scale). We will discuss the

TWE and holistic scoring in more detail in Chapter 12.

> At the end of the ten minutes, the editing test was collected and the essay test was administered. The essay test prompts consisted of three choices, and students were given thirty minutes to write on the essay topic of their choice. Directions for the test were written in English and were as brief and simple as possible. The results did not indicate any misunderstanding of the task posed on the part of the test-takers—all of the tests were completed according to the instructions. According to the proctor, all sixteen subjects were able to finish the test and check their work, and did not seem bothered by time constraints (p. 3).

> A time limit of thirty minutes was allotted for the essay, in accordance with the *Test of Written English* (*TWE*) guidelines. The subjects were only asked to write approximately one page, and the simplicity of the essay question prompts ensured that relatively little time was required for thought preparation (p. 6).

Based on her previous experience with students at this school, Christine chose three essay topics that were the sort of writing assignments her students were accustomed to dealing with. Here are the three topics:

> Write briefly about one of the topics below, using the space provided.
> 1. A special person in your life (or a pet!)
> 2. Something you like to do in your free time
> 3. Your reason (or reasons) for studying English
>
> You have 30 minutes to complete this section (p. 26).

The topic for an essay task is often referred to as a **prompt.** Hughes (1989) argues that offering only one prompt will increase the reliability of raters' evaluations. On the other hand, giving students a choice of prompts may promote more creativity and a sense of confidence among the test-takers.

Christine goes on to describe the students' reactions to the essay task, and the surprising results of the scoring process:

> For the essay test, students were asked to write using the space provided, which is about one page. Again, the proctor reported that there were no complaints from the students regarding the time limit. Some students complained about the space limitations, however, saying they wanted extra paper because they could easily write three to four pages on their topic (p. 7).

> The essays were scored by two raters, using the six-point *Test of Written English Holistic Scoring Guide.* The two raters trained themselves to evaluate writing according to the scale by going over a series of *TWE* benchmark papers and discussing the criteria laid out in the guidelines. The two raters then worked separately to score the sixteen essays. Surprisingly and happily, the two raters independently assigned the same ratings to every single essay! This yielded a perfect inter-rater reliability coefficient of 1.0, or 100 percent. The subjects' scores ranged from two to four on the six-point *TWE* scale (p. 14).

Let me point out (as Christine acknowledges) that the actual process of being trained as an official *TWE* reader is very rigorous and systematic. Educational Testing Service, the organization that developed and administers the *TWE,* is extremely careful to ensure high reliability and adherence to the rating scale among its raters.

Christine's perfect inter-rater reliability coefficient is, as she notes, somewhat surprising, since she and her colleague were self-trained and had not been through a norming process with other *TWE* raters. Notice that there are two issues of possible concern here, however, in terms of the data derived from Christine's use of the *TWE* scale:

1. She and her corater could have had perfect agreement between the two of them without marking the papers according to the scale. (This sometimes occurs, especially when the same rater pairs work together over a period of time. That case is called **rater drift** because even though the raters' scores can be identical, they may have drifted away from the scale.) There's no evidence that this happened in Christine's case, particularly since there were so few papers to score and the raters worked independently.

2. Since the assigned scores on this set of papers ranged from two to four on the six-point *TWE* scale (i.e., no scores of one, five, or six were awarded), in effect the system had been shortened to a three-point scale. (This fact will have implications for the statistical analysis Christine undertook to determine the relationship between the direct and the indirect portions of her test. We will examine this issue more closely in Chapter 8, when we study the correlation family.)

Christine was appropriately cautious in interpreting her results, given that only sixteen students were involved in her investigation, which has not yet been replicated. (Christine's findings will be discussed in some detail in Chapters 8 and 9.) Further research is needed to investigate the relationship between editing skill and writing ability, as Christine notes:

> Even if it does turn out that good editing tasks can be adequate measures of writing ability, I still believe that direct tests of writing are called for in order to provide beneficial washback to ESL and EFL students. Encouraging students to write is part of building their communicative strengths, and if students and teachers had some extrinsic motivation to do so (in the form of a writing test), so much the better (p. 15).

Christine's final comment is extremely important since we definitely want our assessment mechanisms to promote positive washback. (At the very least, we want to avoid creating tests that generate negative washback!) The crux of the matter for us as classroom teachers choosing between direct and indirect measures of a skill is to decide what we want to measure. Do we wish to focus very tightly on specific aspects of enabling skills? (This might be the case in a diagnostic or a progress test.) If so, an indirect test might be useful. Or do we wish to assess our learners' abilities to use the macroskills in the target language? In that case, a more direct test would be called for.

After designing and analyzing her original test, Christine returned for a summer to work at the English school in Japan. I asked her to write me and tell me about her experiences with assessment there. Here is a portion of her letter:

> I still believe very strongly that a direct test of writing is important to begin to assess students' real communicative ability. This feeling has been reinforced by my observations of student behavior in my writing classes since I've been back here. What I mean is that when I put a "wrong" sentence on the board, most of the students can tell me what's wrong with it, but they make the same mistakes in their own writing all the time. It's hard to say exactly what is going on here that makes them able to spot mistakes but not avoid them when they write—maybe some of it is just plain carelessness. But the point is that there is still a difference between recognition and performance, and I see this on a daily basis.

I'm sure that most language teachers have shared Christine's experience. The question becomes, how can we design our assessment mechanisms so as to promote positive washback? Christine's letter continues:

> I have shared these thoughts with the other teachers and administrators at the school, and while they agree with me, they refuse to try to include a direct test of writing in the placement test. It's not practical, they say. It's too subjective and time-consuming to correct. I explained to them that it was possible to come up with a reliable holistic scoring system and that I'd be willing to set it up and work with everyone on it, but their response was, "Sure, that's fine for this time, while you're here, but after you're gone we won't have confidence in continuing this system by ourselves." For this school, and I think for many others as well, the most important considerations when it comes to test format are speed and ease of correction.

Let me point out, before moving to the "Investigations" section of this chapter, that indirect tests do not necessarily have to be presented in a discrete-point format. There are many ways to assess the enabling skills other than multiple-choice questions. For example, I can develop a cloze passage to test my students' abilities to use tense and aspect correctly in the English verb system. The deleted items could all be verbs. And if I wanted to eliminate the issue of the learners' lexical choice in such a test, to keep the task posed to the learners tightly focused on verb tense and aspect, I could actually supply the verbs in their infinitive forms in parentheses before the blanks. By using a cloze passage in this way, I would still be focusing on verb tense and aspect, but unlike multiple-choice or other discrete-point formats, the more integrative format of the cloze passage would provide at least a paragraph-long discourse context in which students' reading skills were invoked, along with their ability to supply the correct form of the verb.

The point is that the terms *direct test* and *indirect test* do not mean exactly the same thing as *integrative* and *discrete-point* tests. Although most direct tests will be integrative (by definition), indirect tests may range in format from very discrete-point in nature to much more integrative. As teachers with assessment responsibilities, it's up to us to choose from among these various options the appropriate procedures for assessing our students' skills and knowledge.

1 *Select a language test with which you are familiar, or one that you'd like to know more about. Examine the test (and any supporting documents) carefully. Then place an "X" on each continuum below to represent your assessment of the test in terms of these three key concepts:*

Indirect .... *Direct*	
Discrete-point testing .... *Integrative testing*	
Objectively scored .... *Subjectively scored*	

If the exam includes subtests, you may find that different parts of the test fall at different points on these continua.

2 *If you are working with a group of classmates or colleagues, compare your markings on these three continua to their assessments of the same test.*

As an alternative, you and your colleagues could choose two or three different tests that are intended to assess the same construct (for instance, two tests of speaking, or perhaps two different grammar tests). How do the assessment mechanisms differ (or how are they similar) when plotted against these continua?

3 *Share the chapter-opening quotation (from "Alma's letter") with an experienced language teacher. Ask the teacher if he or she has ever faced Alma's dilemma, and if so, how it was resolved. It might be useful to compare the responses of several different experienced practitioners.*

4 *Christine Houba's test consists of a very indirect, objectively scored, discrete-point editing task, and a very direct, subjectively scored, integrative essay task—both of which were intended to assess students' writing skills. Choose one of the other skills and brainstorm, with a group of classmates or colleagues, how you would go about assessing student mastery of the skill both directly and indirectly.*

Suggested Readings

If you are particularly interested in assessment issues in English language teaching in Japan, J. D. Brown and Sayoko O. Yamashita have edited a book entitled *Language Testing in Japan* (1995). Gary Buck's article, "Testing Listening Comprehension in Japanese University Entrance Examinations" (1988), systematically analyzes various types of listening tasks posed to learners in Japanese university entrance exams in terms of their potential for generating positive washback.

One reason for conducting indirect assessments is that they may be more efficient to administer and score than direct assessments. For instance, if there were a valid and reliable indirect paper-and-pencil test of speaking that could be administered to several people at once, it would be more efficient than conducting oral interviews with individual students one at a time. One interesting indirect test of speaking is called the "Conversational Cloze Test." As the name suggests, this is a cloze passage, but the text is based on the transcription of an actual conversation. Research has shown surprisingly high correlations between student performance on direct tests of speaking and scores on conversational cloze tests (see, e.g., D. Brown, 1983, and Hughes, 1981).

Elana Shohamy (1982) has also done some research on using language learners' cloze test scores to predict speaking proficiency.

Sandra Savignon (1983, 253) has an interesting chart that locates a number of test formats along two continua, namely: test tasks (ranging from discrete-point to integrative) and learner's response mode (ranging from discrete-point to global). Grant Henning's book *A Guide to Language Testing* (1987), also discusses the continua explained in this chapter.

7

SOME USEFUL
STATISTICAL TOOLS

One of my favorite cartoons was drawn by S. Kelley in 1994.
It depicts two male high school students walking past the lockers
in the hall outside a classroom. One of the boys is wearing a
letterman's jacket.
*   The first boy says to the other, "So what if seven out of ten*
of us failed math on that new standardized test?"
*   And the second boy responds, "Yeah, that's still less than half."*

I have decided to include a few chapters about some basic statistical analyses in this book. What follows is by no means a thorough treatment of the types of statistics we can use with language test results. Instead, it is a very basic introduction to some important concepts that are useful in doing language assessment and in understanding the reports about language assessment that appear in professional journals, books about testing, and the manuals prepared by publishers of language tests.

Why should language teachers be familiar with the statistics used in language assessment? I can think of several reasons, though of course there may be more.

First—and to my mind, this is the main reason for pursuing statistical analyses—the data we glean by computing and interpreting some statistical procedures provide us with the information we need to insure that our assessment devices are valid and reliable. This is important because our students' lives may be affected by the outcomes of the language tests we use. If the tests are invalid or unreliable, the students may suffer and our judgments may be called into question.

Second, in the cases in which the information we gain from analyzing our test results indicates that we need to improve the test, some statistical procedures yield information that will help us see *how* to improve the tests. This issue will be covered in Chapter 9, which reports on how Christine Houba (whose work was discussed in Chapter 6) used item analysis procedures to help her analyze the pilot test results of an exam she had designed for her school in Japan.

Third, some statistical procedures, specifically the correlation family (see Chapter 8) are extremely valuable in helping us determine the validity and reliability of our tests. For instance, correlations can help us investigate what our tests are measuring, what the relationship may be between different subtests, and whether we, as raters of compositions and students' speech samples, are being consistent in our ratings.

Fourth, statistical data provide us with a way of making comparisons. We can look at how our students did on one exam relative to another later exam and check for significant improvement in their performances. Likewise, we can make comparisons across different groups of students if we wish to—for instance, comparing one section of an intermediate French class with another section of students at that same level. There are simple statistical procedures that enable us to make such comparisons in ways that are understood by language testing researchers everywhere. (This leads to my next point.)

Fifth, the use of statistics provides a convenient, highly standardized means of communication with which to convey our findings to other language teaching and testing professionals—whether they are down the hall or halfway around the world. When you understand the logic and the vocabulary of statistical analyses, you can easily communicate your findings to colleagues in a clear and economical fashion.

Sixth—and the importance of this point should not be underemphasized—the correct use and interpretation of statistical analyses typically impresses administrators, parents, student sponsors, and funding agencies. Many people go in awe of statistical outcomes and accord such results a great deal of respect. (In some cases, such respect for "hard data" is totally undeserved. What matters much more than "number crunching" is that the right procedures have been selected, correctly calculated, and appropriately interpreted.) I encourage my students to develop a healthy skepticism about statistics, while at the same time I encourage them to learn all they can. I believe it is important that we language teachers understand the logic and the reporting discourse of statistical analyses so that we can use them if we wish to, and so that we can detect (and therefore protect ourselves and our students from) errors in other people's use and interpretation of statistics if we need to.

Finally, although you may find this idea rather strange at first, another reason to conduct statistical analyses on our language test results is that doing so is both fun and interesting. Once you learn some of the basic procedures and vocabulary, you'll find that statistical analyses can provide fascinating and useful information that can help you (a) interpret and improve your tests, and (b) communicate with others about the results—both of which are inherently rewarding activities.

In fact, I will argue that learning about statistics is very much like learning a language. Consider the following points:

1. The use of statistics involves learning a variety of visual symbols, just as you would do if you were learning to read and write a language that uses an alphabet or syllabary different from the one(s) you already know.

2. There is a specialized jargon associated with statistical procedures. So, just as in the case of learning a new language, learning to use statistics entails acquiring a number of new vocabulary items (as well as developing new professional meanings for terms that are already in your layperson's vocabulary).

3. There are ordering rules for using statistics that parallel the word order rules we must learn in acquiring the syntax of a new language. Some steps must precede others. Some steps are obligatory and others are optional.

4. There are also cultural values attached to statistical analyses. For instance, some procedures are seen as more prestigious than others because of the types of information they provide. Other statistics are viewed as risky and should be handled cautiously.

As we work through some statistical procedures in this book, it may be helpful for you to keep the language-learning metaphor in mind. Imagine that you are about to visit a fascinating new country and I am offering you a brief "crash course" in basic statistics for travel purposes.

My intent in this chapter is to demonstrate a few basic statistical operations that are commonly used in language testing. We will restrict our discussion to those procedures that can profitably be used with small numbers of test-takers. (We won't investigate many of the statistics used in large-scale test development projects since those procedures typically require very large data sets—test results from more learners than are accessible to most classroom teachers.)

In case you feel an attack of acute math anxiety coming on, let me offer these words of reassurance. The only background knowledge of mathematics you need to process the information in this chapter comfortably and with confidence is (a) how decimals work and (b) the concept of positive and negative numbers. If you can use a calculator with a square-root function key to add, subtract, multiply, divide, square numbers, and find square roots, then you can do statistics. The ideas that follow will be fun and easy to grasp. Furthermore, they will provide you with powerful tools for analyzing and improving the language tests you write.

One more comment: You may be the kind of language learner who is comfortable when a teacher responds to your question about puzzling grammar points by saying "That's just how we say it. There is no rule or explanation." If you are, you may also be quite comfortable accepting statistical formulae without any accompanying explanation about their underlying logic. Feel free to skip this material if you have no conceptual need for it. Let me say, however, that as an author and a teacher, I personally feel compelled to include these explanations for the following reasons:

1. I think that they are interesting and that understanding the logic underlying the statistics will help you feel more confident and do more powerful things with your test data.

2. There almost always *is* a sensible explanation (whether in linguistics or statistics), if we just dig for it.

3. I get very annoyed with people who sell learners short (including teacher-learners) by assuming that they can't learn challenging concepts.

Even if you have a calculator or a computer program that will calculate these formulae for you in an instant, it is still important, both as a consumer and as a producer of statistical information, to understand the underlying constructs.

There are actually two distinct but related meanings associated with the terms *statistic* and *statistics.* The first meaning refers to the procedures, the actual mathematical formulae used to manipulate raw data. (**Raw data** are records that have not yet been processed or statistically manipulated in any way—in our case, usually test scores or raters' assessments of students' work.) The second meaning refers to the results of applying those formulae (i.e., the outcome of the calculations). So, for example, I can calculate the average of three test scores (85, 90, and 95 on a 100-point test). You can see that the scores themselves (85, 90, and 95) are the raw data, and also that the average of these three scores is 90 points. To say that the average equals 90 points illustrates the second meaning above: This statistic (i.e., 90 is the average) is the result of applying a mathematical formula to our raw data. In a sense we have "cooked" the raw data by converting the three separate test scores into a single average score.

MEASURES OF CENTRAL TENDENCY

Think about the mental processes you just used. How did you compute this average? To reconstruct your mathematical logic you might say something like this: "To calculate an average, you just add up all the scores and then divide that total by the number of scores you added." So in this case we have 85 + 90 + 95 = 270. Then we divide 270 by 3 and we get 90. So the result (i.e., that the average is 90) illustrates the second meaning of *statistic*—the outcome of the application of a formula.

Here is the actual formula (the first meaning of *statistics* given above) used in calculating an average:

$$\bar{x} = \frac{\sum x}{n}$$

Given what you already know about computing an average, can you figure out what these symbols stand for? Let's try this task as a four-item vocabulary matching quiz. Draw a line connecting each symbol in the left column with its corresponding concept in the right column:

x	*the average*
n	*the individual scores*
$\sum$	*the number of scores*
x̄	*sum what follows*

In statistical jargon, the average is typically called the **mean.** It is often represented by the symbol $\bar{x}$, which is sometimes called "X-bar." The **x** without the bar represents the individual score(s), ***n*** stands for number, and $\sum$ means "sum what follows" or "the sum of."

It is important to realize that when we compute a mean like this, it tells us something about the group, but it subsumes and therefore masks information about individuals in the group. The mean is one measure of what's called **central tendency**—that is, the patterns of how scores in a data set group together, often with some cluster of scores in the middle. There are two other measures of central tendency: the **median** (the middle score in a data set), and the **mode** (the most frequently obtained score in a data set). Among these three measures of central tendency, the mean is used most often in issues related to language assessment.

MEASURES OF DISPERSION

How the scores spread out in any particular data set can be just as informative as how they cluster together. So, as you might imagine, in addition to the measures of central tendency, there are also **measures of dispersion about the mean** (or simply **measures of dispersion**). These are statistics that provide information about how spread out the scores are in a given data set. Let's look at an example.

Imagine that you are a secondary school teacher with three intermediate French classes. Suppose you give all three classes the same fifty-point midterm examination. Let us further assume that something unusual happens and that the mean for each class turns out to be 35 points. Would this indicate that the three classes were identical in their performance on the French test? Not necessarily. Here are the individual students' imaginary scores for the three different classes. For ease of interpretation I have rank ordered the scores in each class from highest to lowest.

Table 7.1: Imaginary Midterm Scores for Three French Classes

9 A.M. Class	11 A.M. Class	2 P.M. Class
46	49	50
45	42	49
45	41	47
43	40	45
42	39	42
41	36	41
40	33	40
37	30	38
32	29	36
31	28	35
29	27	26
28	26	25
25		20
22		16
19		15

What do you notice right away about these three sets of test scores? You probably will have noticed that the 9 A.M. class and the 2 P.M. class both have fifteen students, while the 11 A.M. class has only twelve students. You also probably noticed that the highest scores and the lowest scores achieved by the three classes are not the same.

The difference between the highest score and the lowest score in any set of test results is called the **range.** If the range of scores for the 9 A.M. class is 19 to 46, and the range of scores for the 11 A.M. class is 26 to 49, you can see that the range of the 9 A.M. class is somewhat lower than that of the 11 A.M. class.

What is the range for the 2 P.M. class?

How does it compare to the ranges for the other two classes?

If you said the range for the 2 P.M. class is 15 to 50, that is correct. You probably also noticed that the range for the 2 P.M. class extends further than either of the other two ranges: The top score is higher and the bottom score is lower than in the other two data sets. By comparing the ranges of the three classes, we can see that although the means are identical, the performances of the individuals in the three groups actually varied considerably.

In fact, **variance** is the technical term that captures the collective amount of the "differentness" in any given set of scores. Variance (usually symbolized by a lower-case s^2) is defined as "a measure of dispersion around the mean" (Henning, 1987, 198). Or as Jaeger (1990, 384) put it, "Variance is an indicator of the spread of scores in a distribution" (a **distribution** being a set of scores). However, there is a related concept that is used even more often than *variance* in discussing and interpreting test results, the concept of *standard deviation*. Before we look more concretely at what standard deviation represents, let's put it into a wider context: As you may have guessed, the three measures of dispersion are range, variance, and standard deviation.

Mathematically speaking, **standard deviation** is defined as the square root of variance. Because variance is symbolized by s^2, standard deviation (the square root of s^2) is symbolized by lower case s. But what does *that* mean? Such an abstract definition probably won't help you much if you have just encountered the concept of variance for the first time. Let's situate the idea in a familiar context.

Table 7.2 is reproduced from a form that is familiar to many teachers. It is an example of a student evaluation of teaching (SET) form, of the sort universities often use for students to evaluate teachers and courses, typically at the end of a term. You will see that the content of each question on the form is summarized in the left-hand column, and the right side of the chart shows how many students awarded the teacher a rating at each level on each question. In this rating system, 1 = poor, 2 = fair, 3 = average, 4 = very good, and 5 = excellent.

Table 7.2: STUDENT EVALUATIONS OF TEACHING

QUESTION	1	2	3	4	5
1. Clarity and progression of topics	0	0	4	6	7
2. Integration of different aspects of course	0	0	4	6	7
3. Usefulness of texts, readings, and assignments	0	1	6	4	6
4. Quantity of assignments	0	3	3	3	8
5. Methods of assessment and grading	0	0	3	7	6
6. Course objectives clearly related to profession	0	1	3	8	5
7. Overall course organization	0	0	5	4	8
8. Interest in subject matter	0	2	3	5	7
9. Knowledge of subject matter	0	1	5	9	2
10. Clarity of presentation	0	1	3	6	7
11. Preparation	0	0	0	7	10
12. Stimulation of thought	1	1	2	7	6
13. Response to student work	0	0	1	6	10
14. Overall instructor performance	0	1	1	7	8
15. Knowledge or skill with subject matter	0	0	3	8	6
16. Interest in the subject matter	0	3	3	7	4
17. Desire to pursue the subject further	2	1	5	5	4
18. Overall contribution to your learning	0	2	3	8	4
19. Respect for student opinions and concerns	0	0	2	3	12
20. Responsiveness to questions and comments	0	0	1	3	13
21. Openness to criticism	0	0	0	1	15
22. Availability outside class time	0	0	1	3	12
23. Overall instructor relationship	0	0	1	2	14

The data entered in the right columns are referred to as **frequencies,** because they show how frequently each rating level was selected by the respondents. So, for example, in the first item, which assesses the "clarity and progression of topics" in the course, none of the students chose 1 (poor) or 2 (fair). Four students felt the instructor's performance in this category was average, six felt it was good, and seven categorized it as excellent. Oddly enough, exactly the same ratings were given on item 2, although we don't know for sure if the same people gave the same ratings.

FREQUENCY POLYGONS

This sort of information can be portrayed visually in a bar graph called a "histogram." A **histogram** consists of a matrix in which the vertical axis represents the number of scores and the horizontal axis represents the value of those scores. A vertical bar is drawn above each score value to the point that represents the number of people who got that score on the test, or—as in this case—who awarded that rating. Here's an example of a histogram based on item 1:

Figure 7.1: **Histogram for Item #1 in the SET Data**

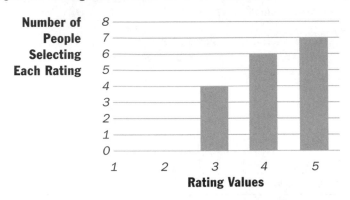

You can see that for the rating categories of 1 (poor) and 2 (fair) no bar has been drawn, because no one selected those ratings. Bars have been drawn, however, indicating that four people chose 3 (average). The process continues for the six people who chose 4 (very good), and the seven people who chose 5 (excellent).

Such bar charts are useful visual representations, but a form of display that is more common in language testing is called a "frequency polygon." The basic logic of the layout is the same: The vertical axis represents the number of people (or scores, or measurements) and the horizontal axis represents the measurements, score values, or rating levels. Instead of a bar representing the frequencies, a dot is placed where the top of the bar would be. The line that is drawn to connect these dots completes the **frequency polygon,** which is, in effect, a line graph representing the frequency with which each score or rating was received.

In Figure 7.2 (on page 96) is a frequency polygon representing the data from item 1 in Table 7.2. You can see that the same information we saw in Figure 7.1 is being presented, but that the frequency polygon provides a slightly different format.

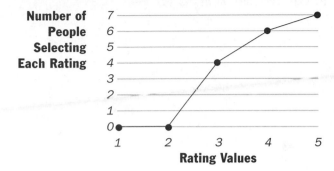

Frequency polygons are important in a variety of statistical procedures. Indeed, this format of data display is the basis of the bell-shaped curve, which is also called the **normal distribution.** (We will return to this concept below.)

> What would the histogram look like for the data represented in item 2?

> What would the frequency polygon look like for the data represented in item 2?

If you said these displays should be identical in appearance to the histogram and the frequency polygon for item 1, that's correct. The pictures don't show us *which* people selected the various ratings—only *how many* people selected each rating.

I hope this example makes clear how to read the data in Table 7.2; I'm going to use these data to illustrate some interesting points. Please skim the ratings and find the one item on which the students had the *highest agreement* about the teacher's performance (i.e., locate the item on which there was the least disparity among the ratings).

If you read all the way down the chart, you'll see that on item 21, "openness to criticism," the students' ratings were very consistent: Fifteen people awarded the teacher a rating of 5 (excellent) and only one person marked 4 (very good). No one selected ratings of 1, 2, or 3. In other words, with one exception, the students agreed that the teacher was excellent in this category. Figure 7.3 shows a frequency polygon representing the data from item 21.

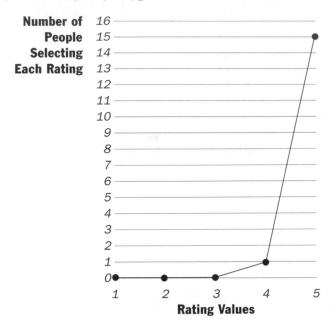

Figure 7.3: **Frequency Polygon for Item 21 in the SET Data**

Why is this frequency polygon so tall and skinny? The answer lies in the concept of *measures of dispersion about the mean.*

Look at Table 7.2 again, but this time locate the item with the *greatest disagreement* among the ratings. I think you'll find, after a few moments of scrutiny, that item 17, which measures the students' "desire to pursue the subject further," received the most mixed reactions:

(1)	POOR	2 people
(2)	FAIR	1 person
(3)	AVERAGE	5 people
(4)	VERY GOOD	5 people
(5)	EXCELLENT	4 people

You can see that the students' reactions to this factor are spread out across the entire scale. Figure 7.4 shows a frequency polygon depicting the data from item 17:

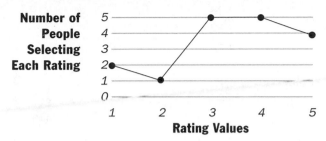

As with the frequency polygon for item 21, you can see that a point has been entered at each score value, representing the number of people who selected that particular rating on item 17. But you'll also notice that the frequency polygon for item 17 is much flatter and more spread out than the one for item 21.

Now, keeping in mind the shapes of the frequency polygons for item 21 and item 17, look at the expanded version of Table 7.2 in Table 7.3. You will see immediately that two columns have been added to the raw data from Table 7.2: one for the mean ($\bar{x}$) and one for the standard deviation (s). Look down the column for standard deviations. Find the smallest number in the standard deviation column, and also the largest number in that column. What items do they represent?

Table 7.3: **Student Evaluations of Teaching**
(Including Means and Standard Deviations)

QUESTION	$\bar{x}$	s	1	2	3	4	5
1. Clarity and progression of topics	4.17	0.78	0	0	4	6	7
2. Integration of different aspects of course	4.17	0.78	0	0	4	6	7
3. Usefulness of texts, readings, and assignments	3.88	0.96	0	1	6	4	6
4. Quantity of assignments	3.94	1.16	0	3	3	3	8
5. Methods of assessment and grading	4.18	0.72	0	0	3	7	6
6. Course objectives clearly related to profession	4.00	0.84	0	1	3	8	5
7. Overall course organization	4.17	0.85	0	0	5	4	8
8. Interest in subject matter	4.00	1.02	0	2	3	5	7
9. Knowledge of subject matter	3.70	0.74	0	1	5	9	2
10. Clarity of presentation	4.11	0.89	0	1	3	6	7
11. Preparation	4.58	0.49	0	0	0	7	10

12. Stimulation of thought	3.94	1.10	1	1	2	7	6
13. Response to student work	4.52	0.60	0	0	1	6	10
14. Overall instructor performance	4.29	0.82	0	1	1	7	8
15. Knowledge or skill with subject matter	4.17	0.70	0	0	3	8	6
16. Interest in the subject matter	3.70	1.01	0	3	3	7	4
17. Desire to pursue the subject further	3.47	1.24	2	1	5	5	4
18. Overall contribution to your learning	3.82	0.93	0	2	3	8	4
19. Respect for student opinions and concerns	4.58	0.69	0	0	2	3	12
20. Responsiveness to questions and comments	4.70	0.57	0	0	1	3	13
21. Openness to criticism	4.93	0.24	0	0	0	1	15
22. Availability outside class time	4.68	0.58	0	0	1	3	12
23. Overall instructor relationship	4.76	0.54	0	0	1	2	14

I think you'll find that the smallest number and the largest number in the standard deviation column represent items 21 and 17, respectively. Do you see how standard deviation relates to the frequency distribution of scores? It is a summary, if you will, or a numerical index, of the amount of differentness, or variability, in a given set of scores.

Just as in learning a new language you must understand how to use the verb *to be* or its equivalent, these two key statistical concepts (mean and standard deviation) must be mastered to use the language of statistics effectively. The concepts of mean and standard deviation show up again and again in statistical formulae.

In fact, the mean and the standard deviation (as well as the mode and median, and the range and variance) are part of a group of basic procedures called *descriptive statistics*. Almost all statistical procedures used in language assessment entail an understanding of descriptive statistics. The procedures are called **descriptive statistics** because they *describe* a set of data.

Let's return now to the imaginary midterm exam results from our three intermediate French classes listed in Table 7.1. Table 7.4 reports the value for the average and for the standard deviation of each class. While the means remain the same across the three sections of intermediate French, the standard deviations vary: 9 versus 7.27 versus 11.81. What do these values tell you about the three different data sets?

Table 7.4: Means and Standard Deviations on an Imaginary Fifty-point Midterm Exam for Three French Classes

	9 A.M. Class (n=15)	11 A.M. Class (n=12)	2 P.M. Class (n=15)
Mean	35	35	35
Standard Deviation	9	7.27	11.81

You can see that although the three means are identical, the three standard deviations are quite different. Indeed, the standard deviations capture and summarize the differences we observed above when we noticed the disparities in the ranges of the three data sets.

Now let's rewrite our definition of standard deviation in terms that are more concrete. **Standard deviation** is a statistic that summarizes the average amount of difference from the mean in any given data set. It is an extremely informative and widely used statistic that has many applications, including those of reporting and interpreting language test results.

DEGREES OF FREEDOM

There is another important concept you'll need to know to understand many statistical formulae. That is the concept of *degrees of freedom* (usually symbolized by *df*). Since degrees of freedom is a rather abstract notion, I will illustrate it with two examples before trying to explain the concept.

Suppose you are teaching a class with twenty students enrolled and exactly twenty seats in the room. As you begin class, sixteen students are present and seated, so there are four empty chairs. As the remaining students enter the room, each of them faces a certain number of chairs and a certain number of choices about where to sit, as follows:

1. When the seventeenth student enters the room, there are four chairs and four choices.

2. When the eighteenth student enters the room, there are three chairs and three choices.

3. When the nineteenth student enters the room, there are two chairs and, hence, two choices.

4. Finally, when the twentieth student enters the room, there is only one chair left. Therefore, there are *no* choices.

It is the end of this list that illustrates the concept of "degrees of freedom": The twentieth student sees *one* chair and has *no* choice. There is only one chair remaining, so there are no options as to where he or she may sit. (I am grateful to Ray Clifford for showing me the chair example to explain degrees of freedom.)

Let's take another, slightly more math-oriented example from basic algebra. Can you figure out what number is represented by the question mark in the following equation?

$$30 = 20 + 4 + 1 + ?$$

The first mental step is to figure out how many numbers out of thirty are already accounted for, so we add $20 + 4 + 1$ and get 25. (In our example of the chairs in the nearly full classroom, this step amounts to checking which seats are already taken.)

$$30 = 25 + ?$$

Then our logic (and perhaps our mathematical knowledge) tells us we can figure out what the question mark represents if we subtract the known commodity of 25 from the total of 30:

$$30 - 25 = ?$$
$$30 - 25 = 5$$

So our unknown commodity is 5. Is there anything else it could be in this equation? No.

These two examples (the classroom seats and the algebra problem) both exemplify the concept *degrees of freedom*. I gave the examples first because the typical definition of degrees of freedom is somewhat abstract. For instance, Grant Henning defines degrees of freedom as "the number of units of analysis after loss due to statistical computation" (1987, 191). Put in more straightforward terms, **degrees of freedom** refers to "the number of quantities that can vary if others are given" (Hatch and Lazaraton, 1991, 254).

The degrees of freedom construct shows up in many, many statistics. In fact, it is an important part of the formula for standard deviation. It is usually represented by the mathematical term *n*-1. In other words, whatever the number of scores is *minus one* is a part of several procedures we'll use with our own test results. (In a few situations, degrees of freedom will be equal to n–2, but you won't encounter this case until you work with correlations.) I went through these illustrations in such detail because the degrees of freedom idea comes into play when we calculate standard deviation.

CALCULATING STANDARD DEVIATION

The formula for standard deviation combines several elements you have already encountered. Here is the formula:

$$s = \sqrt{\frac{\Sigma(x - \bar{x})^2}{n - 1}}$$

One of the important issues here is the sequence of operations. (Remember we're working with the metaphor that learning statistics is like learning a language, so I'm just alerting you to the fact that syntactic rules are important in this case.)

Let's "unpack" this formula. We have to start with the term inside the parentheses, so what does it mean when you see these symbols?

$$(x - \bar{x})$$

You will recall that x represents the individual score and $\bar{x}$ stands for the mean. So this term is telling us, literally, "subtract the mean from each score." What this operation represents conceptually is that we are determining the *distance* on the measurement scale between each score in a distribution and the mean score of that distribution. This distance or difference of scores is often represented by a D (or a d) in statistical formulae.

What will happen *every time* you do this step is that some scores are higher than the mean and some scores are lower than the mean. Think about the case in which we had three scores—85, 90, and 95 on a 100-point test. We have already determined that the mean was 90. So our computations in figuring out the standard deviation start like this:

x		$\bar{x}$		D
95	–	90	=	5
90	–	90	=	0
85	–	90	=	–5

Now, you may wonder, what do we do next? Is it time to sum these values (following the Σ sign), or is it time to square these values? There is a logical way to decide. What would happen if we added these three differences between each of the three scores and the mean score (i.e., the values in the D column)? You can see that

$$5 + 0 + (-5) = 0$$

because the 5 and the -5 cancel each other out. That's why the step of squaring the differences is in the formula: It allows us to get rid of the minus signs before we sum the difference. (This procedure is followed in many statistical equations: Values are squared first to get rid of any minus signs, and then later we find the square root in order to offset the earlier squaring.) So the next step is to add a column for D^2, and to square each D value as follows:

x		$\bar{x}$		D	D^2
95	–	90	=	5	25
90	–	90	=	0	0
85	–	90	=	–5	25

Now when we sum the D^2 values, we get 50. Let's put this value into the numerator of our formula:

$$s = \sqrt{\frac{50}{n-1}}$$

For this small data set, $n = 3$, so the $n - 1$ term in the denominator comes out to 2:

$$s = \sqrt{\frac{50}{2}} = \sqrt{25} = 5$$

Like many examples in books explaining statistics, this particular illustration is much tidier than real data usually are. But if you think back to our raw data, you will see how this sample calculation of standard deviation illustrates the definition. We defined standard deviation as a statistic that summarizes the average amount of difference in any given data set. The mean in this case was 90, and the three individual scores were 85, 90, and 95. So you can see why it makes sense that 5 is the value of the standard deviation in this case.

STANDARDIZED SCORES

Now that you are familiar with means and standard deviations, there is one more set of statistical procedures that you should know about. These are two very useful formulae for what are called "standardized scales." It will be helpful for you to learn these procedures because you may need to explain them to students or parents to help them interpret some test results. Also, there may be times when you yourself need to use standardized scores for various reasons, as I will illustrate in the "Teacher's Voice" section of this chapter.

Imagine that you have been working as an EFL teacher in a rural area of a small, developing nation whose currency, the *mfuti,* is not widely known in other countries. One day, due to a sudden political upheaval, you must be evacuated by helicopter to another country. The helicopter deposits you safely in another small developing nation whose political situation is more stable, but again the local unit of currency, the *zhygleri,* is not well known to the outside world.

In order to buy food and supplies in your new host country, you need to exchange your hard-earned mfuti for zhygleri. Unfortunately, the money changers have never had to deal with mfuti before so they don't have an established exchange rate for buying your mfuti. One solution is to compare both the mfuti and the zhygleri to a different, better-known currency in order to establish their relative values on some other, better-understood scale. (I will use the U.S. dollar to develop the example, since that's the currency scale I understand best.)

If you and the money changers found, for instance, that these currencies were selling at ten mfuti to one U.S. dollar, and twenty zhygleri to one U.S. dollar, you could use the U.S. dollar as a standard against which to compare the values of mfuti and zhygleri to each other:

10 mfuti = U.S. $1 = 20 zhygleri

Given this agreed-upon exchange rate between you and the money changers in your new host country, how many zhygleri could you buy with one mfuti? with 1,000 mfuti? If you said two and 2,000 respectively, that is correct.

There is a statistical procedure that allows us to do much the same thing with test scores. It is called the **z score transformation** (Hatch and Lazaraton, 1991, 196–201); the formula looks like this:

$$z = \frac{x - \bar{x}}{s}$$

I hope all these terms are familiar to you and that you feel quite confident about interpreting this formula. It simply says that to compute z scores for a particular distribution of scores, you find the distance between an individual score and the mean score (the numerator), and then divide that value by the standard deviation of that particular distribution (the denominator). This process is repeated for every score in the data set.

But why, you may be asking yourself, would you ever want to do this? Let's go back to the introductory example we used for standard deviation. There were three students who had taken a 100-point test and received scores of 95, 90, and 85. We had determined that $\bar{x} = 90$ and $s = 5$ in this small distribution. Now let's suppose that these three students had each completed a project that had been evaluated on a ten-point scale, with grades of 3, 6, and 8 respectively, and that you wanted to base the students' final grades on equal weightings of their test scores and their project grades. One way to do this is to convert both the test scores and the project grades into percentages (and indeed, percentages are a kind of standardized scale). However, even though percentages are often sufficient, the z score transformation is useful to know because there are so many things you can do with it. (For instance, this little formula will be very important in Chapter 8, when we study the correlation family.) I am going to convert the three students' scores on the 100-point test and on the ten-point project into z scores to illustrate the process. Here's how we start, using the students' scores on the 100-point test.

ID #	x		$\bar{x}$		D		s		z
1	95	−	90	=	5	÷	5	=	1
2	90	−	90	=	0	÷	5	=	0
3	85	−	90	=	−5	÷	5	=	−1

The next step is to convert the scores on the ten-point project to z scores. But looking at the z score formula you'll see that first we need the mean and the standard deviation for that distribution. The mean is 5.67 and the standard deviation is 2.45 in this set of scores. So now we can use the same column headings to compute the three students' z scores on the ten-point project:

ID #	x		$\bar{x}$		D		s		z
1	3	−	5.67	=	−2.67	÷	2.45	=	−1.09
2	6	−	5.67	=	0.33	÷	2.45	=	0.13
3	8	−	5.67	=	2.33	÷	2.45	=	0.95

Now we can compare the students' performances on a standard scale. (This step is the same conceptually as converting mfuti and zhygleri to their U.S. dollar values.)

ID #	z Scores on 100-Point Test	z Scores on 10-Point Project
1	1	−1.09
2	0	0.13
3	−1	0.95

At this point you can either sum each student's two z scores to get a total, or you can do that and then divide by two (for the score on the 100-point test and the score on the ten-point project) to get a mean, as illustrated below:

Student ID #	z Scores on 100-Point Test	z Scores on 10-Point Project	Combined z Scores	Mean z Scores	Rank
1	1	−1.09	−0.09	−0.045	3
2	0	0.13	0.13	0.070	1
3	−1	0.95	−0.05	−0.025	2

As it turns out, when you combine the values of the 100-point test and the ten-point project on the z scale, student 2 comes out to be the first-ranked student, even though he was the second ranked on each of the two assignments. Student 1 turns out to be the lowest-ranked student even though he had the highest score on the 100-point test. And student 3 did so well on the ten-point project, with a score of 8 out of 10 points possible, that he became the second ranked student overall, even though he had the lowest score on the test.

There are two problems with z scores, however, which make them a bit cumbersome to use: They include lots of decimals and minus signs. A computer can handle these minor inconveniences with ease, but if you are calculating these values by hand, the decimals and minus signs introduce many opportunities for making errors. To remove these problems there is one more simple conversion we can make once we have the z scores, and that is referred to as **T-scale scores**. Here's the formula:

$$T = 10(z) + 50$$

Multiplying the z score value by 10 gets rid of a decimal place, and adding 50 gets rid of any minus signs. I will illustrate this process with the z score values we just calculated:

Student ID #	z Scores on 100-Point Test	X 10	+ 50 = T Score	z Scores on 10-Point Project	X 10	+ 50 = T Score
1	1	10	60	−1.09	−10.90	39.1
2	0	0	50	0.13	1.30	51.3
3	−1	−10	40	0.95	9.50	59.5

You can see that it is more convenient for us to add and/or average the students' scores using the T-scale scores than it was using the z scores:

Student ID #	T Score on 100-Point Test	T Score on 10-Point Project	Combined T Scores	Mean T score	Rank
1	60	39.10	99.10	49.55	3
2	50	51.30	101.30	50.65	1
3	40	59.50	99.50	49.75	2

One convenient thing to know about T-scale scores is that they are consistently easy to interpret: The T-scale always has a mean of 50 and a standard deviation of 10, by definition. (For readers who want more detail on this topic, clear discussions can be found in the reference books by J. D. Brown [1988] and Hatch and Lazaraton [1991].)

Standardized scores such as z scores or T-scale scores can be plotted neatly on the patterned frequency distribution called the "normal distribution." This frequency polygon looks like a perfectly symmetrical hill, whose sides taper off gradually on both sides, or like the classic shape of a bell (the source of its other name—the "bell-shaped curve" or just "the bell curve"). The bell-shaped curve has some interesting properties that are important in reporting and interpreting language test results. Here is a drawing of the bell-shaped curve, which locates the mean, the standard deviations, and the z scores and T-scale scores relative to one another.

Figure 7.5: The Normal Distribution or Bell Curve

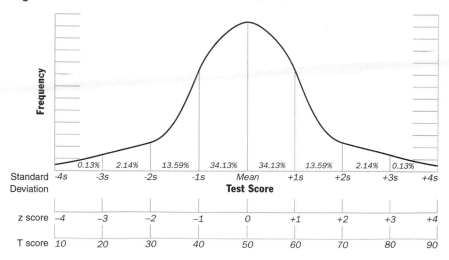

In a normal distribution like the one pictured in Figure 7.5, the mean score falls at the 50th percentile. A score one standard deviation above the mean falls at the 84th percentile, and a score two standard deviations above the mean falls at the 98th percentile. Likewise, a score one standard deviation below the mean falls at the 16th percentile, and so on. This is because, as shown in Figure 7.5, the areas in the parts of the curve delineated by the standard deviation lines encompass predictable percentages of the scores in the distribution. For example, 34 percent of the scores are located in the area of the curve between the mean and one standard deviation above the mean. Because the curve is symmetrical, 34 percent of the scores are also located between the mean and one standard deviation below the mean. Thus you can see that it would be very unlikely for a student to get a score three standard deviations above the mean just by chance. That would place him at the 99th percentile! In order to score that high, the student would normally have to know the material on the test very well (or cheat very skillfully, or be an excellent test-taker or guesser).

In the "Frameworks" section of this chapter we have investigated a number of statistical concepts: measures of central tendency (especially the mean), measures of dispersion (especially standard deviation), degrees of freedom, and standardized scores. In the "Teachers' Voices" section of this chapter I will relate two incidents from my own work where these statistical procedures allowed me to deal with two perplexing assessment dilemmas.

Teachers' Voices

One semester I taught two sections of our introductory research and statistics course, and I was very pleased that the two groups of students seemed equally balanced. Although there were some differences in the composition of the two classes, the students in both groups seemed equally well motivated, bright, and hardworking. The two classes were able to cover the material at the same pace, and no one appeared to be lost in either class. My initial impression, based on in-class discussions, office-hour conversations, and informal quizzes, was that both groups were doing quite well.

When it came time for the midterm exam, I wrote a carefully constructed test in which all the test items were couched in detailed descriptions of language learning and teaching situations. These highly contextualized word problems were the sorts of material we had covered in class and the students had done as homework.

You can imagine my surprise, then, when I was correcting the students' midterm exams and found that the people in the afternoon class were getting lower scores than I'd expected of them, and that their scores were much lower than those of the students in the morning class. To see if this impression was accurate, I calculated the means and the standard deviations for the two groups. Here are the results:

Table 7.5: Means and Standard Deviations on the Midterm Exams of Two Classes

Group	$\bar{x}$	s
Combined classes (n = 25)	82.90	12.06
Morning class (n = 14)	87.90	9.87
Afternoon class (n = 11)	78.90	12.46

Next I tried to determine the reason for this difference in the two groups' performance. (The statistics won't tell you this—you must decide for yourself.) Several students in the afternoon section had left parts of the test unfinished, which suggested a possible explanation for the observed differences in the two sets of scores: The morning section was made up of mostly native speakers of English and the afternoon section was made up of mostly nonnative speakers of English. Because of my lengthy descriptions and carefully contextualized situations in the word problems, the midterm exam had become, in part, a measure of the test-takers' reading speed. This inadvertent result of my good intentions had posed a more serious challenge (and accidentally created a more difficult test) for the nonnative readers. In other words, being able to interpret the means and standard deviations had alerted me to a possible problem (in this case, a source of invalidity) in the test I had created.

For the final exam, I cut back substantially on the amount of material the students had to read during the in-class exam and wrote stimulus materials in which the problems were shorter and easier to read than they had been on the midterm. I am happy to report that the scores of the two groups on the final exam were much more similar than they had been on the midterm.

In another context, I was helping to design an oral communications course for international students (nonnative speakers of English) who were (or wished to be) teaching assistants at the University of California at Los Angeles (UCLA). There had been many complaints from American undergraduates at the school that their international teaching assistants (ITAs) didn't speak English well enough to teach the undergraduate courses.

In trying to understand the situation, those of us working to design the oral communications course wanted to collect relevant information about the ITAs. So we requested their SET data from the departments that hired ITAs. We ran into a problem, though, when we found that the SET data for most departments were based on UCLA's regular instructor evaluation form, which used a nine-point scale, but that the Math Department (one of the largest employers of ITAs on campus) used its own five-point SET scale. You can see that a score of 4.5, for instance, would mean something quite different, depending on which scale it was derived from—a mean rating of 4.5 would be approaching "excellent" on the five-point Math Department scale, but in the nine-point UCLA-wide system, a mean rating of 4.5 would be much lower on the scale. This was an ideal situation for using the z scale transformation and then T-scale scores to make the data from the two systems comparable. That's exactly what I did (Bailey, 1982), and these data were, in fact, useful in our efforts to design the course.

The "Investigations" in the next section have been designed to give you practice with the descriptive statistics discussed in this chapter. I hope you will find this knowledge helpful, whether you see yourself as primarily a consumer of statistical information, or as someone who will actively use these tools in working with your own language assessment data.

---

1 *Try calculating the mean and standard deviation for any of the three sets of French class midterm exam data (Table 7.1, page 92). See if you obtain the same results I did. For calculating the standard deviation by hand, it will be helpful if you set up a worksheet with column headings as follows:*

Investigations

x	x̄	D	D²

Enter each student's score in the x column and the mean in the $\bar{x}$ column. When you subtract the mean from each score, enter each difference in the D column. (Remember, some of these values will be negative.) Then when you square each D value, enter the results in the D^2 column. It is the values in *that* column that you will sum.

---

2 *With some colleagues or classmates, use the raw data from the SET questionnaire given in Table 7.2 to draw frequency polygons and calculate means and standard deviations. Compare your frequency polygon for any particular item with that of a friend who chose the same item. Compare the means and standard deviations you computed with those given in Table 7.3.*

---

3 *Try drawing a frequency polygon for the imaginary French class midterm that displays the data from all three sections (Table 7.1). You'll need to use three different color pencils (or perhaps a dashed line, a dotted line, and a bold line) to make the contrast clear. The frequency polygon will be easier to draw if you use graph paper.*

You'll notice that when your drawing includes all three lines (representing the three different sections of intermediate French) the spread of the base of each line (which represents the respective ranges in the three sections' midterm scores) is related to the standard deviation. That is, the greater the standard deviation, the wider the range of scores as depicted in the frequency polygon: $s_{11am} < s_{9am} < s_{2pm}$. (Actually, the logic in that explanation draws on the empirical evidence of the display. The mathematically logical explanation is that the greater range of scores contributes to the greater standard deviation.)

---

4 *Compile the results from all three of the imaginary French classes. Then, using the combined test scores, try the following steps:*

1. Draw a frequency polygon representing the distribution.
2. Compute the mean of the distribution.
3. Calculate the standard deviation.
4. Calculate three or four students' z scores and T-scale scores.

You can compare these data with the scores from the three groups of French students to see how the mean and standard deviation provide useful summary information. You can also compare this aggregated frequency polygon with those for the three separate classes.

Suggested Readings

There are a number of books and articles available that can provide you with more information about the topics covered in this chapter. Here are some of my favorites.

J. D. Brown's (1988) book *Understanding Research in Second Language Learning,* provides an introduction to the statistics most commonly used in the field. It includes a chapter specifically geared to the procedures used in language testing. This particular book is aimed at an audience of teachers primarily as consumers of research results: It is geared mostly to helping you read and interpret research reports rather than conducting research yourself. It has an excellent explanation of the types of standardized scoring scales often used in reporting language test results. Brown's more recent book, *Testing in Language Programs* (1996), includes many useful statistics directly related to language assessment.

Brown (1991, 1992) has also written a helpful two-part article in which he uses the metaphor of "statistics as a foreign language." His goal in writing the article was to help teachers read statistical language studies more confidently and accurately.

Another useful book is *The Research Manual* by Evelyn Hatch and Anne Lazaraton (1991). This is more detailed and more technical than Brown's introductory text, but it provides helpful, step-by-step examples of statistical calculations in research situations derived from language learning and teaching. Its goal is to help in conducting original research, and many of the statistics it describes are useful in language assessment contexts.

Statistics in Language Studies, by Anthony Woods, Paul Fletcher, and Arthur Hughes (1986), is also intended to help in conducting original research. It has very clear charts and figures, but you may find that the logic is a bit more mathematically technical than is the case with the other books suggested here.

Two of my favorite resources for learning about statistics come from outside this field. Richard Jaeger's (1983) book *Statistics: A Spectator Sport* is designed for teachers as consumers of research reporting. His examples come from general education and psychology rather than applied linguistics, but I find his incremental explanations easy to follow, and his figures and tables are very clear.

The second text that I find extremely valuable is Richard Shavelson's (1988) book, *Statistical Reasoning for the Behavioral Sciences.* I was fortunate enough to have Dr. Shavelson as my very first statistics professor, and his book is written just as he teaches. The principles are laid out in very straightforward prose, the logic underlying the procedures is clearly explained, and sample problems are printed in shaded boxes for easy access.

David Nunan's (1992) book *Research Methods in Language Learning,* has a chapter on the experimental method, which puts many of these statistical procedures into the broader context of experimental science.

8

THE CORRELATION FAMILY

*As I was writing this chapter, I tried to be sensitive to the
fact that many people are uncomfortable with the symbolism and
logic of math. I can remember hating math before I took
Dr. Shavelson's statistics course as a master's candidate at UCLA.
When I ask myself later why I had once hated math so much, I
thought back to the last math class I had taken ten years earlier.*

*Algebra II: the last required course, after algebra I and
geometry, in the college-preparatory curriculum in California
secondary schools. I had been fascinated by algebra I and geometry
but later decided not to take trigonometry or calculus because
algebra II was so horrible.*

*Mr. P was a coach at my high school. He was not a talented
algebra teacher. In fact, he seemed to dislike both the subject
matter and the students. I remember swearing that I'd never study
any form of mathematics again the day I left his classroom for
the last time.*

*As a reality check, I asked my old friend Rudy Spano if he
had taken trigonometry or calculus after we had studied algebra
with Mr. P. He had not. He, too, remembered Mr. P. and said,
"I thought algebra was over my head. Now I wonder how much of
that was me, and how much of it was that the teacher didn't make
the material interesting. I think Mr. P. had to teach algebra in order
to be a coach." Rudy and I also talked about our earlier math
teacher, Mr. C., who had taught geometry. Rudy recalled, "Mr. C.
had more of a love for what he was teaching than Mr. P. did. He
made it a better learning environment. Mr. P was at home with the
guys on the football field. Mr. C. was at home in the classroom."*

*These recollections led me to a parallel with language learning.
I often ask teachers in training to write an autobiography of their
own language learning experiences. Invariably they identify teachers
who inspired them to learn languages as well as teachers who made
them hate language learning. So it was with me and mathematics.*

Think about a situation in which several people are standing at the front of
a classroom. We could divide those people into groups labeled "tall,"
"medium," and "short." Saying that people are tall, of medium height, or short
is making a statement about what sort of category they fit into. It doesn't tell us
how tall a person is, nor does it tell us who is taller than whom (except that we
can assume that the people in the medium category are taller than those in the
short category, and that those in the tall category are taller than all the people
in the other two categories).

We could, however, ask these people to arrange themselves in order of height, from the tallest to the shortest. (Imagine them standing in a line and comparing their heights with one another, and then rearranging themselves appropriately.) If they did so, we would lose the sharp divisions between the three categories, but we would gain information in the sense that we could see which individuals were taller than which other individuals, relatively speaking. Notice that with statements such as "Yukiko is shorter than Marie, who is shorter than Dieter" and so on, we do not have exact measurements telling us how tall each person is. We only have an indication of their height relative to one another. We don't know, for instance, whether the difference between Yukiko's and Marie's heights is the same as the difference between Marie's and Dieter's heights.

But if we ask each person to tell us his or her height (whether we use the metric system or feet and inches), we then have very specific information about each individual. We can tell how much taller Dieter is than Marie, and whether this is more or less than the difference between Marie's and Yukiko's heights. Because inches (or centimeters) are precise increments on a set scale, we can make clear comparisons. For example, we can say that the difference between five-feet-three inches tall (Yukiko's height) and five-feet-seven inches tall (Marie's height) is the same as the difference between five-feet-seven inches tall (Marie's height) and five-feet-eleven inches tall (Dieter's height).

TYPES OF DATA

The three situations about comparing people's heights illustrate the distinction between three important types of data that are commonly used in language assessment:

1. **Categorical data** (such as "tall" and "medium" and "short") divide people or things into categories. This type of data is also sometimes referred to as **nominal data,** because the labels serve to name the classes of people or things we are discussing. So, for instance, after language assessment procedures have been administered, children in a bilingual education program might be categorized as LEP (limited English proficient) or FEP (fluent English proficient).

2. **Ordinal data** derive their name from the fact that the people or items in a series are rank ordered in terms of some quality or attribute (such as height). So, for example, if students' university identification numbers are listed in the order of their scores on an important final exam, from highest to lowest (or lowest to highest), that list constitutes ordinal data. (The actual scores are not listed.)

3. **Interval data** are so termed because they are measurements derived from scales in which the intervals between one unit and the next on the scale are equal for the entire length of the scale. (An inch is an inch, whether the distance falls between the marks indicating 13 inches and 14 inches on the scale, or between those indicating 35 inches and 36 inches on the scale.)

These distinctions are very important in language assessment because they will determine, in part, the nature of the claims that we can make on the basis of our data. The type of data we are working with will also determine, to a certain extent, the types of statistical analyses we can legitimately conduct.

There is one tricky area to be aware of, however, and that is the gray area between ordinal and interval data. This is an issue that concerns us in language assessment because we so often use rating as a way of assigning scores (especially in direct tests of speaking and writing). A **rating** is an assessment made by an evaluator using a scale, which may or may not be accompanied by explicit descriptors of the scale levels. For instance, in Chapter 12 we will look at the descriptors for the *TWE* scale, which Christine Houba used to analyze her students' essays (Chapter 6). Those level descriptors are explicit. In other cases, the poles of a scale may simply be annotated as "poor" to "excellent." The question arises as to whether the various points on the scale are truly interval in nature. Hatch and Lazaraton (1991, 179) explain the problem like this, using as an example the familiar Likert scale format:

> The numbers show 1 = strongly disagree, 2 = disagree, 3 = neither agree nor disagree, 4 = agree, 5 = strongly agree.

> The question is whether the scale is equal-interval. How large an interval is there between *agree* and *strongly agree*? Between *neither agree nor disagree* and *agree*? Are these intervals the same? Can we use a mean score as a measure of central tendency for such data?

> If we believe the intervals are equal, we should be able to compute a mean and a standard deviation for the responses. If not, then it makes no sense to compute these measures.

However, there is some contention about this issue, as Hatch and Lazaraton point out (180):

> Statisticians most often argue in favor of treating rank-order data as though it were interval data. They see ordinal scales as being continuous (with the mean as the appropriate measure of central tendency). Many argue that statistically it makes no real difference and that it is best to treat ordinal and interval as the same. In many cases we believe it is better to consider them as ordinal rather than as interval data, and especially so if the data are not normally distributed.

The point here is that it is important for you to be clear about whether you are working with categorical data, ordinal data, or interval data. We will use these technical terms to discuss data in talking about the three main types of correlation coefficients that are used in language assessment.

I will use the pilot test results from the two subtests in Christine Houba's writing test to illustrate an important family of statistics that are used in many ways in language testing. (You may wish to glance back at Chapter 6 to refresh your memory of Christine's test at this point.) The general procedure we will now study is known as *correlation,* and the technical meaning of the term is closely related to its use in nonstatistical language.

Basic Correlation Concepts

Let's start by thinking about a situation that is *not* derived from language testing. In general, what would you say is the typical relationship between people's height and their weight? You'll probably say something like the taller a person is, the more he or she will weigh. (Of course, there are exceptions to this generalization: There are tall people who are very slender and therefore don't weigh much in relation to their height, just as there are also shorter people who are heavy.) We cannot claim that height *causes* weight exactly, and certainly weight does not cause height. But there is some relationship between height and weight, and that relationship can be expressed both conceptually and mathematically as a correlation.

When a correlation is expressed mathematically, it is often symbolized by a lower-case *r*. (I think of this symbol as representing *relationship*.) The value of *r* can range from -1.00 to 1.00, but whether it is positive or negative (see below) the *strength* of the relationship (referred to as the **magnitude**) is indicated by the value of *r*: The closer that value is to the whole number 1.00, the stronger the relationship between the two variables. So, for example, as rough guidelines we can say that *r* values of 0.85 to 0.99 would be considered "strong." Correlation coefficients of about 0.70 to 0.84 are "moderately strong," and those in the 0.45 to 0.69 range are "moderate" and *r* values below 0.45 may be considered "weak to moderate" correlations. However, these interpretations are somewhat impressionistic and depend on several factors, including the number of measurements that entered into the correlation.

Using our height and weight example, let's work with some (fictitious) data to illustrate the concept of correlation. Imagine that I asked 30 adults to tell me their height in inches and their weight in pounds. (In the tradition of experimental science and quantitative data with which correlation procedures are most closely associated, I will refer to each individual person as a "subject," identified by a code number.) Here's what the data might look like:

Table 8.1: Raw Data for Thirty People's Heights and Weights

Subject	Height (inches)	Weight (pounds)
1	60	105
2	65	120
3	72	180
4	73	200
5	62	105
6	68	150
7	67	160
8	67	150
9	60	103
10	63	110

11	60	125
12	62	140
13	72	160
14	74	180
15	75	210
16	66	220
17	70	200
18	69	155
19	69	160
20	69	153
21	78	220
22	78	200
23	67	160
24	61	102
25	63	105
26	63	120
27	76	145
28	66	120
29	64	130
30	68	170

Even though these data are clearly displayed, it is not easy to see from the column format whether there is a patterned relationship between height and weight. One helpful format to check for such a relationship is called a *scatterplot* (or *scattergram*). It works like this.

We will represent weight on the vertical axis (formally called the *y* axis) and height on the horizontal axis (or *x* axis) of a grid whose two axes meet at the lower left corner of the field:

Figure 8.1: Framework of the Scatterplot of Height and Weight Data

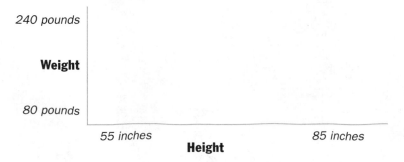

So far we have the backdrop onto which we can map (or "plot") our data. The two axes represent the two variables, height and weight, so by entering the data representing each individual's height and weight, we can see if there's a patterned relationship between these two variables. Subject 1 was sixty inches tall and weighed 105 pounds, so we enter a dot at the point where the lines representing 60 inches and 105 pounds would intersect. If we repeat this step for each person's data, the results should look like Figure 8.2.

Figure 8.2: Scatterplot of Height and Weight Data

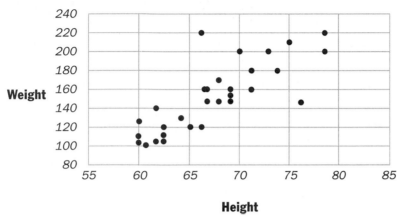

Now do you see why the completed grid is called a **scatterplot**? The data points plotted against the space defined by the axes that represent the two variables provide a graphic depiction of the relationship. The scattered dots provide a pictorial representation of the relationship between the variables height and weight in this data set.

You will have observed that the dots in this scatterplot cluster around an invisible line leading from the lower left corner to the upper right corner of the chart. You will have also seen that a few dots are positioned somewhat away from the line. Can you locate the dot that represents the height and weight of person 16? What about the dot that represents the height and weight of person 27? By reading the data in Table 8.1, we can see that person 16 is relatively short and heavy, whereas person 27 weighs relatively little for his height. But by looking at the scatterplot, we can see more clearly where the data for these two people fall relative to the data for the other people in the group. You'll see that the two dots representing person 16 and person 27 fall outside the cluster of dots representing the rest of the group. Data points like these that fall outside a clear pattern of correlation on a scatterplot are called **outliers.**

In general, what would you say is the relationship between height and weight, now that you have seen this scatterplot? As before, you'll probably say that the taller a person, the more he will weigh. (Again, this is a generalization that doesn't always hold true, as evidenced by our outliers.) This statement is, in effect, a claim about a **positive correlation**—a situation in which, as scores on one variable increase, so do the scores on the other variable. Likewise, as scores on one variable decrease, the scores on the other variable will also decrease.

PEARSON'S CORRELATION COEFFICIENT

The concept of correlation is extremely important in language testing. Let's return to the question of the relationship between the enabling skills, or sub-skills (such as vocabulary and grammar), and the macroskills (such as reading and writing). As a teacher, you may believe that mastery over vocabulary and grammar will contribute to your students' abilities to read and write in the target language. There are four possible hypotheses of positive correlation that we can write to express these beliefs:

1. There will be a positive correlation between scores on a grammar test and scores on a reading test.

2. There will be a positive correlation between scores on a grammar test and scores on a writing test.

3. There will be a positive correlation between scores on a vocabulary test and scores on a reading test.

4. There will be a positive correlation between scores on a vocabulary test and scores on a writing test.

All of these hypotheses predict that in a group of students, as scores on the sub-skill test (grammar or vocabulary) increase, so will scores on the test of the macroskill (reading or writing). If these hypotheses were supported by the data from the four subtests, the scatterplots would look something like our visual image in Figure 8.2, representing the relationship of height and weight. That is, the dots would cluster in such a way as to make a pattern grouped around that invisible diagonal line running from the lower left corner to the upper right corner of the scatterplot. The more tightly clustered the dots are to the invisible diagonal line, the stronger the relationship between the two variables being correlated.

There are also some instances where you may encounter a **negative correlation**. A "negative" correlation isn't bad, nor is a "positive" correlation good. These terms simply refer to the direction of the relationship. Let's look at an example of a hypothesis that predicts a negative correlation. How do you think students' vocabulary knowledge in a foreign language relates to the time it would take them to read a 500-word passage in that language? If vocabulary is indeed an enabling skill underlying the reading macroskill, then the hypothesis might be worded something like this:

5. There will be a negative correlation between scores on a target language vocabulary test and the length of time needed to read a 500-word passage in the target language.

In other words, the prediction is that the broader a student's vocabulary is, the faster he will read.

Now imagine what the scatterplot would look like if you actually conducted tests to generate the data to test hypothesis 5. What would the distribution of data points on the scatterplot that would support this fifth hypothesis look like? The axes on the scatterplot would be labeled as in Figure 8.3.

Figure 8.3: Framework for the Scatterplot of Vocabulary Scores and Reading Time

If you pictured an imaginary diagonal line running from the upper left corner to the lower right corner of the scatterplot, you are correct. This pattern is called a "negative correlation" because as scores on one variable increase, scores on the other variable decrease.

All of the data we have been using in these examples are from interval scales (inches, pounds, test scores, and minutes). When we are trying to correlate two variables that have been measured on interval scales, the particular formula we use is called "Pearson's correlation coefficient," or its full name, "Pearson's product-moment correlation coefficient," or just "Pearson's r." (We will examine its formula in the "Investigations" section of this chapter.)

Pearson's r is the most widely used member of the correlation family in language assessment. This is partly because so many hypotheses that are tested in this field use interval data, and partly because Pearson's results allow us to use an interesting construct known as "overlapping variance."

OVERLAPPING VARIANCE

Suppose we wish to correlate the results of two tests to see to what extent they are measuring the same trait. (This is a commonly used procedure for checking reliability and validity.) We would expect the results of two different tests of writing to correlate much more strongly than, say, the scores from a writing test and the scores from a pronunciation test because we believe writing and pronunciation to be different constructs. Suppose we found the following (fictitious) correlation coefficients by making these comparisons:

Writing Test 1 and Writing Test 2: $r = 0.90$

Writing Test 1 and Pronunciation Test: $r = 0.50$

Writing Test 2 and Pronunciation Test: $r = 0.30$

If we used Pearson's correlation coefficient to derive these r values, we can go one step further and square the correlation coefficients to get a measure of *overlapping variance*. You will recall from our discussion of measures of dispersion in Chapter 7 that variance is "an indicator of the spread of scores in a distribution" of scores (Jaeger 1990, 384). The pronunciation test and the first and second writing tests all had a variety of scores in their data sets. When we use the Pearson's r formula to correlate the students' scores on the various tests, we can square the resulting r values to find the overlapping variance of the three tests.

Overlapping variance is represented by r^2. This value is interpreted as the extent to which the two tests being correlated measure the same construct. In fact, it is sometimes called "shared variance" or "shared variance overlap." Using our writing and pronunciation data, we can illustrate this concept:

Writing Test 1 and Writing Test 2: $r = 0.90$ $r^2 = 0.81$

Writing Test 1 and Pronunciation Test: $r = 0.50$ $r^2 = 0.25$

Writing Test 2 and Pronunciation Test: $r = 0.30$ $r^2 = 0.09$

You can see from the values in the r column and the r^2 column that the stronger the magnitude of the correlation, the greater the overlapping variance will be.

This kind of analysis is useful in several different kinds of applications. One practical context would be if you were trying to determine the relationship between a direct test and an indirect test of the same construct, as Christine Houba was; another would be if you wished to substitute a shorter, more practical test for a lengthy test. The r^2 value would be an indication of the extent to which the two different tests measure the same thing.

In fact, Pearson's correlation coefficient is often used to help establish the validity of a test. There are many different types of validity, but you will recall that the basic definition of the concept is the extent to which a test measures what it is intended to measure. So if you are administering a language test that contains subtests to measure students' skills in reading, listening, grammar, and vocabulary, for instance, you would hope that these different subtests are measuring different things. That is why many commercial test publishers will include correlation tables in their test manuals showing that there is a low correlation among the various subtests. The low correlation coefficients indicate that the subtests are indeed measuring different areas of the students' language skills.

Another important application of the correlation statistic in developing a test is to administer the new test and an older, accepted test to the same group of people, and then correlate the two sets of scores. The resulting correlation coefficient is considered to be an estimate of the new test's **criterion-related validity,** where the accepted test is taken as the criterion. (For further information about the various kinds of validity that are important in test development, see Alderson, Clapham, and Wall, 1995; Bachman, 1990; and Brown, 1996.)

SPEARMAN'S RANK-ORDER CORRELATION

The second most commonly used correlation statistic in language assessment is called "Spearman's rank-order correlation coefficient" (after its inventor). It is also referred to as "Spearman's rho" (after the Greek letter, rho [ρ], which is used to represent the concept), or simply as "Spearman's r." The concept is similar to that of Pearson's correlation coefficient, but in this case instead of using interval data (such as test scores) we will use ordinal data (such as rankings of students' essays relative to one another).

Spearman's rho is useful in cases in which we have two sets of rank-order data we want to correlate, or one set of rank-order data and one set of interval data. (The interval data can easily be rank-ordered so they can be correlated with ordinal data.) Here are some examples:

1. Two different teachers have ranked a group of ten students from most to least communicatively competent. You want to see to what extent the two teachers' rankings correlate with one another.

2. The students in your English grammar class take the *Practice TOEFL*. You have your own opinions of which students are better in the skills measured by the *Practice TOEFL*, so prior to scoring the exam, you list the students' names in order from most to least proficient. You want to see how closely your assessment parallels the students' *Practice TOEFL* scores.

3. Several students of French are competing for cash prizes in a speech contest. Two judges independently rank order the five finalists from first to fifth. You want to see how well the two judges' evaluations correlate.

4. Using an objective scoring system, you score your students' essays. Then, just to see how a nonteacher would react to the same essays, you ask your friend to read the papers and stack them in a pile from best to worst. You want to see how closely your ratings correlate with your friend's rankings.

I hope you noticed that examples 1 and 3 used two sets of ordinal data, whereas examples 2 and 4 both involved one set of interval data (the *Practice TOEFL* scores in 2 and the objective essay scores in 4) and one set of ordinal data. Given these examples, you can see that if we have interval data, it can easily be converted to rank-order data. (Remember the example of relative heights given above.) But rank-order data cannot be turned into interval data legitimately if we don't know the precise measurements that led to the rank ordering.

There are two important things to remember about using Spearman's rank-order correlation coefficient. The first is that it does not handle tied ranks very well, which was a problem for Christine Houba with her data, as we will see below. The second is that the resulting value of the correlation coefficient cannot be squared to give you an estimate of the variance overlap, which is one of the useful functions of the Pearson's correlation coefficient. For these reasons (and others), Spearman's rho is considered a less powerful statistical test than Pearson's correlation coefficient. But it is still useful, and it shows up quite often in the professional literature on language learning (especially on second language acquisition). It is also easy to calculate as we will see in the "Investigations" section of this chapter.

POINT-BISERIAL CORRELATION COEFFICIENT

The third most common kind of correlation is called the point-biserial correlation coefficient, and it has a very important use in language assessment. The odd name is a reflection of the kind of data used in this correlation procedure. With a point-biserial correlation coefficient, one set of data is interval data (e.g., test scores—the series) and the other is **dichotomous categorical data** (that is, categorical data with only two categories—hence the *bi* in biserial).

To illustrate the point-biserial correlation coefficient, here are some data from a study I conducted with Frances Butler Hinofotis and Susan Stern.

Nonnative speakers of English who were candidates for teaching assistantship positions at the University of California were videotaped explaining a concept from their major field in English (their second language) to a mock student (me). Raters then observed the same videotapes of ten different speakers on two different viewing occasions and evaluated them on a scale of one to nine in terms of their oral English proficiency.

In addition to rating the candidates' oral English on a nine-point overall impression scale, the raters answered yes or no to the question of whether the candidate should be a teaching assistant at UCLA. We then used the point-biserial procedure to correlate the mean scores on the overall impression question with the raters' yes/no responses on the TA question. As you can see, the yes/no answers are dichotomous data, and the raters' evaluations of the candidates' English on a nine-point scale may be considered to be interval data. The question is, to what extent are the ratings on the nine-point scale related to the raters' yes/no decisions? To answer this question, we used the point-biserial correlation coefficient. We found some interesting inconsistencies (1981, 116–117):

> In order to determine the degree of correspondence between the overall impression scores and the *yes/no* answers on the TA question a point-biserial correlation coefficient (r_{pb}) was computed for the first and second viewing. Correlations of 0.79 for the first viewing and 0.70 for the second viewing were obtained . . . The coefficient indicates the extent to which the score on a continuous variable (the nine-point global scale) correlates with the "score" on the dichotomous variable (the *yes/no* answer on the TA question).

These correlation coefficients (0.79 and 0.70) are positive but not terribly high. (They may be considered "moderately strong.") However, when we calculated the point-biserial correlation coefficient for each individual rater, using their ratings for all the videotaped subjects, we found considerable variation among the raters, as shown in Table 8.2.

Table 8.2: Point-biserial Correlation Coefficients (r_{pb}) for Nine Raters' Acceptability Decisions vs. Overall Scores[3]

Rater	First Viewing	Second Viewing
1	—4	0.73
2	0.72	0.71
3	0.58	0.89
4	0.91	0.87
5	0.76	0.60
6	0.58	0.37
7	0.86	0.32
8	0.88	0.70
9	0.79	0.71

3. This table was originally printed as Table 12 in Hinofotis, Bailey, and Stern (1981, 117).

4. In the first viewing, no r_{pb} could be computed for Rater 1 because he awarded "yes" answers to all the subjects on the TA question.

In a sense, these point-biserial correlation coefficients may be interpreted as measures of the systematicity of the relationship of each rater's yes/no responses to the TA question and the scores they awarded on the nine-point overall scale: The higher the value of the point-biserial correlation coefficient, the stronger the relationship. We will return to this important procedure in Chapter 9, when we learn about its use in item analysis.

Regardless of whether the correlation value is derived from Pearson's formula, Spearman's rank-order formula, or the point-biserial formula, the resulting correlation coefficient is read in the same way: The range of values is from -1.00 to +1.00. The minus or plus indicates the direction of the relationship (negative or positive). The strength of the relationship between the two variables is indicated by the magnitude of the correlation: The closer the number is to the whole number, ±1.00, the stronger the relationship is between the two variables.

Teachers'
Voices

As we saw in Chapter 6, one of Christine Houba's (1996, 7) original questions was "What is the relationship between what indirect tests measure and what direct tests measure?" In order to answer this question, Christine correlated the sixteen students' scores on the editing task (the objectively scored, discrete-point, indirect test) with the ratings assigned to their essays (the integrative, direct test of writing) on the six-point holistic *TWE* scale. Here's what she found:

> The correlation between the two tests was 0.81 . . . When the coefficient of 0.81 is squared, we see that there is about 66 percent variance overlap between the two tests, which means that they probably measure something somewhat similarly (p. 10).

As you will recall from our discussion of magnitude, an *r* value of 0.81 is strong, especially for such a small group of test-takers. And, as Christine points out, the shared variance of the two tests was 66 percent, or about two-thirds. Remember, though, that correlation does not indicate causality. These results do not tell us that editing skills *cause* people to be good writers (as measured by the *TWE* scale). Nor do they lead to the conclusion that being able to write well necessarily means one can locate errors well in one's own writing. The finding simply indicates that for this group of test-takers, there was a relationship between their holistic ratings on the essay and their objective scores on the editing task. Here is Christine's comment:

> I was surprised to find such an indication of a positive relationship between editing skills and writing skills. I was really expecting to find the opposite, which would support my belief that editing and writing are very different skills. I have long felt that the two skills should not be used in tests as if they were the same. Although the results from this particular pilot test are not generalizable, they do indicate that there may be a stronger correlation between the two skills than I had thought. I am interested in doing further research on the subject, and in revising the editing subtest to increase the consistency of measurement (pp. 14–15).

Now bear with me here for a bit of statistical analysis based on Christine's situation. You will recall from our examination of data types that one key issue is what sort of data you are working with. You must decide on this issue *before* you select a statistical procedure for analyzing your data. You will also recall that there are three very important correlation formulae that are widely used in language assessment, and that the choice among them depends in part on the nature of your data.   Let's review briefly:

1. **Pearson's correlation coefficient** (also called Pearson's *r* or Pearson's product-moment correlation coefficient) uses two sets of interval data.

2. **Spearman's correlation coefficient** (also called Spearman's rho after its Greek letter, [ρ], or Spearman's rank order correlation coefficient, or simply Spearman's *r*) uses either
   a. two sets of ordinal data, or
   b. one set of ordinal data and one set of interval data (easily converted into ordinal data).

3. The **point-biserial correlation coefficient** (symbolized by r_{pb}), is used when you are working with one set of interval data and one set of dichotomous categorical data. (We will return to point-biserial correlation coefficients in Chapter 9, when we consider item analysis.)

Given what you know about Christine's data, what would be the appropriate statistic for her to use to analyze the relationship between her twelve-item editing task and her essay task?

If we make the assumption that the twelve items on the editing task are equally weighted (both linguistically and mathematically), then we can say that the twelve points possible on the editing task are interval data. The problem arises when we look at the six-point *TWE* scale (or any other holistic rating scale for that matter). The descriptions on the *TWE* scale (see Chapter 10) do not guarantee that the difference between a rating of four and a rating of five, for example, conveys the same interval of difference as that found between ratings of one and two, or even two and three. (Indeed, if you were to be trained as an official *TWE* rater, one of the first decisions you would learn to make is the crucial distinction between a level three paper and a level four paper.) In other words, holistic scales may represent ordinal distinctions rather than true intervals: Certainly a rating of 5 is higher than a rating of 4, but is it the same amount higher as a rating of 4 relative to a 3, or a 3 relative to a 2? Unless we can make firm claims about equidistant intervals between the contiguous points on a scoring system, we cannot confidently state that it represents an interval scale.

I think you can see where I'm going here, since some people might feel that Christine's essay ratings would be more properly categorized as ordinal data than as interval data. So you're probably thinking, "Aha! She should have used Spearman's rho, not Pearson's *r*, to examine the relationship between her editing task and her essay task." Well, okay, maybe, but there's another problem here and frankly, this is the kind of stuff that drives first-year research students (and their graduate advisors) crazy. The problem is that the formula for Spearman's rank-order correlation coefficient does not accommodate tied ranks very well, especially when there are several ties and you are doing the calculations by hand. (Hatch and Lazaraton [1991, 453] recommend the use of a statistic called Kendall's tau if you have several tied ranks in your ordinal data.) Consider Christine's essay test scores: Of the sixteen students who took her test, four received a score of two, seven received a score of three, and five received a score of four. (No essays were rated as ones, fives, or sixes.) In other words, four people tied for ratings of two, seven people for ratings of three, and five people for ratings of four. In this case, the Spearman's rank-order correlation coefficient could not have accommodated the test data. But we also know that the point biserial correlation coefficient was not appropriate because Christine's *TWE* data consisted of three rating levels (out of the possible six)—not just two. So she was left with Pearson's Correlation Coefficient as her choice to analyze the relationship between her editing task and her essay task, even though the procedure wasn't an ideal match with the data. In fact, she checked to see that the scores were normally distributed (one of the assumptions underlying Pearson's *r*) and then proceeded. We will walk through the steps of her computations in one of the tasks below.

---

1 *Look at the data in Table 8.2. Given the point-biserial correlation coefficients, which rater was the most consistent in terms of the relationship between his yes/no answers and his overall scores? Which rater was the least consistent? (If you said rater 4 and rater 7, respectively, that is correct.)*

Investigations

If you want to see the formula for the point-biserial correlation coefficient, I suggest you look at Hatch and Lazaraton's book (1991, 448). However, the point-biserial correlation coefficient is extremely tedious to calculate by hand. (In Chapter 9 I will show you a shortcut procedure which is useful in language test development.) If you do need to calculate point-biserial correlation coefficients, it's best to use a computer program.

---

2 *Below is the raw score formula for Pearson's correlation coefficient. We're going to walk through this formula step by step, to "unpack" it. The lengthy formula looks intimidating, but if you look closely you will see that it consists of only a few elements that are used repeatedly in various combinations:*

$$r_{xy} = \frac{N (\Sigma xy) - (\Sigma x)(\Sigma y)}{\sqrt{[N\Sigma x^2 - (\Sigma x)^2][N\Sigma y^2 - (\Sigma y)^2]}}$$

We have encountered all of these symbols before, so let's begin by examining the formula's denominator more closely. Although it looks rather imposing at first glance, there is a pattern to it:

$$\sqrt{[N\Sigma x^2 - (\Sigma x)^2][N\Sigma y^2 - (\Sigma y)^2]}$$

If we remove the square root sign for the moment, you will see that we have two very similar mathematical terms:

$$(1)\ [N\Sigma x^2 - (\Sigma x)^2],\quad \text{and } (2)\ [N\Sigma y^2 - (\Sigma y)^2]$$

What is the difference between these two mathematical terms? (Keep in mind that we're learning a language here. Imagine that I'm asking you to compare two similar sentences—"She made the cookies" versus "She ate the cookies," for instance.)

If you look closely, you'll see that these two "sentences" are identical except that the first "sentence" uses x twice in the same slots where the second uses y twice. You will recall from our earlier discussion that in correlation, the symbol x represents the variable on the horizontal axis and the symbol y represents the variable on the vertical axis of the scatterplot. (In the case of Christine's data, the scores on the editing task would be the x variable and the scores on the essay would be the y variable.) You also probably remember from our discussion of the formula for the mean that Σ indicates we must sum what follows.

It is crucial to remember at this point that statistical operations often involve ordering rules, just as learning a new language involves syntactic rules. In this case, it is important to know that Σx^2 and $(\Sigma x)^2$ mean two different things. (Think of them as minimal syntactic pairs.) What do these two terms mean?

1. Σx^2 is translated as the sum of x^2—in other words, square each score and then sum the results.

2. $(\Sigma x)^2$ is translated as the sum of x, squared—meaning that you sum all the scores and then square the result. It is the parentheses that tell you to sum the scores before squaring them.

Believe it or not, this subtle distinction results in vastly different numbers when you calculate the formula.

The next step is to recall that the first terms inside both the left and right brackets were preceded by an N (for *number*), and the terms in both brackets were under the square root sign, as follows:

$$\sqrt{[N\Sigma x^2 - (\Sigma x)^2][N\Sigma y^2 - (\Sigma y)^2]}$$

So the next thing we need to do is multiply the first value inside each bracket by the number of scores being correlated (so N is the same value in each set of brackets).

So far we have analyzed the component of the formula summarized in the symbols $[N\Sigma x^2 - (\Sigma x)^2]$—what we called the first "sentence" above. I expect that you can now explain the sequential procedures involved in calculating the following term: $[N\Sigma y^2 - (\Sigma y)^2]$.

Now you should have four numbers, two in each set of brackets. The brackets indicate that the second term in each bracket (i.e., the term in parentheses) needs to be subtracted from the first term. Once you have done this subtraction you will have two numbers—one inside the brackets that were surrounding the x side of the denominator, and the other inside the brackets representing the y side of the denominator. The two sets of adjacent brackets are telling us we now need to multiply these two numbers.

At this point, if you are calculating Pearson's r by hand, it's very important *not* to forget to find the square root of the product you've just obtained by multiplying the two numbers. When you've done that, you'll have your denominator.

Compared to what you've already done, the numerator seems quite straightforward:

$$N(\Sigma xy) - (\Sigma x)(\Sigma y)$$

Interpreting the parentheses correctly is the key to working this part of the equation. What is the difference between (Σxy) and $(\Sigma x)(\Sigma y)$? The first term, (Σxy), is telling us to multiply each person's score on the x variable by the same person's score on the y variable, and *then* sum the results. (So in the case of Christine Houba's data, we would multiply each student's score on the editing subtest by that same person's score on the essay. When we had done that for all sixteen students, we would total the results.) The total is then multiplied by the number of students involved. The second term, $(\Sigma x)(\Sigma y)$, is telling us to add all the scores on the x variable (e.g., the editing subtest scores), add all the scores on the y variable (e.g., the essay scores), and then multiply the two totals. After you do the subtraction, you will have completed the numerator of the equation.

At this point you must divide the numerator by the denominator. If you get a negative number, it means the two variables are negatively correlated (i.e., as scores on one variable increase, scores on the other decrease). However, if you get a number greater than the whole number 1.00, it means there is a mathematical error somewhere in your calculations.

These days many pocket calculators will compute Pearson's correlation coefficient, and any reasonable statistics package on a computer will include at least this correlation formula. However, if you are doing the calculations by hand (or if you are trying to explain to your colleagues how correlations work), it's useful to set up a worksheet with column headings that reflect the steps in the formula.

Table 8.3 shows the students' scores on the twelve-point editing task and the six-point essay (as rated on the *TWE* scale) from Christine Houba's data. We will use these data to illustrate the suggested worksheet format and work through a correlation problem.

Table 8.3: Students' Scores on Christine Houba's Editing Task and Essay

Student number	Editing Task (x)	x²	Essay (y)	y²	xy
1	4		3		
2	3		2		
3	5		3		
4	4		2		
5	10		4		
6	6		4		
7	8		4		
8	5		3		
9	5		3		
10	3		3		
11	5		3		
12	8		4		
13	2		2		
14	4		4		
15	5		3		
16	6		3		
	$\Sigma x =$	$\Sigma x^2 =$	$\Sigma y =$	$\Sigma y^2 =$	$\Sigma xy =$

If you insert the values you obtained into the Pearson's r formula, you should get the same correlation coefficient that Christine got — $r = 0.81$. What would the value of r^2 be?

---

3 *Below is the z score formula for Pearson's correlation coefficient. You will recall that we use the z score transformation if the scales we are working with are not equivalent:*

$$r_{xy} = \frac{\Sigma(z_x z_y)}{N - 1}$$

Compared to the Pearson's raw score correlation formula above, the z score correlation formula seems very straightforward. Remember, you'll need the original z score transformation formula to be able to derive the numerator in the equation above. That formula, which we saw in Chapter 7, is:

$$z = \frac{X - \bar{X}}{s}$$

For practice, try converting Christine's two sets of data to z scores and T-scale scores. In fact, since she was working with one set of data from a twelve-point scale and another from a six-point scale, Christine used the z score formula when she calculated the correlation.

---

4 *In case you are working with ordinal data, remember that you need to use the formula for Spearman's rho instead. Here is the formula for Spearman's rank-order correlation coefficient:*

$$\rho = 1 - \frac{6(\Sigma d^2)}{N(N^2 - 1)}$$

Compared to the formula for Pearson's correlation coefficient given above, this equation is pretty straightforward. It uses only two new symbols: ρ (rho) represents the correlation; d stands for the difference between the ranks. Once again, in computing this formula, we must pay attention to the ordering rules. The numerator, $6(\Sigma d^2)$, tells us to perform the following steps in the following order.

1. Square each difference, d, between the rankings;

2. sum the values of d^2; and

3. multiply that sum by six.

The number 6 here is what's called a "constant." It doesn't change, regardless of the number of scores in your data set. There is also a required order in calculating the denominator: $N(N^2 - 1)$. Can you tell what that order should be? (If you said square the number, subtract one from N^2, and then multiply the result by N, you are correct.)

If you saved the scores from your cloze-test investigation (Task 4 in Chapter 5), you could now try either or both of the two correlations:

1. Use the Pearson's r formula to correlate your test-takers' scores derived from the exact-word scoring method and the acceptable-word scoring method.

2. Use the Spearman's r formula to calculate the value of rho based on the two rank-ordered lists (of the exact-word scores and the acceptable-word scores).

What is the difference, if any, between the two resulting correlation coefficients?

5 *If you have access to two different sets of test scores for the same students, you can compute the correlation coefficient to determine the relationship between the two tests. (Remember to decide first whether you're working with ordinal or interval data. If it's ordinal data, watch out for tied ranks.) How would you interpret your results?*

Suggested Readings

John Oller's (1979) book *Language Tests at School* includes an interesting chapter called "Statistical Traps." It contains an especially informative section on common misinterpretations of correlation data.

Good explanations of the various kinds of correlations used in language assessment can be found in reference books by Brown (1988); Hatch and Lazaraton (1991); Woods, Fletcher, and Hughes (1986); and Shavelson (1988). Donna Johnson's (1992) book *Approaches to Research in Second Language Learning* also has a helpful chapter on correlation.

J. D. Brown (1983) wrote a very clear explication of problems associated with Spearman's rank-order correlation coefficient. His examples are selected from morpheme acquisition research on second language acquisition. Although that paper appeared in a somewhat obscure anthology, it is well worth reading.

The fifth chapter in Henning's (1987) book covers the correlation statistics that are often used in language assessment. It includes some additional procedures I have not addressed here.

9

MULTIPLE-CHOICE TESTS AND ITEM ANALYSES

Then Jephthah gathered together all the men of Gilead, and
fought with Ephraim: and the men of Gilead smote Ephraim,
because they said, Ye Gileadites are fugitives of Ephraim among
the Ephraimites, and among the Manassites.
*   And the Gileadites took the passages of Jordan before the*
Ephraimites: and it was so, that when those Ephraimites which
were escaped said, Let me go over, that the men of Gilead said
unto him, Art thou an Ephraimite? If he said, Nay;
*   Then said they unto him, Say now Shibboleth; and he said*
Sibboleth: for he could not frame to pronounce it right. Then they
took him, and slew him at the passages of Jordan: and there fell
at that time of the Ephraimites forty and two thousand.

[Old Testament: Judges 12, 4–6]

This famous passage from the Book of Judges describes the use of a pronunciation contrast, /š/ versus /s/, to distinguish between members of two groups of people: the Ephraimites (the test-takers) and the Gileadites (the test administrators). The exam was a one-item, single-word repetition test in the discrete-point tradition. The stimulus material was the instruction, "Say now *Shibboleth.*" The task posed was to perceive and produce the phoneme /š/ correctly. The test-taker's response was to produce the single word, *Shibboleth,* in the oral mode. The scoring criteria were *right/wrong,* with the production of the phoneme /s/ counted as a wrong answer with dire consequences. (Some people feel that language testers today are cutthroat, but we certainly don't compare to the Gileadites!)

The example of the Gileadites forcing the Ephraimites to pronounce the word *Shibboleth* presents an interesting problem. Thinking back to the discussion in Chapter 3, would you say it was a norm-referenced test or a criterion-referenced test? I'd say the score interpretation was criterion-referenced (*right* versus *wrong* on the pronunciation of /š/ versus /s/) even though it was a very discrete-point (albeit direct) test of speaking. Now we can add our earlier contrast to the list of contrasting continua we developed in Chapter 6:

1. indirect tests versus direct tests;

2. discrete-point testing versus integrative testing;

3. objective scoring versus subjective scoring; and

4. norm-referenced score interpretation versus criterion-referenced score interpretation.

In other words, although standardized tests tend to be indirect, discrete-point, objectively scored, and norm-referenced, not every test must use this particular combination of elements. It's up to us as teachers to understand these alternatives and to select among them carefully and appropriately. For example, both the *ACTFL Oral Interview* and the *ILR OPI* (described in Chapter 11) claim to be standardized, direct, integrative, criterion-referenced tests. Their scoring criteria are objective rather than subjective, to the extent that (a) the criteria are clearly stated, (b) rater preparation involves rigorous training and careful norming, and (c) the raters are carefully monitored to insure high rater reliability and to prevent rater drift.

Biblical consequences aside, there are times when, for various reasons, we teachers may choose to write very focused test items, in the tradition of discrete-point testing, as discussed in Chapter 6. Using such specific test items can help provide information that is particularly useful in diagnostic testing, and may also be helpful in placement testing and achievement testing, if the items are clearly related to specific objectives of a program.

Unfortunately, in my experience, individuals or teams of teachers often choose to write discrete-point items, particularly multiple-choice items, without fully understanding the many pitfalls associated with this approach. In this chapter I will discuss some of these problems and to describe the procedures that must be used in order to develop and analyze a viable discrete-point test. I will use the familiar multiple-choice format as a case in point because it is so controversial.

MULTIPLE-CHOICE TESTS

Paradoxically, my goal in discussing the multiple-choice format is not to promote its use, but rather to caution you about the dilemmas presented by this approach. Oller takes a very firm stance on this topic (1979, 233). He states

> . . . [T]he preparation of sound multiple choice tests is sufficiently challenging and technically difficult to make them impracticable for most classroom needs. . . .The formidable technical problem of item analysis done by hand will. . . all but completely eliminate multiple-choice formats from consideration.

Given this word of caution, why do teachers, schools, and assessment organizations use multiple-choice items so often? The following reasons come quickly to mind:

1. Multiple-choice tests are fast, easy, and economical to score.
   In fact, they are machine scorable.

2. They can be scored objectively and thus may give the test the appearance of being fairer and/or more reliable than subjectively scored tests.

3. They "look like" tests and may thus seem to be acceptable by convention.

4. They reduce the chances of learners guessing the correct answer, in comparison to true-false items.

However, if you are going to write multiple-choice items, there are at least three things you need to know. The first is that although multiple-choice items can indeed be objectively scored, a great deal of subjective judgment goes into their development. The second point is that though they may be practical to score, good multiple-choice items are extremely labor-intensive to write. These two concerns alone almost counteract the assumed benefits of objectivity and practicality described above.

The third point—and this is the most important—is that there are also major concerns about the likely negative washback of using the discrete-point testing philosophy in general and the multiple-choice format in particular. In fact, Oller (ibid.) has written that

> . . . [T]he multiple choice format is intrinsically inimical to the interests of instruction. What multiple choice formats gain in reliability and ease of administration, in other words, is more than used up in detrimental instructional effects and difficulty of preparation.

Hughes (1989, 3) also criticizes the multiple-choice format:

> Good multiple choice items are notoriously difficult to write. A great deal of time and effort has to go into their construction. Too many multiple choice tests are written where such care and attention is not given (and indeed may not be possible). The result is a set of poor items that cannot possibly provide accurate measurements.

In fact, Hughes (60–62) makes six sweeping criticisms of multiple-choice tests and devotes some discussion to each point:

1. The technique tests only recognition knowledge.

2. Guessing may have a considerable but unknowable effect on test scores.

3. The technique severely restricts what can be tested.

4. It is very difficult to write successful items.

5. Backwash may be harmful.

6. Cheating may be facilitated.

What is it about multiple-choice items that arouses such strong reactions? Let's examine the format more closely.

Every multiple-choice item consists of a **stem** (the beginning of the item) and either three, four, or five answer **options** (with four options being the most common format). One, and only one, of the options is correct, and that is called the **key.** The incorrect options are called **distractors.**

As the term suggests, the purpose of the distractors is to distract the inattentive, unsure, or ill-prepared test-taker—in effect, to lure him away from the key (or to provide plausible alternatives if he is guessing). Once again, Oller (1979,

256) eloquently relates the philosophy underlying the construction of multiple-choice items to problems with negative washback:

> While multiple choice tests have rather obvious advantages in terms of administrative and scoring convenience, anyone who wants to make such tests part of the daily instructional routine must be willing to pay a high price in test preparation and possibly genuine instructional damage. It is the purpose of the multiple choices offered in any field of alternatives to trick the unwary, ill-informed, or less skillful learner. Oddly, nowhere else in the curriculum is it common procedure for educators to recommend deliberate confusion of the learner—why should it be any different when it comes to testing?

In other words, to relate these ideas to the conflicting assessment goals we considered in earlier chapters, the multiple-choice format provides a classic illustration of the dynamic tension between reliability and assumed practicality on the one hand, and validity and positive washback on the other.

If you're going to develop a multiple-choice (or other discrete-point) test—especially one that will remain secure and be used repeatedly—there are some procedures you must be familiar with to be sure your test is working well and providing you with the information you need. These procedures are known collectively as "Item Analyses." (Actually, some of them are equally useful with more integrative tests, as we will see shortly.)

There are two main kinds of item analysis that we will discuss in this chapter: *item facility* and *item discriminability*. We will also look at examples of a *distractor analysis* and a *response frequency distribution*, both of which are specifically related to multiple-choice testing. Each procedure will be examined in turn, and we will illustrate these ideas by using data from Christine Houba's editing task, which was introduced in Chapter 6.

ITEM FACILITY

Item facility (often abbreviated I.F. in tables and research reports) is an index of how easy an individual item was for the people who took it. I.F. is a number, typically printed as a decimal, ranging from 0.0 to 1.0. It represents the proportion of people who got the item right (out of all the people who took the test). The formula is very straightforward:

$$\textbf{I.F.} = \frac{\text{\# of test-takers answering the item correctly}}{\text{\# of test-takers}}$$

For instance, if forty people take a test and only twenty of them answer item 1 correctly, then we would say that item 1 has an I.F. of 0.50 (i.e., 50 percent of the test-takers got it right), because 20 ÷ 40 = 0.50.

What does it mean if an item has an I.F. of 0.0?

What about an item with an I.F. of 1.00?

If you said an I.F. of 0.0 means everyone missed the item, and an I.F. of 1.0 means everyone got it right, you are correct.

Now maybe you're thinking to yourself, "But wait a minute! As a teacher I would be happy if all of my students got all the answers right on material I had taught them!" True. That's because whether or not you knew the terminology, many of the assessment procedures we teachers use—especially achievement tests—are criterion-referenced tests. But whether you are working in the norm-referenced or the criterion-referenced tradition, item facility values can be very informative.

In Table 9.1 are listed the item facility data for Christine Houba's (1996) editing task, which was printed in full in Chapter 6. Due to length restrictions, in this chapter I will only reprint the texts of those items whose data suggest they'd bear further scrutiny.

Table 9.1: Item Facility (n = 16)

Item	Students who answered item correctly	I.F.
1	8	0.50 (50%)
2	4	0.25
3	11	0.69
4	8	0.50
5	1	0.06
6	12	0.75
7	3	0.19
8	8	0.50
9	9	0.56
10	4	0.25
11	7	0.44
12	8	0.50

Here is Christine's interpretation of her I.F. results:

> The item facility chart [Table 9.1] shows the percent of students who answered each item correctly. Oller (1979, 247) says "items falling somewhere between about 0.15 and 0.85 are usually preferred"; generally speaking, items with an I.F. near 0 percent or 100 percent do not yield enough variance to be useful test items. According to Oller's criteria, all the items in my editing test except for number 5 (0.06) are of acceptable difficulty (although item 7 also looks a little suspicious at 0.19). Half of the items appear to be in the medium difficulty range, from 0.44 to 0.56, two items are in the lower difficulty range, at 0.25, and two are rather high, at 0.69 and 0.75. It might be a good idea to replace items 5 and 7 with one high difficulty and one low difficulty item.

DISTRACTOR ANALYSIS

Although I.F. data can be computed with many kinds of test formats, a "Distractor Analysis" is a procedure specifically related to the multiple-choice format. Item facility indices present us with interesting information relative to the entire group of test-takers on each individual item. But in order to improve a multiple-choice test, it's important to see how each individual distractor is functioning. Christine explains:

> One important aspect affecting the difficulty of multiple-choice test items is the quality of distractors. Some "distractors," in fact, might not be distracting at all, and therefore serve no purpose. We can find out which distractors are functioning as they should by doing a distractor analysis.

Remember that the function of the distractors is to sort out those test-takers who know the correct answer (with some degree of certainty) from those who don't know it (or who aren't sure). This approach assumes that there is variability among the test-takers' skills and/or knowledge, and that a main function of the test is to uncover that variability. (I hope this line of thought is reminding you of our discussion of *variance* in Chapter 7.) That's why Christine said that distractors that don't distract anyone serve no purpose in the norm-referenced approach to assessment.

Table 9.2 shows how many people selected each option in Christine's twelve-item multiple-choice editing task. An asterisk denotes the *key*, or correct answer.

Table 9.2: Distractor Analysis (n = 16)

Item	A	B	C	D
1	8*	4	0	4
2	4*	3	5	4
3	3	2	0	11*
4	1	8*	2	5
5	5	6	1*	4
6	2	0	2	12*
7	2	10	3*	1
8	1	2	8*	5
9	9*	5	0	2
10	1	8	3	4*
11	7*	4	2	3
12	2	8*	6	0

Again, here is Christine's interpretation:

> Looking at the zeroes in the Distractor Analysis [Table 9.2], we can see that some distractors were not selected by any of the test-takers. In the philosophy of the multiple-choice format, this

indicates that these distractors should probably be changed. Distractor C for Item 1, distractor C for Item 3, distractor B for Item 6, distractor D for Item 9, and distractor D for Item 12 do not seem to be doing any distracting.

ITEM DISCRIMINATION

Remember that one goal of norm-referenced testing is to uncover the variability in skills and/or knowledge that is assumed to exist in a group of test-takers. For this reason, a comparison of the good students and the poor students, in terms of how they perform on each item, provides useful information in the discrete-point, norm-referenced approach to testing.

But who's to say which are the good students and which are the poor students? If we rely solely on our judgment as teachers, we may be unduly influenced by factors such as who works hard, who comes to class on time, and so on. So in terms of item analysis, the assumption is made that the student's total test score on a specific exam is the best estimate of how good a student he is in terms of whatever knowledge and/or skill that particular exam is measuring.

What would you think about a test item that all your best students missed, even though several of your poorer students got it right? You might take a long hard look at that item to see if you could determine why the good students missed it. Was it perhaps perceived as a "trick question"? Was it ambiguous in some way? Were there two potentially correct answers? These questions are addressed with an item analysis procedure called **item discrimination.** Christine summarizes the logic of this procedure as follows:

> Item discrimination (I.D.) provides a more detailed analysis of the test items than does item facility, because it shows how the top scorers and lower scorers performed on each item. This allows us to investigate whether the item with a low I.F. is actually difficult, or if other factors might be contributing to the low rate of correct response for that item. (For example, if most of the high scorers miss item 1, but several low scorers answer item 1 correctly, this would alert us to the fact that extraneous variables may be affecting the results.) I.D. values range from +1 to -1, with positive 1 showing a perfect discrimination between high scorers and low scorers, and -1 showing perfectly wrong discrimination. An I.D. of 0 shows no discrimination, or no variance whatsoever. The lowest acceptable values are usually set at 0.25 or 0.35 (Oller, 1979).

If you have a computer program that will calculate point-biserial correlation coefficients, that is the most appropriate way to determine item discriminability. You will recall from our discussion of correlation in Chapter 8 that the point-biserial correlation procedure involves one set of dichotomous categorical data and one set of continuous interval data. In the case of item discriminability, the dichotomous variable is whether the students got a particular item right or wrong. The continuous variable (i.e., the interval data) consists of the students' total scores on the test.

Oller (1979, 250–252) describes a short-cut for calculating item discrimination that is easy (though tedious) to do by hand. This is called "Flanagan's method," named for its inventor (1939). Flanagan demonstrated that this shortcut provides a good approximation of the actual correlation coefficient. Following are the steps in Flanagan's method of computing item discriminability:

1. Score the exams. Rank order the papers from highest to lowest score.

2. Take the top 27.5 percent of the exams and the bottom 27.5 percent of the exams from the top and bottom of the pile of papers. These two subsets of the exams will be referred to as the "high scorers" and the "low scorers," respectively. (Set the middle group aside for the moment.) So, for instance, if you have 100 test papers to evaluate, you'll use the top 28 papers and the bottom 28 papers in this step.

3. Then, to compute the I.D. value for each item, you use the following formula:

$$\text{I.D.} = \frac{[\text{\# of high scorers who got the item right}] - [\text{\# of low scorers who got the same item right}]}{27.5\% \text{ of the total number of students tested}}$$

Oller points out that it's probably not worthwhile to calculate I.D. values for groups smaller than 25 or so. However, to illustrate Flanagan's method we will use Christine's editing task to calculate approximate I.D. values. Christine had only sixteen students in her pilot test group, so we decided the best way to approximate Flanagan's method was to use the top 25 percent and the bottom 25 percent of her students to identify the high and low scorers, respectively. In other words, out of the pilot test group of sixteen students, the top four were designated the high scorers and the bottom four the low scorers. If you choose to do this, you need to adjust the denominator in Flanagan's formula accordingly. So Christine used 25 percent instead of 27.5 percent in the denominator of her calculations.

In computing Flanagan's discriminability, tally the number of right answers for both the high scorers and the low scorers for each item. Here is an illustration using Item 1 from Christine's editing task. Pluses indicate correct responses to the item and minuses indicate incorrect responses.

Item 1: Score Tally

High Scorers (n = 4)		Low Scorers (n = 4)	
HS1	+	LS4	–
HS2	+	LS3	–
HS3	–	LS2	–
HS4	+	LS1	+
Total	3	Total	1

We then insert the values 3 and 1 into the I.D. formula:

$$\text{I.D.} = \frac{3 - 1}{25\% \,(16)} = \frac{2}{4} = 0.50$$

Keep in mind that if you alter the formula in this way, you are making Flanagan's approximation somewhat less accurate. Still, the results may provide you with interesting information that should help you interpret your test results and evaluate your test items.

Table 9.3 shows the I.D. values for the twelve items on Christine's editing task. She computed these values using the approximation of Flanagan's method described above.

Table 9.3: Item Discriminability (n = 16)

Item	High scorers (top four) with correct answers	Low scorers (bottom four) with correct answers	I.D.
1	3	1	0.50
2	0	0	0.00
3	4	2	0.50
4	4	1	0.75
5	0	0	0.00
6	4	2	0.50
7	2	1	0.25
8	4	3	0.25
9	3	0	0.75
10	2	0	0.50
11	4	0	1.00
12	2	2	0.00

Based on her item discrimination analysis, in which three items displayed zero discriminability, Christine reached the following conclusions:

In looking at the data, it appears that items 2, 5, and 12 should probably be rewritten, since they do not discriminate at all between high and low scorers:

2. Some famous people will admit that they <u>are</u> a serious disease such
A
   as AIDS <u>or</u> Alzheimer's', but <u>others</u> probably want to keep <u>it</u> a secret.
   B   C   D

5. Sherlock Holmes is <u>a detective who</u> is only interested in <u>the facts,</u>
                        A   B
   and works hard <u>for finding</u> a clue, like footprints <u>on the stairs</u>.
                     C   D

12. <u>Upon hearing</u> the report that the famous actor <u>was died</u>, fans
       A   B
    <u>the world over</u> were overwhelmed <u>with sadness</u>.
       C   D

Of course, the statistic will not tell us *why* the students select particular options. For that we must rely on our experience with our students and on our understanding of interlanguage development and contrastive analysis. No matter what we judge the source of the problem to be, items with I.D. values of 0.00 need to be changed if we are developing a norm-referenced test. (If you are designing a criterion-referenced test, there are situations in which I.D. values of 0.00 would not be problematic. For instance, if all the test-takers missed an item prior to instruction, there would be no variance, so the I.D. value of 0.00 would indicate a need for instruction. Likewise, if all the test-takers got an item right after instruction, the I.D. value would be 0.00, but this could indicate their mastery of the item's content.)

Item discriminability can also point out which items are working quite well. Here is an example from Christine's data.

Item 11 is the best item, with a perfect I.D. value:

11. <u>One of the investor</u> predicts <u>a rise</u> at the end of the first term, after
　　　　　A　　　　　　　　　B
<u>an improvement in</u> <u>the supply and demand</u> relationship.
　　　　C　　　　　　　　D

Indeed the structure "one of the [plural noun]" is difficult for learners of English as a second or foreign language, and seems to be a late-learned structure. Christine's I.D. results for item 11 support this idea. Christine's interpretation of her I.D. values continues:

The other values are fairly solid, with the exception of items 7 and 8, which are just at the lowest acceptable cutoff line and should therefore be reviewed.

7. They <u>were scheduled</u> to take a trip to <u>the Philippines</u> last January,
　　　　　A　　　　　　　　　　　　　B
<u>but met an accident</u> <u>in December</u>.
　　　C　　　　　D

8. In order to join <u>the</u> Entrepreneur Association, you have to be
　　　　　　　　　A
<u>the inventor</u> of <u>the new business</u>, and be <u>successful at it</u>.
　　B　　　　　C　　　　　　　D

Computing I.D. values may seem like a big hassle to you. John Oller called it a "formidable technical problem" (1979, 233). But if you plan to use multiple-choice items, it is important that you can demonstrate that they work well—and part of what that means is that such items discriminate between the high scorers and the low scorers on a norm-referenced test. Professional test developers and publishers always analyze item discriminability. In fact, if your school or program is considering buying a commercially developed test, you should ask for (or even demand!) the I.D. statistics if they are not provided with the test manual.

RESPONSE FREQUENCY DISTRIBUTION

Item discriminability, like item facility, can be conducted with many different test formats. But there is one more variation on this theme that could be useful to you if you are developing or using multiple-choice tests, the response frequency distribution. Again, we will use Christine's data to illustrate.

The response frequency distribution [Table 9.4] gives us an even more detailed look at how the distractors are functioning. This table shows which options were chosen by high scorers and low scorers for each item. The results here also support those in the I.D. table [Table 9.3], in which we noted that items 2, 5, and 12 did not discriminate at all, and items 7 and 8 showed only borderline variance. Looking at the response frequency distribution, we can easily see why this is the case: In items 2 and 5, no one in either group answered correctly, and in item 12, the two groups (high scorers and low scorers) chose identical responses.

In other words, the response frequency distribution combines information from both the distractor analysis and the item discrimination analysis.

Table 9.4: Response Frequency Distribution on the Item Editing Task

		A	B	C	D
Item 1	High Scorers	3*	0	0	1
	Low Scorers	1	2	0	1
Item 2	High Scorers	0*	0	2	1
	Low Scorers	0	2	1	1
Item 3	High Scorers	0	0	0	4*
	Low Scorers	1	1	0	2
Item 4	High Scorers	0	4*	0	0
	Low Scorers	1	1	1	1
Item 5	High Scorers	0	2	0*	2
	Low Scorers	3	0	0	1
Item 6	High Scorers	0	0	0	4*
	Low Scorers	1	0	1	2
Item 7	High Scorers	0	2	2*	0
	Low Scorers	1	2	1	0
Item 8	High Scorers	0	0	4*	0
	Low Scorers	0	0	3	1
Item 9	High Scorers	3*	0	0	1
	Low Scorers	0	3	0	1
Item 10	High Scorers	0	1	1	2*
	Low Scorers	1	3	0	0
Item 11	High Scorers	4*	0	0	0
	Low Scorers	0	2	0	2
Item 12	High Scorers	0	2*	2	0
	Low Scorers	0	2	2	0

Each zero in Table 9.4 indicates that no one selected that distractor. The difference between this table and the distractor analysis (Table 9.2) is that in the earlier table all data from all the test-takers were included. Here we see only the data from the top 25 percent and bottom 25 percent of the examinees, since we were using an approximation of Flanagan's method, given the small number of test-takers in Christine's pilot study. Christine continues:

> It is interesting to see what distractors attracted the high and low scorers. In item 5, for example, no one selected the correct answer, but the high scorers and low scorers differed considerably in the distractors they chose:

5. Sherlock Holmes is <u>a detective who</u> is only interested in <u>the facts</u>,
                              A   B
and works hard <u>for finding</u> a clue, like footprints <u>on the stairs</u>.
                      C   D

	A	B	C	D
High Scorers	0	2	0*	2
Low Scorers	3	0	0	1

In item 8, it seems that only option D was functioning as a distractor, and only for one member of the low-scoring group:

8. In order to join <u>the</u> Entrepreneur Association, you have to be
                          A
<u>the inventor</u> of <u>the new business</u>, and be <u>successful at it</u>.
       B   C   D

	A	B	C	D
High Scorers	0	0	4*	0
Low Scorers	0	0	3	1

These kinds of observations can be very helpful when the test developer is thinking about making revisions, as they show which distractors are functioning for which groups of subjects.

Teachers' Voices

In this section we will hear the voices of two teachers who have used item analyses in their test development efforts. One is the voice of Christine Houba, whose data and reflections we have been using throughout this chapter. The other is the voice of Peter Hicks, who teaches in an adult school ESL program in central California.

You will recall from Chapter 6 that Christine wanted to introduce a direct test of writing into her school's placement examination. When she returned to Japan after studying for her master's degree, she hoped to apply some of the knowledge and skills she had gained. Here is an excerpt from a letter she wrote to me from Japan:

It is difficult to get people to change a system they are used to, even if they know that the change is probably for the better. In such situations, it often seems that the familiarity of the format takes precedence over the quality of the content. This is something I had noticed before, but this time it was particularly frustrating to me because they put me in charge of making the placement test for this term. "Oh, Christine, since you've been studying testing in America, we'd like you to oversee the making of the placement test and share with us what you've learned," they said. I thought that this was a great opportunity for me and a good chance to improve the placement test, but then when I really started doing things, I realized that nobody really wanted to change the testing procedures.

The kind of inertia Christine describes is fairly typical in assessment. It seems to me that testing often (though not always) lags behind teaching, and is in some regards inherently conservative. Why should that be the case? Here are a few possible reasons:

1. Creating tests is hard work. Once a test has been generated and piloted, people hate to let go of it. This is especially true if the tests have been kept secure so that they can be reused.

2. Test results, especially those used in making important decisions, are often seen as immutable. People feel such test procedures are sacrosanct and view change with suspicion (since it might make the test harder or easier).

3. Creating tests is expensive and time-consuming. Developing new items or prompts, pretesting new stimulus material, training and norming teachers with new scoring procedures, and producing new test booklets all take time and money—resources that could be applied to other parts of the program.

Christine's parting comment provides a classic illustration of these factors at work:

In the end, we made the same kind of test we always make, which means that everything was multiple-choice (and therefore easy to score). Of course multiple-choice tests have their place, but if in an entire placement test—reading, writing, listening, speaking—all these sections are only multiple choice, it makes me wonder how much this test can really tell us about what a student can do with English. Sometimes what these decisions come down to is administrative policies. Disappointing, isn't it?

It is possible to bring about change in assessment procedures, but it often demands a team effort and administrative support, as well as knowledge and skill on the part of individual teachers. My friend Peter Hicks surprised himself by getting quite interested in assessment issues while he was completing his master's degree, so I thought it would be valuable to include Peter's comments in this chapter on item analysis, particularly as so many of his remarks indicate the teamwork involved in his setting. Below are Peter's answers to questions I posed to him in an e-mail conversation:

Kathi: What exactly is your job, especially as it involves assessment?

Peter: My job in assessment includes writing exit tests for all of our ESL levels at Salinas Adult School. We have written grammar tests so far, and plan to do reading next. It is also my responsibility to do the item analysis of new items and to provide the statistics on the results of the tests. I am working closely with the teachers and the ESL coordinator.

Since I had been Peter's teacher for courses on language assessment and research, I was both pleased and amused by this comment. I asked him for more information on the kinds of procedures he was using.

Kathi: Do you use descriptive statistics (like the mean and standard deviation and range) in your work? If so, how?

Peter: I use means and standard deviations to compare how different groups are performing on our tests. Intensive classes, for example, tend to have higher mean scores than regular ESL classes, perhaps due to the length of instruction time.

Kathi: Do you ever use correlation in your work? If so, how?

Peter: I have not used correlation yet, but I will soon be using correlation to see if learners' performance on Form 2 of the new grammar tests correlates well with their Form 1 performance. If the correlations are high, this would indicate that the two forms are equivalent. If not, more revision of Form 2, and perhaps Form 1, will be necessary.

I was glad to hear that Peter was learning to do new analyses and also that he was doing the appropriate procedures to try to ensure the quality of their tests. I asked him about his work with item analyses:

Kathi: When we talked, you mentioned point-biserial correlations, so it sounds like you're doing some item analyses. What procedures do you do and why?

Peter: So far, I have done item discrimination analyses, to see if each item was discriminating between the high and low thirds of the subjects. This was very useful in a level exit or achievement test. Item facility was calculated to weed out items which were too easy or too hard. I also did a response frequency analysis to see how the distractors were performing. We changed numerous distractors based upon information from this analysis. I worked closely with the coordinator on the revisions. New items were piloted and analyzed in the same manner.

It struck me that the interest in assessment that Peter had developed was exactly the sort of reaction I'd hoped for from people reading this book. So I asked him what ideas he'd have for other teachers who might wish to pursue an interest in testing. I think the advice he offers is very sound:

Kathi: Do you have any advice, suggestions, cautions, etc., for teachers getting involved with assessment—especially those just learning to use statistical analyses on their data?

Peter: I recommend beginning with the basics to those just getting started. Be careful of taking on too much work in testing if you still are teaching. Test writing and analysis are time-consuming, so I think it's a good idea to plan carefully to avoid an accumulation of data to be analyzed.

I also recommend getting as much input from the instructors as possible. At Salinas Adult School, we began with instructors each writing a set of items for their prospective levels. This provided us with a set of core items to start with. We wrote more items based on our course outline, which has been "aligned" with the Model Standards for the State of California.

In using statistical analyses, it is important for us to remember that most teachers do not have an extensive awareness of statistics. I often find it necessary to explain basic statistical terms, such as standard deviation, to other teachers and coordinators. When you use item analyses and statistical procedures, be prepared to explain, as clearly as possible, what procedures you are using and why. My supervisor, for example, did not see the value in a response frequency analysis until she saw the data presented in a visual (chart) format.

At a recent testing conference in San Diego, the catchword for the year was "Accountability." This could be good news for those interested in beginning work on testing. Administrators are very keen on showing that their programs are working, and that students are actually learning. In this political climate, support for teachers as test writers, in the form of paid hours, is much more likely.

Peter's parting comment echoes Christine's experience. Sometimes dissatisfaction with the status quo leads to the beginnings of change:

Kathi: Do you have any other ideas or comments for the teachers who will read this chapter?

Peter: Teachers, if you are interested in testing, speak up at staff meetings and other forums. You might be surprised to find that people are really listening. My work in testing began when I got upset over our assessment system and complained at a staff development meeting. Several other teachers echoed my concerns, and soon our staff began to develop a site-based achievement test battery.

I hope the "Frameworks" and "Teachers' Voices" in this chapter have helped you learn how to interpret and calculate item analyses. This is a very important part of developing reliable and valid tests, particularly if you are using the multiple-choice format. This knowledge should also help you scrutinize the commercially produced tests you may consider using in your program.

Investigations

1 *Do you remember the graduated dictation we saw in Chapter 2? Jennifer Lin, the person who developed that graduated dictation, computed an item facility analysis on her data. The results are shown in Table 9.5 (Lin, 1982, 123):*

Table 9.5: Item Facility Values for Jennifer Lin's Graduated Dictation

Item No.	I.F. Values
1	0.78
2	0.51
3	0.84
4	0.63
5	0.54
6	0.46
7	0.36
8	0.49
9	0.49
10	0.25
11	0.28
12	0.30
13	0.27

You will recall that the higher the I.F. value, the easier the item was for the collective group of test-takers whose data fed into the computation of the I.F. statistic. You may also recall that an assumption underlying the graduated dictation is that the longer the bursts become, the more difficult they will be. Lin's data reveal some interesting results. Use the spaces in Table 9.6 to rank order the items in Lin's graduated dictation from easiest to most difficult. The first two have been done as examples. (To find the number of words in each burst, refer to Table 2.1 in Chapter 2.)

Table 9.6: Rank Ordering of Bursts in Lin's Graduated Dictation

	Item No.	I.F. Value	Number of Words
Easiest	3	0.84	3
	1	0.78	2
Most Difficult			

If the difficulty of each item depended only on the number of words in the burst, then the item numbers should correspond directly to the item facilities. But as you can see, there are some discrepancies in the rank ordering of the bursts in terms of difficulty.

1 > 3 > 4 > 5 > 2 > 8, 9 > 6 > 7 > 12 > 11 > 13 > 10

Why do you think the tenth burst turned out to be the most difficult?

___

2 *Table 9.7 shows some data derived from Table 7 in J. D. Brown's study of different ways of scoring cloze passages (1980, 315), which we discussed in Task 5 of Chapter 5. In addition to the familiar exact word and acceptable word approaches to scoring cloze passages, Brown also devised a multiple-choice format that was machine scorable because the test-takers selected one of four printed options to fill each blank in the cloze passage. See if you can interpret these data, given what you now know about item facility and item discriminability. Remember that the ideal range for I.F. values is between 0.15 and 0.85. I.D. values should be at least 0.25, preferably between 0.35 and 1.00 (with values closer to the whole number 1.00 indicating better discrimination).*

Table 9.7: Item Analyses for Three Different Methods of Scoring Cloze Tests

Scoring System	Exact Word	Acceptable Word	Multiple Choice
Mean item facility	0.30	0.51	0.64
Mean item discrimination	0.44	0.61	0.42

As Brown points out, with the exact word scoring system, the mean I.F. value (0.30) shows that, on the average, about 30 percent of the students taking the test got each item right. A mean item facility of 0.50 is considered ideal. Remember, too, that in interpreting I.D. values, numbers closer to the whole number 1.00 indicate better item discrimination.

Which scoring system seems best, in terms of item facility?

Which scoring system has the best item discriminability index?

If you said the acceptable word method is best in terms of both item facility and item difficulty, you are correct. This is good news for those of us who favor the acceptable word scoring method in terms of its potential for positive washback.

---

3 *Following are the data from the Response Frequency Distribution table about two items from a multiple-choice reading test developed by a teacher named Pat Bolger. (Pat's test will be discussed in more detail in Chapter 11.) Use these data to calculate the I.F. and I.D. values for these two items.*

Once again, the asterisk indicates the key.

Item 9

	A	B	C	D*
High Scorers (top 25%)	0	0	0	3
Mid Scorers (middle 50%)	0	1	2	3
Low Scorers (bottom 25%)	1	2	0	0
	I.F. = _____		I.D. = _____	

Item 10

	A	B*	C	D
High Scorers (top 25%)	0	0	0	3
Mid Scorers (middle 50%)	0	1	1	3
Low Scorers (bottom 25%)	2	0	1	0
	I.F. = _____		I.D. = _____	

You will notice immediately that Pat's numbers are even smaller than Christine's (a total of twelve people in his pilot test), so we must be cautious in interpreting these results.

Suggested Readings

John Oller (1979, 245–254) describes these item analysis procedures in more detail than I have used here. He includes several clear examples and explains Flanagan's method.

The appendix to Arthur Hughes's (1989) book *Testing for Language Teachers* includes a brief section on item analysis. It covers item facility, item discriminability (which Hughes calls "item-test correlations"), and distractor analysis. It also shows how to set up item analysis record cards for item banking.

Kyle Perkins and Sheila R. Brutten conducted an interesting study of a reading comprehension test in which they related students' background knowledge, which we examined in Chapter 4, to the item discriminability of the test. They found that "reading comprehension items which depend heavily on a reader's background knowledge" did not discriminate well among the test-takers (1988, 7).

Roberta Abraham and Carole Chappelle conducted an interesting study (1992) on the item difficulty of cloze test scores. Their work builds on research by Lyle Bachman (1985), which we considered in Chapter 5.

The topic of item analysis is covered quite well in Chapter 4 of Grant Henning's (1987) book *A Guide to Language Testing*. It includes a helpful section on how to minimize problems at the original item-writing stage, which should be read by anyone writing multiple-choice items.

J. D. Brown's book (1996) *Testing in Language Programs* has an excellent section on developing criterion-referenced language tests.

10

Measuring Meaning: Dictocomps and Strip Stories

On an episode of Star Trek: The Next Generation, *Captain Jean Luc Picard and Ensign Wesley Crusher are traveling together through space in a shuttlecraft. Ensign Crusher is en route to his preliminary Star Fleet examinations.*

Captain Picard asks the ensign, "Did you read that book I gave you?"

Wesley looks slightly sheepish and replies, "Parts of it."

Captain Picard responds in a somewhat sarcastic tone, "That's reassuring."

Wesley says that he hasn't had much time to read lately, since he's been preparing for his exams. Captain Picard says, "There is no greater challenge than the study of philosophy."

Wesley replies, "I don't really think William James will be on my Star Fleet exams, sir."

Captain Picard sighs audibly and responds, "The important things never are."

The conversation between Ensign Crusher and Captain Picard provides an example of perceived negative washback: Wesley hasn't been reading philosophy because he's been studying for his Star Fleet examinations. Picard's reaction, that the really important things are never included on exams, represents the point of view of many frustrated teachers.

One source of teachers' frustration with language tests is the lingering sense that sometimes the really important things are not typically assessed. Teachers often see a mismatch (as Ellie Mason did in Chapter 3) between the skills they address in their classrooms and the material that is covered in exams, especially standardized multiple-choice tests.

With the advent of communicative language teaching as a widely used approach, language teachers have become especially aware that many traditional testing formats emphasize form over meaning. In this chapter we will examine two teaching and testing procedures. The first one, the dictocomp, focuses almost exclusively on meaning. As mentioned in Chapter 2, the dictocomp procedure is related to dictation, but the scoring criteria are quite different. The first "Teacher's Voice" section of this chapter will report on my use of a dictocomp with one particular group of ESL students. The second procedure discussed in this chapter, the strip story, invokes the learners' understanding of lexical meaning, but also demands an understanding of coherence and cohesion in discourse. The second "Teacher's Voice" reports on an experience I had in trying to get my writing students to connect form and meaning using a strip story.

Some years ago my friend Penny Partch was teaching a course of intermediate ESL students. Since she wanted them to have exposure to different people speaking English, she asked me if I would visit her class. Here the first "Teacher's Voice" you hear will be my own, acting as a visiting teacher, describing a task I developed and administered in her class. Penny and I agreed that I would do a dictocomp exercise with her students, since they had been working on listening for meaning, and on writing.

For purposes of illustration, this chapter first uses the dictocomp as a sample technique. It is a variation on the traditional dictation procedure, in which the teacher reads a paragraph or a short story several times while students listen carefully. Typically the paragraph contains vocabulary and grammar structures studied in the course. After the teacher has read the paragraph for the last time, the students write the ideas as they remember them, staying as close as possible to the original meaning and sequence of events. The students do not write while the teacher is reading the paragraph. They write only after the complete paragraph or story has been read and understood. To the extent the students write what they remember exactly, this activity is similar to a traditional dictation exercise, but to the extent that they have to fill in the memory gaps, making sense of the story contextually, this is a creative composition exercise (Wishon and Burks, 1968, 10). In scoring a dictocomp we emphasize the students' grasp of meaning.

I chose to read a story (reproduced below) partly because I thought it would interest the students since they were familiar with the setting. But I also thought it would be fun since Penny herself had been a character in the story even though she had never heard it before. I read the story aloud to the students three times, at their request. They listened and then wrote a summary of the story.

In terms of Wesche's framework, the stimulus material here is the story of how an extraordinary person, Dick Hedge, performed a secret kindness. The events described in the story had taken place many years before, but Dick's kindness had never been revealed to his classmates, of whom Penny was one. Needless to say, Penny was very surprised when she heard the story told in full for the first time.

You will notice that the text includes a number of words that were probably beyond the students' vocabulary development (*dominated, pilfer, slush fund, sabbatical, recognizance, profusely,* etc.). If you are using the dictocomp technique for teaching purposes (as I was), you may wish to explain some vocabulary or allow the students opportunities to ask about the unfamiliar words. If you are using a dictocomp for assessment purposes, you must decide if part of the task posed to the learners is to discern the meaning of unfamiliar lexical items from the context. As you read this story, imagine how you yourself would summarize it.

Every year the Monterey Institute of International Studies (MIIS) hosts a dinner dance the night before graduation. As a faculty member, I am expected to attend such functions, but the TESOL students don't usually go. The party is always dominated by IPS and IM students.[5] So every year I end up sitting and drinking and watching other people dance, and wishing I weren't there.

One year I asked my students in advance if any of them were going. Molly said, "I'd like to go, if anyone else is going." Dick said, "I'd like to go." Penny said, "I'd like to go, but $20.00 a ticket is too expensive." I said, "Well, if you'd like to go and the cost is holding you back, come see me and we'll pilfer some money from the departmental budget."

Nobody said anything more about the graduation dinner dance until the tickets went on sale. Then Dick came to my office and asked me if anyone had followed up on the offer for financial assistance. I said, "No, but I guess it's a good thing. The departmental slush fund is pretty low now that it's the end of the academic year."

Now you need to understand about Dick. He was an experienced school teacher who used his sabbatical year to come back to school and do an MA in TESOL. Since his career was well established, he didn't have some of the financial difficulties faced by most of the other TESOL students. He was also a quiet leader in the group, sensitive and thoughtful, and very kind.

Well, Dick said he'd been thinking about the graduation dance and he didn't want anyone to stay home who wanted to go. He wanted to buy tickets for the group, but he didn't want them to know about it. He asked if I'd let the students think that the department was buying tickets. I said, "Dick, we're talking $20 per person." He said, "I know, but I want to do it." So he began calling his classmates and telling them that I was buying tickets for everyone who wanted to go to the dinner dance.

In the end, Dick bought tickets for 13 TESOL types. Three others showed up on their own recognizance. We sat together at two big tables for the dinner, talking and laughing. When the dancing started, we were the first on the floor and the last to leave. We danced all night and seemed to set the tone of the party. A rumor began circulating that our department had gotten free tickets. Dick and I just laughed. When the party was over, the students all thanked me profusely. Penny said, "You know, we wouldn't have been able to come if it hadn't been for a certain very special person." I laughed and winked at Dick and said, "You're absolutely right!" Dick just smiled.

What are the key variables in the stimulus material that you think should be included in a successful summary of this story? To answer this question, you could either try to write a summary of the story yourself or underline or high-

---

5. IPS stands for International Policy Studies, and IM for International Management—two of the programs at MIIS. Also, this story talks only about our TESOL program because it predates our Master of Arts in Teaching Foreign Languages (TFL) Program.

light the key bits of information in the text that you think would need to be included. Here are the twelve key concepts that I, as the author of the story, thought would be essential in a summary:

1. There is a yearly graduation dinner dance at the Monterey Institute.

2. Kathi must attend the dinner dance but doesn't enjoy it much.

3. The TESOL students don't usually go.

4. They don't go because the tickets are too expensive.

5. Dick offered to pay for the TESOL students' tickets.

6. However, he wanted to do so secretly.

7. Dick bought tickets for several TESOL students (thirteen, to be exact).

8. The TESOL group had a great time at the dinner dance.

9. A rumor began circulating that the TESOL students had gotten free tickets.

10. The TESOL students thanked Kathi, because they thought that she had bought the tickets.

11. Kathi didn't reveal that it was actually Dick who had bought the tickets.

12. Dick was pleased.

Each of these twelve concepts contains one or more propositions. According to the *Dictionary of Applied Linguistics,* a **proposition** is "the basic meaning which a sentence expresses. Propositions consist of (a) something which is named or talked about (known as the argument or entity) and (b) an assertion or predication which is made about the argument" (Richards, Platt, and Weber, 1985, 233). A sentence may consist of one proposition (such as 12, above, "Dick was pleased") or of several. For instance, sentence 1, above, "There is a yearly graduation dinner dance at the Monterey Institute," includes the following propositions:

1. There is a dance.

2. The dance is held at the Monterey Institute

3. The dance is held every year.

4. The dance celebrates the graduation.

5. The dance includes dinner.

You need to decide, in setting the scoring criteria for a dictocomp, how specific you will be. Do you want to identify broad concepts that you consider important as indicators of the students' understanding? (This is what I did in identifying the twelve key ideas listed above.) Or do you want to do a tight propositional analysis of the stimulus material? The choice depends, in part, on your assessment purpose(s).

In order to see how native speakers and proficient nonnative speakers would perform the dictocomp task, I asked ten language teachers to write summaries of this story. Here are two examples:

> Every year at MIIS a dance is held before graduation. One year several TESOL students considered going, but the ticket price was a financial burden for many, and the potential for a dull evening further decreased their conviction. A certain faculty member suggested to the students that funds could be available from the departmental budget for those who were serious about going. Eventually, after no one came forth, an affluent student confided to the professor that he wouldn't mind paying for the TESOL students, even though the total cost was considerable. He had one caveat, however: The students were to think that the department was paying. In the end, the TESOL students had a surprisingly wonderful evening at the dance, all assuming that their admittance was "on the school." (Paul Firth)

> The annual graduation dinner/dance at the Monterey Institute is not usually attended by TESOL students because of the financial cost. One year, a TESOL student offered to buy the $20 ticket for any other TESOL student interested in going. He was a financially secure, experienced school teacher on sabbatical to do his MA in TESOL. He did not want the other students to know about his generosity, so he told them that the department would cover the cost of the tickets. On the night of the dinner/dance, sixteen TESOL students ate, talked, laughed and danced the night away. All of the students enjoyed the party and were very thankful for the "free" tickets "provided" by the department. (Diane Malamut)

You will notice that although these summaries differ, they both include several of the key elements of the story (points 1, 3, 4, 5, 6, and 8). Paul's summary includes point 9, but not 2, 7, 10, 11, or 12. Diane's summary includes point 10 but not 2, 11, or 12. In other words, neither of my native speakers included points 2, 11, or 12. How do their choices of the key points compare to the ones you identified or to the summary you wrote?

Here are the summaries written by three of Penny's students. Their spelling and grammar have been reproduced exactly as in their original versions.

Amy (Chinese)

There is a graguate daicig part will be given in Monterey. Tesol students want to take part in the party, but they have no enough money. Finally they solved the promblem and took part in the party.

Amy's summary, the shortest in the class, includes points 1 and 4, and a rather vague solution that doesn't exactly match the facts. Indeed, I wonder whether Amy (a) even understood that Dick had bought the tickets for his classmates, or (b) understood the story but couldn't summarize the key points and/or reproduce them in writing. She was the least proficient student in the class, and this story may have been too difficult for her.

Shiho (Japanese)

Every year TESOL students at MIIS has a party of graduation. This party's cost is 20 dollers, so somebody wants to go the party, but somebody doesn't want to go the party. Because 20 dollers is expensive.

13 people goes to the party. The teacher looks at students. They sit, drinks, eat and dancing. The party is all night and is over. Penniy, one of the students, said "The party was very good."

Shiho's summary contains more information than Amy's, including some specific facts (20 dollars, 13 people). Shiho correctly included propositions 1, 3, and 4 (but note that he inappropriately stated that "every year the TESOL students at MIIS has a party . . ."). Shiho omitted propositions 5, 6, and 7 (except for the numeral *thirteen*), and all of the information about Dick as a central character and a moving force in the story. The conclusion Shiho wrote is not exactly wrong, but it strikes me as interestingly vague.

Hafez was the only student in the group who provided a title for his summary. You can see that, although there are several spelling inaccuracies in his dictocomp, Hafez captured the gist of the story.

Hafez (Arabic)

Money is No Object

In the TESOL department, Kathi was very unhappy because there is a party witch run every year and her students don't show up, so she always sit and, drink, watch and wich that she wasn't there.

One ther is student named Dick who decided to buy the ticket because the students though that $20 is very big money, so the can't afford. But Dick bought 13 tickets for the student and told them that the department bought it. So TESOL students went to the party and the were the first in dans floor and the last who leave the party.

At the end they thank Kathy very much because the didn't know who did it. So Dick safe the departmant at that time.

In fact, referring to our list of essential ideas, Hafez included at least some elements of 1, 2, 3, 4, 5, 6 (implicitly), 7, 8, 10, and 12. In other words, in terms of sheer numbers of key ideas, Hafez included ten out of twelve key ideas from my list—more than were included in my two native speakers' example summaries.

With the widespread development of communicative language teaching in the 1980s, there was a general feeling among language teaching professionals that assessment had not kept pace with changes in curricula and methodology. Typical tests seemed to be too indirect, too form-focused, and too inauthentic to measure language as it is really used for communication.

An interesting test development project in Canada at the time I was working with Penny's students had a profound impact on my thinking about testing. A team at the Ontario Institute for Studies in Education (OISE) wanted to design an assessment battery for Anglophone secondary school students of French. The resulting test, *A Vous la Parole,* is an integrative, direct, four-skills test based on a theory of communicative competence (Canale and Swain, 1980).

In the process of devising this test, the OISE team articulated four principles of communicative language test design. These ideas seem valuable to me, and I'd like to illustrate them with examples from the use of the dictocomp story with Penny's ESL students.

1. **Start from somewhere:** This idea means that assessment should be based on sound theoretical principles. It entails having a clear understanding of the construct we are trying to measure and designing our assessment procedures to match that understanding.

2. **Concentrate on content:** The content (in terms of both topics and tasks) of assessment devices should be appropriate in terms of the age, proficiency level, interests, and goals of the learners.

3. **Bias for best:** Tests should be designed so as to elicit the best possible performance from the test-takers. So, for example, in the writing portion of *A Vous la Parole,* students are allowed to use dictionaries, just as they would if they were writing in a nontest situation.

4. **Work for washback:** Assessment procedures should be designed and used so as to promote positive washback. This goal involves clearly defining our scoring criteria, as well as making them available to students and teachers alike. It also demands a clear alignment of course objectives and test content, especially in placement and achievement tests.

In choosing a dictocomp to use with Penny's students, my intent was to provide them with practice listening to an unfamiliar native speaker and subsequently reproducing the speaker's meaning in the written mode. The underlying theory in the choice of a dictocomp is the idea that conveying and capturing meaning, regardless of one's accuracy, is a key component of communication. So the "somewhere" I started from was the separation of meaning and accuracy. I realize, of course, that accuracy is also important, and that often clearly communicating one's meaning demands accurate utterances. However, here my intent was to focus on the bits of meaning the learners could produce without dealing with accuracy as part of the scoring criteria.

The principle "concentrate on content" is illustrated by both my choice of stimulus material and the intended learner's response. The story about Dick's secret kindness was relevant to the students because it involved their teacher as a character in the story and because it took place within the culture of their school. In addition, the intended learner's response—to get the gist of the story and write a summary of the key ideas—was an appropriate task for these students, most of whom were studying English for academic purposes.

The "bias for best" principle is illustrated in the fact that because the story was rather challenging relative to the students' proficiency level, I read it to them three times (at their request). In addition, they were able to ask about unknown vocabulary items if they wished. Also, because this was the first time they had done a dictocomp, their performances did not influence their course grades.

"Working for washback" is illustrated in Penny's wanting the students (many of whom were on their first visit to an English-speaking country) to have the experience of talking with a new native speaker, to ask questions, to focus on meaning, and to express their ideas in writing. All of these were goals in her course, as well as goals for this particular activity. If we had been evaluating the students' performances, the assessment emphasis would have supported the course goals.

We will return to these four principles of communicative language test development again after we consider another meaning-oriented activity, the strip story. This procedure is interesting because it forces learners to focus on both form and meaning at the discourse level in order to complete the task.

Once when I was teaching an advanced writing class I was having some trouble getting the students to understand the need for coherence and cohesion from the reader's point of view. My students were all advanced nonnative speakers of English who had completed the required sequence of ESL courses at the University of California at Los Angeles. They were all enrolled in credit-bearing graduate or undergraduate courses in their own disciplines, and they all had faced a variety of written assignments—lab reports, essay exams, term papers, summaries, and so on—as part of their education. As sophisticated as they were, however, I couldn't seem to get them to recognize the importance of coherence and cohesive devices, and to use these systems consistently in their academic writing.

Teachers' Voices

Cohesion is produced by "the grammatical and/or lexical relationships between the different elements of a text" (Richards et al., 1985, 45). For example, the use of an appropriate pronoun to refer to a previously mentioned noun creates cohesion. The related concept of **coherence** involves "the relationships which link the meanings of utterances in a discourse or of the sentences in a text. These links may be based on the speakers' shared knowledge" (Richards et al., 1985, 45). So, for instance, the following conversation exhibits coherence even though there are no cohesive devices:

Speaker 1: "Can you pick up Melissa?"

Speaker 2: "I have a class."

Speaker 2's response is taken to be a refusal of Speaker 1's request, based on their shared understanding that Speaker 2's attendance at his class would interfere with his ability to pick up Melissa.

The students in my advanced writing class seemed to be unaware of the extent to which cohesive devices in particular can help the reader follow an author's train of thought. I wanted to find some way to sensitize them to this important part of communicating their intended meaning in writing.

One day I watched my friend Thom Hudson teach a lower-intermediate class in our ESL series. Thom's class was working on the structure of the paragraph and, in fact, the ability to write a well-organized paragraph was a stated goal for that level of instruction. Thom used an activity called a "strip story" to help his students understand the logical structure of the paragraph. A **strip story** is a speaking/listening activity in which every student is given a strip of paper with one sentence from a story written on it. This activity can also be used with a single student who arranges the strips of paper in order on a table, but when it is used interactively, the sentences are randomly distributed to various students on strips of paper. Each student gets one and only one sentence, and the sentences are given out in a jumbled sequence.

Thom had written a paragraph with enough sentences for each student to have one. The students' job was to sort out the best order for the sentences to form a logical paragraph. I had never seen the strip story activity used interactively before, though as an individual task, it was a common procedure for teaching and testing paragraph structure and the logical sequencing of events.

When you use a strip story as an interactive activity, each student has a few minutes to memorize his or her own sentence. The students may question the teacher about the vocabulary or the pronunciation of the words in their sentences, but they may not show the strips to one another. After the teacher collects the strips of paper, each student says his or her sentence aloud and the group tries to sort out the correct order to assemble the entire story logically. (It is important that you collect the strips of paper; otherwise the students will just read them aloud, instead of striving to recite them clearly. Also, students may stop communicating with one another and resort to simply arranging the slips of paper on a desk or table.) Often students will choose to physically arrange themselves in the sequence of the sentences they represent (like a living paragraph). The teacher's role in this process is to keep quiet and let the students work at it, but it's a good idea to monitor their progress carefully and sometimes to provide some coaching if a student forgets his or her sentence or repeats it incorrectly. You may need to repeat a student's sentence loudly and correctly or have him or her repeat it if his or her classmates have not understood it properly. The task is complete when the class can jointly render the story in its proper sequence.

Prior to the strip story activity, the teacher's responsibilities are to:

1. select or write a story of appropriate difficulty and interest for the students;

2. divide the story into segments that are long enough to be challenging but not too long or too complex (syntactically or semantically) to memorize;

3. get some native speakers (or fluent nonnatives) to try arranging the segments first to make sure there is only one possible correct order;

4. revise the story as needed if alternative orders appear in step 3; and

5. reproduce the revised story and cut it into pieces so the individual strips of paper each contain a sentence (or a portion of a sentence).

The story needs to be long enough for every student to have his or her own sentence. It is a good idea to have some sentences (perhaps marked with an asterisk, as in the example below) that can be deleted without damaging the story line, but nevertheless have a single specified place in the story. These can be omitted if any students are absent, or they can be distributed as needed if anyone enters the classroom late.

The strip story process can also be done with some poems, jokes, and songs, though they must be chosen carefully. This activity uses Johnson's "jigsaw principle" and "task dependency principle" (1982) because (1) students must exchange information in the target language, (2) in order to complete the task of assembling the story correctly. Although reciting the memorized sentences does not involve any original language production, the students do use a great deal of creative language in the process of negotiating the sentence order to reconstruct the story.

Watching Thom Hudson's lower-intermediate class inspired me to try out the strip story technique with my own students. I tried to find or create a text that would be suitable for my advanced students in the composition course. Because I was working with a large group, I wrote a long story. The result was the following narrative, based on a familiar folk tale. It contains 32 obligatory sentences and 10 optional sentences. The individual sentences in the story are reproduced below in random order, in the hopes that when you read them, you will have a mental experience similar to that experienced by the participants in the interactive strip story activity.

Sample Strip Story for Advanced ESL or EFL Students

(Sentences marked with an asterisk [*] are optional and can be deleted in case someone is absent or added if someone arrives late.)

The baby was laughing and rolling in the spilled sausage grease, while the dog licked everything in sight—the pan, the floor, the stove, and the baby.

*The little girl was just two years old and had recently learned how to walk.

"I, on the other hand, must feed the pigs and hoe the corn and do all sorts of back-breaking work."

(as the proverb might have said) "Man works from sun to sun, but woman's work is never fun."

One night the farmer said to his wife, "I'm exhausted from working on the farm all day. I wish I could do women's work."

*She would follow it around all day, cooing and laughing and reaching for its tail.

The moral of this story is, "The grass is always greener on the other side of the fence," or—

The woman looked at her sobbing husband and then glanced through the window into the kitchen, where the floor was covered with water and sausage grease.

"Have a nice day and don't forget to feed the pigs!" the happy farmer called after her from the front porch.

He grabbed the dog by the collar and dragged it outside as it began to howl.

*The farmer said, "Oh, wonderful! I'll have a delightful day of rest."

The dog howled and the farmer began to yell and to tear off his clothes and cough violently.

*"Now," he thought to himself, "I'll have another cup of coffee and relax—maybe even take a nap."

After breakfast the next morning, the woman took the farmer's hoe and walked out to the cornfields.

*At the back of the house she found the dirty baby rolling in the mud with the smelly dog.

"Very well," said the woman, "tomorrow morning I will go to the fields and you will stay home and do women's work."

There he found the soapy baby happily rolling in the dirt with the dog licking her face once more.

*At that remark, the woman smiled her quizzical smile again.

*Meanwhile his wife stayed home and cooked and took care of the baby.

But as he turned to go back into the house, he heard a loud crash in the kitchen.

Once upon a time there was a farmer who raised pigs and grew corn.

*The skunk was breaking open the chicken eggs to eat the yolks, and the chickens were furious.

The farmer yelled, "Hey, you dumb mutt! Look at the mess you've made in here!"

The farmer had just begun to wash the baby when he heard the dog barking and the chickens squawking out in the yard.

"Because all you do is stay home all day and play with the baby," the farmer said.

The baby was startled by her father's yelling and the dog's howling, so she began to cry.

He ran outside to see why the animals were making such a fuss, and there he saw a skunk in the chicken coop.

As he ran back to the house to wash the terrible odor from his hair and skin, the farmer realized that he'd left the baby sitting in a tub of soapy water.

The farmer came back to the kitchen, all covered with dog hair, and picked up the greasy, crying baby to give her a bath.

He lived in a farmhouse with his wife and their baby girl and a large dog.

*As she walked into the yard going toward the house, she could see the broken eggs in the chicken coop.

The dog was growling and barking and snapping at the skunk as the farmer ran up to the coop.

He ran to the bathroom, but the baby was gone and there was water all over the floor.

*She loved the dog, which was a big, clumsy, furry thing that was always shedding its hair.

He ran to the kitchen and saw that the dog had knocked the frying pan off the stove.

Just at that moment the farmer's wife came back to the house for the mid-day meal.

He followed a trail of puddles down the hall and out through the back door of the farm house.

The family was basically happy, but every morning the farmer left for the fields, grumbling about how hard he had to work.

His wife looked at him with a quizzical smile and asked, "Why do you say that, dear?"

The naked, foul-smelling farmer sat on the back step with his head hanging and dog hair clinging to his body as he began to cry.

Then she smiled and set down her hoe and asked, "When will lunch be ready, dear?"

At that moment the skunk got annoyed and sprayed them all—the dog, the chickens, and the farmer—with his foul-smelling scent.

It took my advanced writing students nearly an hour to work out the proper order of the sentences in this story. In doing so they first memorized and recited all the sentences out loud, one at a time. Everyone listened intently because each person had to figure out where his own piece of the puzzle belonged. Of course, the person whose sentence began, "Once upon a time . . ." immediately realized that he had the formulaic beginning of the tale, and those who had the moral realized that their sentences belonged at the end. (Their formal schemata helped them recognize the discourse pattern of a folk tale.) But figuring out the sequence of the other sentences was not so easy.

First the students milled around for a while and tried to arrange the entire story. Then they decided to gather themselves together in groups, in cases where they felt their sentences were related to common themes or scenes (e.g., the sentences about the chickens, the skunk breaking the eggs, the dog barking at the skunk, etc., all relate to the scene with the crisis at the chicken coop). In this way they were able to discover how topic-relevant sentences formed the various episodes, which they quickly realized would be represented by paragraphs—physical divisions in a written version of the tale.

What linguistic elements did the students attend to in order to sort out the single best sequence of sentences? Here are just a few of the linguistic cues the students used when they tried to arrange the sentences in this strip story:

1. **Formulaic expressions:** such as "Once upon a time" and "The moral of the story is . . .";

2. **Pronominal references:** especially *he, him, she, her, your, yours, they, them, theirs* and *it*, but also *his, her, your, its,* and *their*: "*She* would follow *it* around all day cooing and laughing and reaching for *its* tail.";

3. **Transitional expressions:** "I, *on the other hand,* . . ." or "*Because* all you do . . ."

4. **Indefinite and definite articles indicating specificity:** "*The* baby was laughing and rolling in the spilled sausage grease, while *the* dog licked everything in sight—*the* pan, *the* floor, *the* stove, and *the* baby . . ." or ". . . there he saw *a* skunk in *the* chicken coop. *The* skunk was breaking open *the* chicken eggs . . .";

5. **Adverbs and adverbial phrases:** "*There* he found the soapy baby . . .", "*Meanwhile* his wife stayed home . . . ," or "*At that remark* the woman smiled her quizzical smile *again* . . ."; and

6. **Tenses and aspect in verb phrases:** "The farmer *had just begun* to wash the baby when he *heard* the dog barking . . ." and "But as he *turned* to go back to the kitchen, he *heard* a loud crash . . ." or "As he *ran* back to the house to wash the terrible odor from his hair and skin, the farmer *realized* that he*'d left* the baby . . ."

By attending to these linguistic elements, as well as to their shared background knowledge about men's and women's traditional roles in agrarian societies, my students sorted out the correct sequence of sentences and also realized the importance of cohesion and coherence in discourse.

Once more we will use Wesche's framework (1983), this time to analyze the strip story activity. It is easy to identify the first three components:

1. **The stimulus material** consists of the individual, randomly ordered sentences of a larger story, but also of the negotiated oral interaction among the learners.

2. **The task posed to the learners** is first (a) to memorize their own sentence, and then (b) to listen to the randomly ordered recitation of the sentences. Then they must (c) attend to the linguistic cues (as well as the content and formal schemata) that signal the appropriate sequencing of the story elements as their classmates recite their own individual sentences.

3. **The learner's response** is to determine (through interaction) the single best order of elements to present a coherent and cohesive story, and to recite (collectively) the story aloud.

So far what we have is an interesting classroom activity that can be completed interactively or individually. But what makes this a possible assessment device? In other words, in Wesche's terms, what are the scoring criteria? The tricky part here is to figure out what you are measuring with the strip story. If you choose to use it as a testing device (instead of as a teaching procedure) you can either have each individual student physically arrange the paper slips on the table himself (and evaluate his ability to arrange them in the right order), or you can take full advantage of the negotiation demanded by the task and evaluate the *group's* ability to sort out the correct order. If you are sure there is only one correct order, you can deduct points for misplaced sentences. Either way, it is your responsibility as the teacher to decide what the scoring criteria will be. When I used this story with my advanced writing class, for instance, I told them they would receive a group grade of *complete* or *incomplete* performance on the task. If they successfully completed the task, I promised I would cancel one assignment.

By the way, the students in my advanced writing class were successful in reconstructing the strip story about the farmer and his wife. When they finally recited their coproduced version of the story, after nearly an hour of intense interaction, it matched the intended sequence. I announced that they had done a beautiful job and that the following week's quiz was canceled. They cheered (in many languages), but the real reward was that thereafter they were more attentive to coherence and cohesive devices in their own writing.

How would you evaluate the strip story procedure using the four principles of communicative language testing described in the Frameworks section of this chapter? It depends on whether you are using the procedure as an individual reading and text-restructuring task or as an interactive reading, listening, speaking, and text-restructuring task. I will use the latter context, as described above in the experience with my writing students.

1. **Start from somewhere:** Linguistically my choice of this procedure was informed both by schema theory and by the constructs of coherence and cohesion in discourse. Pedagogically it was motivated by my belief in experiential learning.

2. **Concentrate on content:** Men's and women's roles in society was a topic we had read about and discussed in class (and one that had sparked a great deal of debate). It was of particular importance to the women from developing nations, so I thought the old folktale based on this theme would be appropriate and interesting for my students.

3. **Bias for best:** Remember that I was using this procedure as a classroom activity in this case, rather than as a formal assessment device. But there were "bias for best" elements built in nevertheless: intentional collaboration among the students, opportunities to ask about unfamiliar vocabulary, and an open-ended time frame.

4. **Work for washback:** This procedure was so different from what we had been doing in our advanced writing class that I prefaced the activity with an explicit explanation about why I was doing it and how it related to problems in the students' academic writing. In addition, in writing the text of the stimulus material I incorporated several of the issues we had studied in class: complex tenses, pronominal reference, transitional expressions, and so on.

The students' successful completion of the strip story task depended on their ability to recite a sentence-length text clearly in front of their peers, to listen to their peers' sentences, and to negotiate the proper sequence based on linguistic cues and their understanding of the content and the discourse structure. It was a highly integrative task that involved three of the four skills (and I would argue that the text-restructuring aspect approximates some component of writing as well).

The "Investigations" section of this chapter is designed to give you more practice with dictocomps and strip stories. I see these two procedures as interesting and versatile activities that can be used for either teaching or assessment purposes, and that have a high potential for positive washback, given their focus on meaning.

1 *Try writing a dictocomp passage of your own to use with your students. If you want the students to retell the entire passage, make it* much *shorter than the story reproduced above.*

If you are going to score the students' dictocomps, you must decide what the key pieces of information are before you read the dictocomp to your class. In other words, what events or facts from your dictocomp passage would the students need to reproduce in order to demonstrate that they have fully understood the meaning of the passage? Decide whether you will do a tight propositional analysis or simply look for key ideas. When you have identified the key bits of information, you will have set up the basis for your scoring criteria.

It may be quite interesting for you (as it was for me) to ask some native speakers or highly proficient nonnative speakers to take your dictocomp for you. You may be surprised at what they choose to include (or exclude).

2 *Here are two more dictocomp summaries written by the students in Penny's class, based on the story about Dick. On your own, score these two summaries in terms of which of the twelve key ideas they contain. (Be alert for extraneous information.) Then compare your scores with those of a colleague who evaluated these two dictocomps independently. How similar are your evaluations?*

Thatit (Thai)

TESOL program want to join the graduation dinner dance but no students come because of the price of admission.

The party was dominated by IPS and IM program.

The teachers want to collect TESOL students by buying them the tickets. Dick was paying the admission ticket because he was a rich man. Well establish, kind, leader among others.

After that TESOL came to the graduate dinner dance and first came on the floor until the end of the party.

The teachers satisfied what happened to them and every student thanked Kathi Bailey.

Marlene (Spanish)

The eventing before student get graduated is every year at the Monterey Institute a diner dance party.

Unfortunately Kathi was every year without any TESOL students of her class at this party and couldn't enjoy it. The party was always dominated by the international students.

The reason because her students didn't go to this party was only the price of $20 for one ticket.

Kathi couldn't get some money from the department budget but a student called Dick bought one year for all students of his class the tickets and let the students know Kathi would had bought them. So everybody from this class could go to theis party and now it was the 1st time it was dominated by the TESOL students. And this was only because Dick sponsored money.

---

3 *The dictocomp technique presents many opportunities for creating positive washback. If you are working individually, try to list four or five ways the dictocomp procedure could be used to link teaching and assessment. If you are working with classmates or colleagues, try brainstorming for about ten minutes to see how many connections you can make collectively. (You may wish to use Melinda Erickson's ideas in Table 2.2 as a starting point.) My own list is included as a postscript at the end of this chapter.*

---

4 *Try the strip story in this chapter with a friend or an advanced language learner, and then with a group of people. I suggest the following series of steps:*

1. Photocopy the sentences of the story and cut the photocopy into individual strips of paper.

2. Set aside the optional sentences (those marked with asterisks).

3. Ask the person to organize the sentences into the best possible order to form a coherent story, and to "think out loud" as he or she does so. (If you tape record these comments you will have the data necessary to transcribe a "think-aloud protocol," as described in Chapter 5.)

4. When the person has finished organizing the obligatory sentences, see if you agree with the arrangement. If not, discuss the decisions with him or her.

5. When you have agreed on the ordering of the basic sentences, give the person the optional strips (those marked with asterisks). Ask him or her to integrate them into the story, again thinking out loud as he or she does so.

6. Repeat step four.

When you feel you have gained all the insights that individual has to offer, and you are reasonably sure that there is one correct sequence of sentences, have a group of language students try to arrange this strip story. (If you are working with a small group of only six or eight students, it may be beneficial to give them the sentences paper clipped into groups of only one episode at a time.)

---

5 *Here is the story about the farmer and his wife arranged in the proper sequence and with paragraph divisions added. The asterisks have been maintained before the optional sentences. Compare your version of the story with this version.*

Once upon a time there was a farmer who raised pigs and grew corn. He lived in a farmhouse with his wife and their baby girl and a large dog. * The little girl was just two years old and had recently learned how to walk. * She loved the dog, which was a big clumsy furry thing that was always shedding its hair. * She would follow it around all day, cooing and laughing and reaching for its tail.[6] The family was basically happy, but every morning the farmer left for the fields, grumbling about how hard he had to work. * Meanwhile his wife stayed home and cooked and took care of the baby.

One night the farmer said to his wife, "I'm exhausted from working on the farm all day. I wish I could do women's work." His wife looked at him with a quizzical smile and asked, "Why do you say that, dear?" "Because all you do is stay home all day and play with the baby," the farmer said. "I, on the other hand, must feed the pigs and hoe the corn and do all sorts of back-breaking work." "Very well," said the woman, "tomorrow morning I will go to the fields and you will stay home and do women's work." * The farmer said, "Oh, wonderful! I'll have a delightful day of rest." * At that remark, the woman smiled her quizzical smile again.[7]

---

6. Notice that among the optional sentences there are obligatory orderings. So for example, the second optional sentence in a row ("She would follow it around all day, cooing and laughing and reaching for its tail") makes no sense without the preceding optional sentence ("She loved the dog, which was a big furry clumsy thing that was always shedding its hair").

After breakfast the next morning, the woman took the farmer's hoe and walked out to the cornfields. "Have a nice day and don't forget to feed the pigs!" the happy farmer called after her from the front porch. * "Now," he thought to himself, "I'll have another cup of coffee and relax—maybe even take a nap."

But as he turned to go back into the house, he heard a loud crash in the kitchen. He ran to the kitchen and saw that the dog had knocked the frying pan off the stove. The baby was laughing and rolling in the spilled sausage grease, while the dog licked everything in sight—the pan, the floor, the stove, and the baby. The farmer yelled, "Hey, you dumb mutt! Look at the mess you've made in here!" He grabbed the dog by the collar and dragged it outside as it began to howl. The baby was startled by her father's yelling and the dog's howling, so she began to cry. The farmer came back to the kitchen, all covered with dog hair, and picked up the greasy, crying baby to give her a bath.

The farmer had just begun to wash the baby when he heard the dog barking and the chickens squawking out in the yard. He ran outside to see why the animals were making such a fuss, and there he saw a skunk in the chicken coop. * The skunk was breaking open the chicken eggs to eat the yolks, and the chickens were furious. The dog was growling and barking and snapping at the skunk as the farmer ran up to the coop. At that moment the skunk got annoyed and sprayed them all—the dog, the chickens, and the farmer—with his foul-smelling scent. The dog howled and the farmer began to yell and to tear off his clothes and cough violently.

As he ran back to the house to wash the terrible odor from his hair and skin, the farmer realized that he'd left the baby sitting in a tub of soapy water. He ran to the bathroom, but the baby was gone and there was water all over the floor. He followed a trail of puddles down the hall and out through the back door of the farm house. There he found the soapy baby happily rolling in the dirt with the dog licking her face once more. The naked, foul-smelling farmer sat on the back step with his head hanging and dog hair clinging to his body as he began to cry.

Just at that moment the farmer's wife came back to the house for the mid-day meal. * As she walked into the yard going toward the house, she could see the broken eggs in the chicken coop. * At the back of the house she found the dirty baby rolling in the mud with the smelly dog. The woman looked at her sobbing husband and then glanced through the window into the kitchen, where the floor was covered with water and sausage grease. Then she smiled and set down her hoe and asked, "When will lunch be ready, dear?"

The moral of this story is, "The grass is always greener on the other side of the fence," or—(as the proverb might have said) "Man works from sun to sun, but woman's work is never fun."

---

7. The same issue (obligatory ordering within the optional sentences) arises again here. The sentence, "At that remark, the woman smiled her quizzical smile again," makes no sense without the preceding statement by the farmer about his plan for a "delightful day of rest." Be careful about including all the necessary pairs of components if you use this story with your students.

If your ordering of this strip story differs from mine, how could you alter the original sentences to insure that there is only one possible sequence?

---

6 *Try creating a strip story, either from an existing text or from your own original prose. Be sure to pilot test the activity with native speakers or proficient nonnative speakers before using it with language learners.*

There are several issues to keep in mind as you select or write the text for a strip story. Are the learners familiar with the vocabulary and grammatical structures in the story? Are they familiar with the concepts in the story? Is the content appropriate for the ages and interests of the learners? If you intend to use the strip story activity for assessment purposes, what is the skill or knowledge you want to assess? (This decision must precede the establishment of your scoring criteria.)

---

7 *Use the OISE team's framework to analyze a test with which you are familiar (or perhaps a test you'd like to learn more about). How does the test measure up to their "four principles of communicative language test development"? In which areas could it be improved?*

Suggested Readings

There are several interesting books and articles available about communicative language testing. Some of my favorites include Mari Wesche's (1983) article, which we first encountered in Chapter 2, and an early paper by Lyle Bachman and Adrian Palmer (1982) that investigated the components of communicative competence. An earlier and influential anthology of research on assessing communicative competence was edited by Adrian Palmer, Peter Groot, and George Trosper (1981).

There have been some attempts to directly transfer principles of communicative language teaching to assessment. For example, the teaching technique known as the "information gap" (K. Johnson, 1982) has been described as a testing procedure by David Bowker (1984).

Several interesting and accessible items have been written about the development of *A Vous la Parole* as an example of communicative language testing. These include the papers by Green (1985); Hart, Lapkin, and Swain (1987); and Swain (1984).

Brendan Carroll's book *Testing Communicative Performance* (1980), although a bit dated by recent research on communicative competence, is still an excellent starting place to read about this topic.

Lyle Bachman's book *Fundamental Considerations in Language Testing* (1990) offers what is probably the most thorough treatment of communicative testing in the literature to date on language teaching and testing.

There are a number of papers now available on washback. These include the articles by Alderson and Wall (1993), Shohamy (1993), and Wall and Alderson (1993), and volume 13 (number 3) of the journal *Language Testing*.

If you have a particular interest in summarizing, you might want to read Andrew Cohen's (1993) article, "The Role of Instructions in Testing Summarizing Ability."

More ideas about strip stories are described in an article by Robert Gibson (1975). Although that paper is over twenty years old, it has some excellent ideas for using strip stories to promote communication.

Ruth Wajnryb's book *Grammar Dictation* (1990), describes the dictogloss, a procedure similar to the dictocomp. She offers an excellent framework for using dictoglosses and several texts teachers can use.

Postscript: Washback Ideas

There are many things that can be done with the students' responses to the dictocomp task, in addition to scoring them for assessment purposes. Here are a few ideas. You will see that some of these parallel the activities Melinda Erickson and her writing students do with dictation (as described in Chapter 2).

1. *After reading the stimulus material, allow the students time to reread their versions and ask questions on the information they feel they are lacking.*
2. *When the students have finished writing their versions, have them compare papers. Very useful negotiation for meaning can result as students notice the differences in their various renditions.*
3. *Tell the students the in-class dictocomp activity will focus entirely on content and meaning. Then, as a homework assignment, have them revise their version of the story with an additional focus on form and accuracy.*
4. *Use the dictocomp stimulus material as the model for the production of a similar but original text by the students. For example, after writing a dictocomp summary based on the story of Dick and the dinner dance tickets, students could write their own stories on the theme of "A Remarkable Person" or "A Secret Kindness."*
5. *Students can select short passages, or even write original texts, to be used as dictocomp stimulus materials with their classmates. This can be done in pairs, or a single student can read his or her story to the entire class, with everyone taking a turn over time. If you try this variation on the dictocomp theme, it is important to set a word limit on the length of the text and to have the student reader identify in advance the key propositions to be assessed.*
6. *If you teach with a book of readings, or if you are working from a theme-based syllabus, you can choose dictocomp topics related to the material the learners have been studying. This tactic promotes practice with the vocabulary and concepts introduced in class. If you use dictocomps in this way for assessment purposes, they function well as progress tests.*
7. *You can use a brief dictocomp before a reading lesson or a writing assignment as a schema activator to get the students thinking and talking about the topic before they tackle a larger piece of discourse (either receptively or productively).*
8. *Try using the same dictocomp as the stimulus material for a listening/writing task both before and after a lesson or a unit. Have each student compare his or her first rendition (prior to instruction and practice) with his or her second.*

11

ELICITING SPEECH SAMPLES IN ROLE PLAYS

Many subjects may feel uncomfortable with "showing off," particularly with role playing. An example of a role-play exercise used in [interviewer] training sessions is as follows: "The interviewer will play the role of your four-year-old child whose kitten has just died. Try to offer the child consolation and a solution to the problem." Such role-playing may be met with resistance from many subjects. Role playing ability can be compared with acting ability, and of course not everyone is a good actor. Nor is being a good actor equivalent to being a good communicator. Furthermore, role playing is a specialized kind of acting, requiring ad-libbing ability. Not every good actor is a good ad-libber. Can these skills therefore be assumed, or are they perhaps culturally and psychologically specific? It is also possible that the interviewee may be intimidated by the interviewer's obvious expertise in role playing. (The interviewer has planned and probably practiced this role play a number of times, and the interviewee is therefore at an unfair advantage.)

This comment about role play as an elicitation device is from Leo van Lier's article "Reeling, Writhing, Drawling, Stretching, and Fainting in Coils: Oral Proficiency Interviews as Conversation" (1989, 502). When Leo was collecting the data for that article (which I consider to be one of the most important pieces ever written about the oral proficiency interview procedure), I was privileged to be part of the data-collection process. With our colleague Deanna Tovar, from the Defense Language Institute, I interviewed Leo in English (which is his third second language).

In Chapter 1 I mentioned the *Interagency Language Roundtable Oral Proficiency Interview (ILR OPI)*—the face-to-face interview procedure used by many U.S. government agencies to test the foreign language speaking proficiency of potential employees. In conducting an official *ILR OPI*, testers must elicit "ratable samples" that allow them to make judgments about each candidate's performance relative to the stated criteria of the rating scale. At the higher levels this includes having the examinee demonstrate his or her command over various registers—an important part of sociolinguistic competence. Although the oral proficiency interview format can include a variety of elicitation devices (translation tasks, direct questions, storytelling, etc.) as the stimulus materials, role play is often used as context for eliciting sociolinguistic variation.

In order to assess register variation, I set up the following role-play situation. I asked Leo to imagine that he and a female companion were traveling across the country. They had stopped at a diner in the middle of nowhere, had supper and coffee, and then driven on. Later Leo's female companion realized that she had lost a valuable earring—perhaps at the restaurant. At that point I removed one of my (not so valuable) earrings, gave it to Leo, and asked him to role-play a situation in which he telephoned the restaurant (after closing time) and convinced the waitress (who was tired and wanted to go home) that she should look for the missing earring. (If I remember correctly, this particular earring was an oddly shaped twisted gold strand. I myself would be hard-pressed to describe it.) After getting the waitress to look for the earring, Leo was to convince her to mail it to him at a forwarding address. As you might have predicted, I was to play the role of the waitress.

Leo *glowered* at me when I had finished setting up the situation. He hates role plays. I know he does, and he knows I know he does. (And we both know that for me to ask Leo van Lier to demonstrate his command over register variation in English during a role play is a bit like a fifth-grade language arts teacher asking Joseph Conrad, a nonnative writer of English, to defend his decisions about where he put the commas in *Lord Jim*.) Leo's distaste for role plays as elicitation procedures fascinates me, because I myself like and enjoy role plays—as a language tester, a language teacher, and even as a language learner. Given the contrast in our viewpoints, I have tried to examine the variables affecting the use of role-play situations as stimulus material.

In this chapter, one "Teacher's Voice" will be that of Michelle Bettencourt, a Spanish teacher who had to participate in some role plays as part of a job interview. However, the first "Teacher's Voice" you hear will be my own. Once again, I will write about a situation in which I was not in the teacher's role. Indeed, in this case, I was the language learner trying desperately to communicate in my much-less-than-perfect second language. I find it is often the case that if I pay attention to what the world is saying to me, I learn a great deal about teaching (and about testing) when I am not in the classroom.

A few years ago during a vacation in Mexico, my friend Les and I decided to take a catamaran trip down the coast. You can picture the brochure: a beautiful boat, tourists sun-bathing on the deck, music piped in on the stereo— and indeed, the beginning of the trip was everything the brochures promised.

Teachers' Voices

We cruised down the coast for about two hours, listening to salsa music, while the first mate's running commentary about the scenery and the history provided a challenge to my lower-intermediate Spanish. The further south we cruised, the more remote and rugged the coastline became, with only occasional beaches punctuating the jungle cliffs.

We arrived at a point south of Puerto Vallarta on the Mexican coast where *el capitán* said that the snorkeling would be great. The water was choppy, so we wore life vests while we snorkeled. We'd only been in the water for about three minutes before Les (*macho* dude though he was) began screaming that he was being bitten and stung as he thrashed in the water, frantically clawing at his back and shoulders. I could see nothing on his back, but as I swept my hands across his shoulders and under the life vest, I felt a burning, gelatinous mass resisting the sweep of my hands. Something had gotten wedged into his life vest. I tried to scrape it away as my own hands began to burn with an electric intensity. Even though I could see nothing, something was definitely in his vest. "We have to get your vest off!" I yelled. "Something's stuck to it!" With burning, semiparalyzed fingers, I tried to untie the sodden knots of his vest as we were both buffeted by the surf. After what seemed like hours we managed to untie Les's life vest and swam back to the catamaran. As we clambered aboard, gasping for air, Les was doubled over in pain and could barely haul himself up the ladder.

The captain met us at the stern of the boat amidst the salsa music and the happy laughter of the other tourists. "What's the problem?" he asked me in Spanish.

"I'm not sure," I answered (fairly confident at this point that I had properly declined the adjective *segura* [*sure*] in the feminine, since "I'm not sure" is a frequently used formulaic chunk in the repertoire of my Spanish/English interlanguage). When I described what had happened, the captain immediately recognized the situation and responded, "*¡Ah! ¡Agua mala!*"

At first I did not fully appreciate the captain telling me that "bad water" was the problem. But then, as the captain began to call for hot limes to rub on Les's shoulders, I realized that he had, in fact, understood me and that the Spanish phrase, *agua mala,* referred to the transparent gelatinous mass that had been a very large jellyfish trapped in Les's life vest. Normally if you have contact with a jellyfish while you're swimming or walking on the beach, your autonomous nervous system kicks into overdrive and causes you to jerk away from the painful contact immediately. In this case, the life vest had kept the poisonous tentacles trapped on Les's skin for about three minutes.

The salsa music played on, the catamaran bobbed lightly in the waves, and the other tourists squealed and thrashed in the water while Les gasped for breath and writhed on the deck. He couldn't sit up and he couldn't lie down for the pain—no position was comfortable. It was clear that I had to get him to a doctor. But we were on the open sea, two hours south of Puerto Vallarta on a large sailing vessel that couldn't put in to shore at that remote beach.

What would you have done at that point if you were me, with my lower-intermediate grasp of Spanish? We're not talking about a role play here. This was not a "for-instance" situation. I *had* to get Les off that boat and to a doctor.

In Spanish I begged the captain to put in to shore, but there was no place he could dock the catamaran. After minutes of intense negotiation he hailed a tiny boat, which pulled alongside the catamaran. Three hard-working fishermen took Les and me ashore, where we stumbled up the beach. We staggered through the nightmare sand, the pain moving down into Les's lower back. I entreated the sunbathers to tell me where I could find a doctor.

No, there was no doctor there. The village had no doctors. The town was over there, they said in Spanish, pointing back to Puerto Vallarta.

But we needed help then and there. I begged a boy standing nearby to run ahead and get a taxi for us. As we staggered up the cascading sands, Les hobbled, bent like a ninety-year-old man because the pain had moved down into his legs. The youth dashed ahead of us through the huts and vegetable gardens, across a plank bridge spanning the drainage ditch, and through the dilapidated back streets, scattering the chickens as he ran. I was holding my throbbing hands above my head, and Les was doubled over in agony.

At the outskirts of the village our high-spirited helper bounced, poised to guide us to the waiting taxi he had caught. We collapsed in the back seat and I explained to the driver—"¡*Agua mala! ¡Al hospital!*" and we were gone—the boy, the sunbathers, the fishermen, and the catamaran full of tourists left far behind us in the billowing dust.

The taxi driver (God bless him!) understood my desperate pleas to get us to a hospital as fast as possible. What followed was the stereotypical chase scene from every adventure movie you've ever seen about Mexico. The cab careened around the curves of the narrow coastal road, winding along the cliffs above the sea. On the uphill stretches, the driver honked wildly as we passed busloads full of multigeneration families, bulky packages, and crates of chickens headed to the market in Puerto Vallarta.

Les groaned in the back seat as the driver accelerated. Did we want the big hospital or the little hospital, the driver wanted to know. We wanted the first hospital as fast as possible, I replied.

After thirty hair-raising minutes, we arrived at the small hospital. Les hobbled into the waiting room, still doubled over in pain. I asked a woman in a white uniform to please help me find a doctor because we needed help quickly. She glanced at Les and said she was the doctor, and then led us into a small, dimly lit room with one chair and one cot.

She and I negotiated in Spanish what had happened, where Les's pain was, and whether he had any drug allergies. She hooked him up to an intravenous tube of antihistamines to counteract the poison and shot him full of painkillers. Then she turned to me and we repeated the same litany of medical questions and answers. My hands had turned a dull brownish purple. They felt like they would explode. I too was dosed with painkillers and antihistamines.

Les and I waited there in the dim, cool back room of the small hospital for about two hours. And as I watched the intravenous drip slowly restore his breathing to normal, two recurring thoughts spun through my drug-numbed head. The first was that Leo van Lier would never believe the role play. And the second was that I'd managed to negotiate the entire experience without the subjunctive, and even without full control over the polite negative and affirmative command forms in Spanish. On the *Interagency Language Roundtable Oral Proficiency Interview* five-point rating scale I had successfully completed a level two survival task without the hypothesized grammatical structures needed to do so.

Now language teachers and testers will probably see that there are at least two fallacies associated with this logic. The first is the possibility that with better control over Spanish grammar, I might have been able to negotiate the whole experience more effectively and more efficiently. And the second is that given the gracious and helpful people we encountered that morning, the same series of events might have transpired even if neither of us had spoken any Spanish! (Upon hearing this story my friend Paul Firth pointed out that if we had not run into such nice people, the events could have turned out much worse.)

After two hours of the intravenous drip treatment the doctor pronounced us free to go, so we took another cab back to our hotel. Later that day, the pounding in my hands diminished and Les's pain gradually subsided. My puzzle remained, however. What would Leo van Lier think of this scenario as a language testing role play? What would you think?

If you were given this scenario as a role play prompt in a Spanish oral proficiency interview, the stimulus material might look something like this:

> Imagine you and your friend, who speaks no Spanish, are on a tourist boat on the open sea about two hours south of Puerto Vallarta, Mexico. Your friend has been badly hurt by a jellyfish while snorkeling. (You yourself are slightly hurt.) The captain of the boat cannot put in to shore here because there is no harbor—only a beach. He hails a small boat to take you and your friend ashore. Your task is to use Spanish to negotiate the following points (with complications to the role play indicated in parentheses). Note that all of the people you interact with as you complete this role play speak only Spanish.

1. Get the men in the small boat to bring you both to shore as quickly as possible. (This will disrupt their fishing trip.)

2. Get the people on the shore to take you to a doctor in the village. (There is no doctor in the village, so you must get them to help you find a taxi immediately.)

3. Get the taxi driver to take you to the nearest hospital as fast as possible. (En route, you must answer all his questions about what happened.)

4. Interpret for the doctor as she asks questions about your friend's physical condition, potential drug allergies, etc. Then answer her questions about your own physical condition.

5. Negotiate payment of the bill as you leave the hospital. (Fortunately, the hospital will accept a credit card.)

Would this be a role-play situation you could enact? Would you find it believable, or totally unrealistic? In some sense it is inherently realistic because it is derived from my personal experience: I was there and it really happened. In another sense this scenario may be "universally realistic" in that getting emergency medical help in unexpected circumstances is something travelers need to be able to do—in whatever language.

This issue of realism intersecting with personal experience is illustrated in a different way by the voice of my friend Michelle Bettencourt. She is a teacher of Spanish but a native speaker of English who had an interesting experience with some assessment role plays. In this case it was Michelle whose language skills were being evaluated when she was applying for a job as a teacher at a large federal language school in the United States. The school's policy is to interview job applicants using the *ILR OPI* in both the target language (i.e., the language the applicant intends to teach) and in English (the administrative language of the school).

Michelle told me that one of the hardest parts of the interview was a role play that the interviewers led up to in an indirect way. They had asked her what she thought the crime situation would be like in the U.S. in the coming decade, and from that question they guided the topic around to the idea that used car dealers are basically legitimized crooks. They then put her in an imaginary situation in which she was to pretend to be a used car salesperson at an awards banquet, where she would be presented with the "Used Car Dealer of the Year Award" and would have to make an acceptance speech to her fellow used car salesmen.

Another role-play situation the testers constructed was for Michelle to speak to her godfather, a close friend of her family whom she had known all her life, about his recent heavy drinking and a rumor in the town that he had been offensive to some women while he was drunk. This role play involved leading her "godfather" (one of the interviewers) to talk about his alleged drinking problem and using appropriate mitigating devices to downplay the seriousness of the situation to get him to address this personally and socially sensitive issue.

I asked Michelle which role play was most difficult and she answered without hesitation: "The used car dealer situation." I asked her why. "Oh," she said, "because I have absolutely no idea what it would be like to be a used car salesman. I couldn't imagine it!"

The drinking godfather scenario, in contrast, Michelle thought was fun, plausible, and easy because it allowed her to use the familiar form of address in Spanish (which is more comfortable for her than the formal register). She also felt the situation of talking to her godfather about the gossip in the town was culturally plausible—she "could get into it" and felt successful doing it, even though the interviewer who played the godfather kept the conversation going, forcing her to respond and continue the interview, thereby eliciting a longer ratable speech sample from her. "He was really good," she said. "I guess that's his job." (This last comment is reminiscent of Leo van Lier's point that interviewers have planned and probably practiced the role-play situations before.)

I asked Michelle if she had the sociolinguistic competence in Spanish to carry out the role play with the godfather. She replied that *that* was no problem. The hard part was giving an acceptance speech for the "Used Car Dealer of the Year Award." The most interesting thing she said to me is that the used car dealer role play was conducted entirely in English—Michelle's native language! Michelle's perceived difficulty with role-playing an unfamiliar situation in her native language (and her comfort in role-playing a different scenario in her second language) underscores Leo's point that role plays may be culturally and psychologically specific.

Michelle's experience with her Spanish/English interview, Leo's resistance to role plays, and the unfortunate encounter with the jellyfish all made me think about role plays as elicitation procedures in language assessment. The "Frameworks" section lays out some of the variables that I see as relevant to these concerns.

A cartoon about the *ILR OPI* training program shows three men standing in front of an audience. A banner across the stage reads, "OPI TESTER TRAINING PROGRAM." One man is wearing a shawl draped over his head and staring blankly at another man. The third man (obviously the trainer) says to them both, "Okay, Willoughby, this time you be Mother Teresa, and Jones, you try to sell her the storm windows."

PLAUSIBILITY AND EXPERIENCE

The question of *real* versus *unreal* or *plausible* versus *implausible* is a particularly difficult issue in designing role-play stimulus materials for language assessment because each test-taker's own personal experience (and willingness to act and ad lib, as Leo van Lier points out) may interact with the stimulus material in idiosyncratic ways. Likewise, in addition to the historical variable of past personal experience, there is also the question of plausible or potentially realistic scenarios. (What if Michelle's acceptance speech role-play scenario had involved winning the "Teacher of the Year Award" instead of the "Used Car Dealer of the Year Award"?) So we can imagine two intersecting continua: that of experience and that of plausibility. In fact, we can discuss Michelle's experience in light of the framework in Figure 11.1.

Figure 11.1: Plausibility and Experience as Factors in Role-Play Scenarios

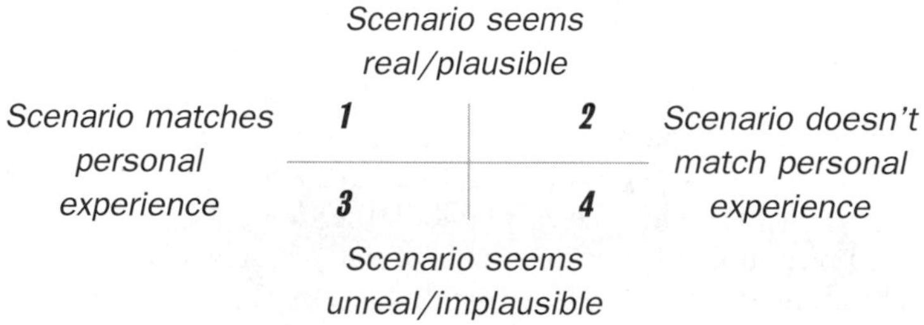

```
                       Scenario seems
                       real/plausible

  Scenario matches        1            2        Scenario doesn't
     personal          ─────────────────────    match personal
    experience            3            4           experience

                       Scenario seems
                      unreal/implausible
```

For Michelle, the stimulus material of giving the acceptance speech for the "Used Car Dealer of the Year Award" falls in quadrant 4: It didn't match her personal experience and it didn't seem like a plausible situation to her. I suggest that if the stimulus material had involved accepting the "Teacher of the Year Award" instead, we would be operating in quadrant 2: Michelle has not yet won such an award, so the scenario wouldn't have matched her previous experience, but it is quite plausible (in fact, I think highly likely) that someday she will.

Presumably the easiest sort of role play would be one that matched the test-taker's experience and seemed plausible (quadrant 1 in Figure 11.1). It would be easier for me to role-play small talk at a party in Spanish than to deliver a lecture on language testing in Spanish. (I've never done that before, but it's possible that I would—hence for me the language testing lecture would exemplify quadrant 2.) It is even less likely that I would deliver a lecture on physics in Spanish. I never have and it's unlikely that I ever would, since I've never even studied physics—so for me this physics lecture scenario would be an example of quadrant 4. I hope that the earring scenario I set up for Leo would fall into quadrant 2: This situation had not happened to him, but it's possible that it might at some point.

There may be the fewest examples of quadrant 3, in which the test-taker has had personal experience with the role-play situation but it still seems unreal or implausible. I submit to you that the incident with the jellyfish in Mexico is a possible example of a role-play scenario in this quadrant. Although that experience did really happen to Les and me, it still seems bizarre. As you read my account of the incident, I hope you were able to sense the nightmare-like feeling of the story as the events unfolded.

I suggest that if you are writing role-play scenarios to use in assessment (or even in teaching), it would be worthwhile to ask at least two questions about each situation you design:

1. Will the role-play scenario match the students' experience?

2. Will the role-play scenario at least seem plausible to the students?

If the answer to question #2 is "No," then we have the case of poor old Willoughby trying to sell storm windows to Mother Teresa. Under such circumstances, if you decide to proceed, I suggest that you be very cautious about using scores based on the role play to make decisions that will affect your students' lives.

UNEQUAL POWER DISCOURSE

Another major concern in using role plays as elicitation devices is trying to manipulate the unequal power discourse issues inherent in the oral interview format. The tester, by definition, typically has more power in the interview context, but in order to elicit sociolinguistic variation, the tester may often wish to manipulate that power differential, to create a context for equal power discourse or even a context in which the tester takes the role of the person of lesser power.

My friend Pat Bolger designed a reading and speaking test for students entering graduate programs at an English-medium school. He tried to set up a role-play situation (based on some passages students had read in an earlier portion of his test) that would generate conversation between equals. He wanted the texts of the reading passages to contribute to the context of the role play. These are the instructions for Pat's test (Bolger, 1996, 19):

> This test is an attempt to measure your English language ability with respect to understanding written passages *and* to working with that information in order to construct arguments. As much care as possible has been given to simulating the environment in classes where you are often given a certain amount of reading material and then asked to discuss this information in the following class period. That is exactly how this test works.

> The first part, reading comprehension, consists of a test booklet and an answer sheet. The test booklet contains six written passages taken from a magazine source. The subject matter is somewhat controversial with respect to the American media. Each of the six reading passages corresponds to exactly two multiple choice questions found on the answer sheet. Each of the questions on the answer sheet concerns the main ideas and/or arguments contained in the corresponding reading passage.

The six passages on the reading comprehension section of Pat's test were taken from the *Utne Reader* in 1993 and were about important news stories that had never been fully covered by the U.S. media. In each passage the author takes an argumentative stance; the author's attitude toward the topics is both implicit and explicit in the various articles. After each passage Pat posed two multiple-choice items. The stems were:

> Which of the following most accurately reflects the main point of the passage?

> Which of the following does the author *not* state or imply in the passage?

These stems were each followed by four options. The instructions continue:

> After completing the reading comprehension section of the test, you will participate in a role play, in which you will try to convince a "colleague" of the importance of one or more of these articles (your choice). The "colleague" will, in fact, be a test administrator.

Notice that Pat's use of quotation marks clearly indicates in print his awareness of the "as if" conditions of the role play. He tried very hard, in creating his role-play scenario, to manipulate the sociolinguistic variables that would create equal power discourse between the interlocutors while at the same time being honest about his real role as the test administrator.

Here are the instructions for the oral communication section of Pat's test. As you read them, try to identify the factors in the stimulus material that are intended to set up a conversation between equals.

> Imagine that you are an editor for a major newspaper. You are concerned about presenting the truth to the public.

> It is 1996 and the stories from 1993 that you just read [i.e., in the reading comprehension section of the test] have not been published in your newspaper and you think that they should be. Unfortunately, your fellow editor and friend of many years, David York, is not so receptive to the stories. He thinks that they are too controversial for the public and are not supported by any data. Moreover, most of the other major newspapers have not covered these stories, so why should he?

> You feel that these news stories, though old, should be covered in one way or another in your newspaper since the public was never really informed of them. So you decide to present your case to David York. Choose one or more of the articles that you feel most comfortable presenting to him and make your case.

I hope you noticed that the relationship between the two interlocutors is clearly established in this scenario. David York, the test-taker's fictitious interlocutor, is described as a "fellow editor and friend of many years." So the intended speech event in this role play is a disagreement between friends who are professional equals and who know each other well.

Pat's interview procedure is an interesting example of speaking for a particular purpose. Clearly the interlocutors are intended to be social equals, but also, the speech act is that of persuasion. So Pat's scoring criteria needed to reflect the intended purpose of the speech event.

SOME ISSUES IN SCORING SPEECH SAMPLES

Table 11.1 shows the scoring criteria Pat used in evaluating the audio-recorded role-play data from his test-takers. He adapted these descriptions from the British Council scale as presented in Hughes (1989, 95–96).

Table 11.1: Holistic Scale for a Speaker's Effectiveness of Argumentation

7	Relevant arguments are presented in an interesting way, with main ideas prominently and clearly stated, with completely effective supporting material; arguments are effectively related to the speaker's view.
6	Relevant arguments are presented in an interesting way; main ideas are highlighted with effective supporting material, and are well related to the speaker's own views.
5	Arguments are well presented with relevant supporting material and an attempt to relate them to the speaker's views.
4	Arguments are presented but it may be difficult for the rater to distinguish main ideas from supporting material; main ideas may not be supported; their relevance may be dubious; arguments may not be related to the speaker's views.
3	Arguments are presented, but may lack relevance, clarity, consistency or support; they may not be related to the speaker's views.
2	Arguments are inadequately presented and supported; they may be irrelevant; if the speaker's views are presented, their relevance may be difficult to see.
1	Some elements of information are present but the rater is not provided with an argument, or the argument is mainly irrelevant.
0	A meaning comes through occasionally but it is not relevant.

Pat and a colleague scored the tape recordings of the students' role plays independently, using the criteria in Table 11.1. Table 11.2 shows the scores that they awarded to the speech samples. How similar are the two sets of ratings?

Table 11.2: Two Raters' Scores

Speaker	Rater 1's scores	Rater 2's scores
A	5	6
B	3	4
C	6	5
D	6	6
E	4	4

F	6	6
G	4	5
H	2	4
I	6	6
J	4	4
K	5	5
L	7	7

Pat and his colleague gave exactly the same rating to seven of the twelve speech samples (those for speakers D, E, F, I, J, K, and L). Most of the other ratings differed by only one score level (e.g., a 5 and a 6 awarded to Speaker A, and a 3 and a 4 awarded to Speaker B). However, the ratings of 2 and 4 given to Speaker H are a matter of some concern, since they represent rather different reactions on the part of the two raters. It would be worthwhile for them to replay the tape of that particular interview together and discuss the features that led to the discrepancies in their ratings.

You will recall that in the quote from "Alma's letter" that opened Chapter 6, Alma explained that she preferred to assess her students' actual English use, rather than give them objectively scored multiple-choice tests. But she worried about the subjective scoring of students' output in direct tests and how she could justify such scoring to parents and colleagues. Indeed, demonstrating that our scoring systems are reliable is an important responsibility in any assessment situation.

We will use Pat Bolger's role-play data to illustrate an important procedure for demonstrating the reliability of our rating systems. There are several different ways to do this, including some uses of correlation. However, I will introduce a statistic called "coefficient alpha," which we have not yet encountered.

COMPUTING RATER RELIABILITY

Let's return briefly to some statistical procedures that are important in language assessment. You will recall that in Chapter 1, a particular dilemma faced by Diane Williams in getting information about her students' speaking skills if she decided to interview them all was the need to be fair and consistent in rating their speech. Such consistency is referred to as **rater reliability** and it generally is discussed in either of two ways.

1. **Intrarater reliability** is determined by having the same person evaluate the same data (usually writing samples or recordings of student speech) on two different occasions and comparing the results to see how similar they are. (We would be unhappy if the rater had been inconsistent and evaluated the data quite differently on the two occasions.) Normally a period of time is allowed to elapse between the two rating occasions and the data are presented to the rater in a different order the second time.

2. **Interrater reliability** refers to the consistency with which two (or more) raters evaluate the same data using the same scoring criteria. Again, it is desirable that the ratings of the same data be identical or very similar.

If Diane had interviewed and tape-recorded her students, she could have calculated intrarater reliability by listening to the tape recordings and scoring the speech samples a second time. In the case of Pat and his colleague independently scoring Pat's data and then checking to see how similar their scores were, we have an example of interrater reliability.

One accepted procedure for comparing the ratings of two different evaluators (or one evaluator rating the same data at two different points in time) is known as the *coefficient alpha*. It is also called *Cronbach's alpha* (after the man who described it, in 1951), and it is symbolized by the Greek letter *alpha,* or α. Here is the entire formula:

$$\alpha = \frac{k}{k-1}\left(1 - \frac{S^2_{r_1} + S^2_{r_2}}{S^2_{r_1 + r_2}}\right)$$

Once again we are faced with an imposing formula, but remember that we have seen some of these symbols before. You will recall that S^2 represents variance. Here the lowercase subscripts r_1 and r_2 are used to represent the two raters if you are calculating interrater reliability (or the two different rating occasions if you are calculating intrarater reliability). So if we look at the threatening beast in parentheses, we see that it says

$$1 - \frac{S^2_{r_1} + S^2_{r_2}}{S^2_{r_1 + r_2}}$$

or, to put the concept into prose, the whole number one, minus the variance of Rater 1 plus the variance of Rater 2 divided by the variance of the summed ratings. In this case (though not always—see Bachman, 1990, 177), the symbol k stands for the number of ratings (two)—Pat's and his colleague's:

$$\frac{k}{k-1} = \frac{2}{2-1} = \frac{2}{1} = 2$$

We will use Pat Bolger's interrater reliability computations to illustrate the use of coefficient alpha. In this case Pat evaluated students' speech samples, but you can use coefficient alpha to determine rater consistency with other kinds of ratings (e.g., composition scores) as well.

The calculation of interrater reliability using Cronbach's alpha involves first computing the variance for the two raters. (This is related to the procedure for computing standard deviation, which we explored in Chapter 7.) You will recall that we first find the mean for a set of scores. We then establish the difference (D) between each score in that set and the mean of that set. We square the difference scores (D^2) to get rid of the minus signs. These steps have been carried out for Rater 1 in Table 11.3. (The mean of Rater 1's scores was 4.833.)

Table 11.3: Variance for Rater 1

Speaker	Raw scores	D	D²
A	5	0.17	0.028
B	3	−1.83	3.360
C	6	1.17	1.362
D	6	1.17	1.362
E	4	−0.83	0.694
F	6	1.17	1.362
G	4	−0.83	0.694
H	2	−2.83	8.026
I	6	1.17	1.362
J	4	−0.83	0.694
K	5	−0.17	0.028
L	7	2.17	4.696

The standard deviation (s) was 1.4668 and the variance (s^2) was 2.152.

The next step is to calculate the variance for the second rater, represented in the numerator of the formula as $S_{r2}{}^2$. The same steps were followed for Rater 2 as those described above. The mean for Rater 2's scores was 5.167. If you calculate the mean based on the data in Table 11.4, I hope you will get this same value. (The way you round off places beyond the decimal in each stage of the calculations may lead to slightly different values.)

Table 11.4: Variance for Rater 2

Speaker	Raw scores	D	D²
A	6	0.83	0.694
B	4	−1.17	1.362
C	5	−0.17	0.028
D	6	0.83	0.694
E	4	−1.17	1.362
F	6	0.83	0.694
G	5	−0.17	0.028
H	4	−1.17	1.362
I	6	0.83	0.694

J	4	−1.17	1.362
K	5	−0.17	0.028
L	7	1.83	3.360

Thus the standard deviation (*s*) was 1.0299 and the variance (*s*²) was 1.061. Again, if you calculate *s* and *s*², I hope you will get these same results.

Just looking at the two means and two standard deviations, how would you compare Raters 1 and 2? If you say that Rater 1 was slightly tougher (as indicated by the somewhat lower mean) and had more variability in his ratings (as indicated by the larger standard deviation), that is correct.

Finally, we must compute the denominator of the term inside the parentheses—that is, the variance of the summed ratings for the two raters. To do this we must add the two raters' assessments of each speaker to come up with a combined raw score. (This has been done in the second column of Table 11.5, below.) Then, once again, we compute *D* and *D*², to find the variance. The mean for the two raters' combined raw scores was 10.

Table 11.5: **Total Variance for Raters 1 and 2**

Speaker	Combined Raw scores	D	D²
A	11	1	1
B	7	−3	9
C	11	1	1
D	12	2	4
E	8	−2	4
F	12	2	4
G	9	−1	1
H	6	−4	16
I	12	2	4
J	8	−2	4
K	10	0	0
L	14	4	16

The standard deviation (*s*) was 2.4121 and the variance (*s*²) was 5.818.

We can now use the variance values for Rater 1 and Rater 2 as our numerator, and the total variance for Raters 1 and 2 in the denominator of the formula for coefficient alpha:

$$\alpha = 2\left[\left(1 - \frac{2.152 + 1.061}{5.818}\right)\right]$$

Now that the values have been plugged into the formula, completing the procedure is largely a matter of addition, subtraction, multiplication, and division. (I told you that you could do this stuff!)

$$\alpha = 2\left(1 - \frac{3.213}{5.818}\right)$$

$$\alpha = 2(1 - 0.55225)$$
$$\alpha = 2(0.44775)$$
$$\alpha = 0.8955$$

Rounded off to the nearest hundredths, $\alpha = 0.90$. What does this alpha value mean? We read it just like a correlation coefficient: The closer the value is to the whole number 1.00, the greater the interrater reliability. In other words, the scores awarded independently by Pat and his colleague were very reliable. They were systematic enough that we can have confidence in their ratings.

In this chapter we have dealt with a few of the issues related to the elicitation and evaluation of speech samples. We considered some problems associated with role play, specifically the concern about the plausibility of role-play topics and how they interact with the test-taker's experience. We also noted that the unequal power discourse situation inherent to the oral proficiency interview makes it difficult to elicit speech in which the test candidate takes a role of equal or greater power in the discourse. Finally, we experimented with a statistic called *coefficient alpha*, which can be used to demonstrate the reliability of our rating procedures. The following tasks are intended to give you practice with these ideas and to further your practical knowledge about eliciting and evaluating speech samples, especially through role play.

 Investigations

1 *Design a series of three thematically related role-play tasks in which you try to systematically vary the relationship of the speakers. Try to design one role play in which the speakers are of equal power. Try to design one in which the test administrator is the character with greater power in the scenario. Finally, try to create a situation in which the test candidate takes the role of the person with greater power. Here is an example of a possible context:*

Have a conversation after a very difficult and important examination in a university course. A student wants the professor to reconsider (change) the grade the student received.

Figure 11.2: Role Assignments for Task 1's Thematically Related Role Plays

Role of the Interviewer	Role of the Test-taker
Student	Student
Professor	Student
Student	Professor

Try to write instructions that clearly spell out the different power roles. Tape record someone role-playing these three situations with you. Afterward, ask your role-playing partner to describe the experience for you, with a focus on whether your attempts to alter the power relationship were successful.

---

2 *Michelle Bettencourt's experience of having to role-play a situation that seemed unrealistic to her, even in her first language, suggests an interesting investigation. If you are currently teaching a language class, you could have pairs of students who share the same first language enact a role play in their first language and then in their second (or foreign) language. Then ask them to explain how the experiences differed—affectively, linguistically, and culturally. This procedure would allow you to explore the extent to which their success as role players was language-independent. In other words, we are questioning the validity of role plays as language elicitation devices: Are we measuring language skills, role-playing abilities, or both?*

---

3 *If you are writing role plays to use as either a testing or a teaching procedure, it is a good idea to try them yourself with a colleague before asking students to participate. Pilot-testing the role-play scenarios can help you discover whether the instructions are clear. It will also give you a feel for the plausibility issue, which is important if the students' speech elicited during the role plays will be evaluated and the results used in decision making.*

Write the stimulus material for a role play and then perform it with a colleague. Afterwards, discuss the experience with your colleague and revise the role-play prompt as needed, based on the discussion.

---

4 *Once you have pilot-tested a role play and feel that it is working well, have three or more groups of students enact the role play (either within or outside one anothers' view). Then ask some colleagues who did not witness the original role plays to evaluate videotapes or audiotapes of the students' output. Be sure you know in advance what the evaluative criteria will be. Then apply the formula for* coefficient alpha *to your data to check the interrater reliability.*

Suggested Readings

There are many procedures other than role plays for eliciting spoken language. For instance, several helpful suggestions can be found in Nic Underhill's (1987) book *Testing Spoken Language: A Handbook of Oral Testing Techniques*. Other references that contain ideas for eliciting spoken language include the books by Cohen (1994), Hughes (1989), and Madsen (1983). Cohen, for instance, discusses the use of dialogues for assessing speaking skills.

Steve Ross (1987) has investigated an interesting idea for eliciting spoken language. He wanted students' speech samples to be comparable and he also wanted to investigate fluency as a component of oral proficiency. So he had Japanese college students view and narrate video cartoons of familiar Japanese folktales. The fact that these were stories every student would know eliminated the problem of students having to generate original ideas. The sound of the videos was turned off and each student narrated the story as it was shown in the video. This procedure allowed him to control the speed of presentation of the stimulus material and also to make sure the learners' responses were of comparable length and content.

Susan Stern (1983) has written an interesting article about the use of drama and role play in language teaching. Some parts of her rationale may be useful to you if you want to implement role play as a part of an oral assessment program.

It may not always be practical to conduct direct face-to-face oral interviews. This has especially been the case with some of the less commonly taught languages, where there may be no trained tester readily available. For this reason, researchers working at the Center for Applied Linguistics in Washington, D.C., have developed tape-delivered tests called "simulated oral proficiency interviews" (or SOPI's). These procedures are sometimes referred to as semidirect tests because they don't entail the interactive spontaneity of an actual conversation, but they do involve the student in speaking to a greater extent than, say, a conversational cloze test or other indirect test of speaking. Charles Stansfield (1991) has written an interesting comparison of simulated and direct oral proficiency interviews that would be useful background reading if you are considering how to assess your learners' speaking skills.

For further guidance on computing and interpreting rater reliability, see Henning (1987) and Bachman (1990).

12

THREE APPROACHES TO SCORING WRITING SAMPLES

I spent the summer of 1974 stuck in a one-room cabin in the tobacco fields outside the little town of Clarksville, Tennessee. (If you remember the Monkees' song, "The Last Train to Clarksville," that's the place.) How I got stuck there is a long story that involves sinking my life's savings into a used Volkswagen van that got burned up one week after I'd rented a cabin way out in the woods, as far away as possible from any public transportation.

Clarksville, Tennessee, in 1974 was a town whose main industries were growing tobacco, producing fertilizer, and making cowboy boots. (In my opinion, Clarksville's main claim to fame is that it was the original home of my friend and dissertation advisor, Frances Butler.) After the fire, I found myself with no car, no job, no money, no television, and no friends (I didn't know Frances then), listening to tornado warnings and country music on the radio, through the long, hot, boring, sticky summer of 1974. Once a month I would splurge on an expensive taxi ride into town to buy supplies and go to the library. I read the classics of English literature, I went for long walks with the neighbors' dog, and I wrote letters.

As you can imagine, I didn't have much to write about. The most exciting thing that happened that summer (after the car burning up) was that I saw my first firefly (or "lightning bug," as they are called in Tennessee). Since I was so bored and so lonely, I would write to my friends and family about the little events of my life, trying to make them sound as interesting as possible, so that someone would write back to me. I wrote about the same mundane things (topics like a recipe that didn't turn out as expected) over and over (this was before the days of electronic mail and word processors), sometimes five or six handwritten letters in a day. And even though I already had my bachelor's degree in English literature, even though I had taken writing courses, even though I'd already been an English teacher, the summer of 1974 was when I really learned to write. The way I knew if I had written something well was that somebody, somewhere, would write back to me.

There are many important issues to consider in assessing language learners' writing skills, but I have tightened the focus a bit in this chapter in order to be able to explore issues related specifically to scoring writing samples.

Furthermore, since my own experience in recent years has been working with learners of English at the tertiary level, this chapter will deal primarily with issues related to assessing the writing of young adults in academic contexts. We will see that the assessment of writing has undergone numerous developments in the past two decades, some of which will be illustrated here.

Some of the many fascinating questions about the assessment of writing that are beyond the scope of this chapter concern the stimulus material: Are students given a simple prompt, as in Christine Houba's essay task in Chapter 6, or is the stimulus material more detailed? For example, do the students read an article and then take a position on the issues it raises? In terms of the task posed to the learner, the prompt may specify only the topic or it may tell the students what to do with the topic (e.g., compare and contrast, discuss the advantages and disadvantages, etc.). The conditions for eliciting writing samples are also a matter of debate: Much of the writing students must do in academic contexts involves long-term assignments done outside class, such as research papers using reference materials, yet in many writing assessment settings, the students' response is to write a very brief essay under timed conditions without access to other sources of ideas for writing. And, as we saw in Chapter 6, for many years, assessing the hypothesized enabling skills (e.g., error identification) through very indirect testing formats, such as multiple-choice items (rather than actually having students compose original essays) was thought to be more reliable, more objective, and more practical than directly testing students' writing.

I am particularly fascinated by the question of how we evaluate students' writing since our collective professional thinking about the teaching of writing has changed so much in my lifetime as a writer and a teacher of writing. While our pedagogic emphases have swung from a strongly product-oriented to a largely process-oriented approach, which involves multiple drafts of papers, our evaluation procedures have lagged behind our pedagogy. How can we promote learners' development as writers when we face institutional requirements to assign grades? How do we evaluate students' writing during the lengthy drafting and revision process? In the Teachers' Voices section of this chapter we will see how one teacher, John Hedgcock, deals with these issues.

When it comes to assessing students' actual production of written texts in a second or foreign language, three approaches have traditionally been used to rate learners' writing. Each of these approaches is defined by the scoring criteria used, rather than by the stimulus material, the task posed, or the learner's response. These three traditional approaches are holistic, analytic, and objective scoring.

Before we examine these three approaches to evaluating writing, it is important to clarify what is meant by *scoring criteria*. Mari Wesche (1983, 44–45) points out that the term **scoring criteria** has two meanings:

> Test tasks should . . . be designed to give not only a "yes" or "no" answer as to whether an examinee can "do" a task, but should indicate how well he or she can do it relative to how well he or she needs to do it.

In other words, the term *scoring criteria* has two meanings: Scoring criteria can identify skills that are demonstrated (or not), but they can also identify the extent to which a skill is demonstrated. The former function is a categorical distinction (presence versus absence). The latter is a qualitative function—a matter of specifying how values are assigned to the task being evaluated. What distinguishes holistic, analytic, and objective scoring systems from one another is how values are assigned to the written product. We will examine each system in turn.

HOLISTIC SCORING

The idea in holistic scoring is that a single scale can be used to describe different levels of writing performance. Raters using holistic scales are trained not to think about the individual components of the writing skill or to count the number of errors that students make. In **holistic scoring,** the reader reacts to the student's composition as a whole: A single score is awarded to the writing. Normally this score is on a scale of 1 to 4, or 1 to 6, or even 1 to 10. Often each level on the scale is accompanied by a verbal description of the performance required to achieve that score (the second meaning of *scoring criteria* given above). For example, the level descriptors for the *Test of Written English (TWE)* are reprinted below (from the *TOEFL Test of Written English Guide,* 1989, Educational Testing Service, Princeton, New Jersey). For discussions about the development of the *Test of Written English,* see Stansfield (1986) and Nevo (1986).

Test of Written English (TWE) Scoring Guide

Readers will assign scores based on the following scoring guide. Though examinees are asked to write on a specific topic, part of the topic may be treated by implication. Readers should focus on what the examinee does well.

Scores

6. **Clearly demonstrates competence in writing on both the rhetorical and syntactic levels, though it may have occasional errors.**

    A paper in this category

    — *is well organized and well developed*
    — *effectively addresses the writing task*
    — *uses appropriate details to support a thesis or illustrate ideas*
    — *shows unity, coherence, and progression*
    — *displays consistent facility in the use of language*
    — *demonstrates syntactic variety and appropriate word choice*

5. **Demonstrates competence in writing on both the rhetorical and syntactic levels, though it will have occasional errors.**

    A paper in this category

    — *is generally well organized and well developed, though it may have fewer details than does a 6 paper*
    — *may address some parts of the task more effectively than others*
    — *shows unity, coherence, and progression*

— *demonstrates some syntactic variety and range of vocabulary*

— *displays facility in language, though it may have more errors than does a 6 paper*

4. Demonstrates minimal competence in writing on both the rhetorical and syntactic levels.

A paper in this category

— *is adequately organized*

— *addresses the writing topic adequately but may slight parts of the task*

— *uses some details to support a thesis or illustrate ideas*

— *demonstrates adequate but undistinguished or inconsistent facility with syntax and usage*

— *may contain some serious errors that occasionally obscure meaning*

3. Demonstrates some developing competence in writing, but it remains flawed on either the rhetorical or syntactic level, or both.

A paper in this category may reveal one or more of the following weaknesses:

— *inadequate organization or development*

— *failure to support or illustrate generalizations with appropriate or sufficient detail*

— *an accumulation of errors in sentence structure and/or usage*

— *a noticeably inappropriate choice of words or word forms*

2. Suggests incompetence in writing.

A paper in this category is seriously flawed by one or more of the following weaknesses:

— *failure to organize or develop*

— *little or no detail, or irrelevant specifics*

— *serious and frequent errors in usage or sentence structure*

— *serious problems with focus*

1. Demonstrates incompetence in writing.

A paper in this category will contain serious and persistent writing errors, may be illogical or incoherent, or may reveal the writer's inability to comprehend the question. A paper that is severely underdeveloped also falls into this category.

Papers that reject the assignment or fail to address the question in any way must be given to the Table Leader. Papers that exhibit absolutely no response at all must be given to the Table Leader.

There are both advantages and disadvantages to holistic scoring. The advantages are that it is fast, high rater reliability can be achieved, and the scoring scale can provide a public standard understood by teachers and students alike.

Holistic scoring systems are also assumed to be widely applicable to many different topics. In addition, many people feel that holistic scoring emphasizes the writers' strengths, rather than their weaknesses. The disadvantages are that the single score may mask differences across individual compositions (i.e., not all papers awarded a "4" on the *TWE* scale, for example, are of identical quality), and do not provide much useful diagnostic feedback to learners or teachers. Furthermore, such broad scales may fail to capture important differences across various writing tasks. For these reasons, there is concern that holistic rating scales may not promote positive washback.

Typically, when people are trained to score compositions holistically, the training begins with familiarization with the scale and then the trainees read several **benchmark** papers. These are papers that are classic examples of the levels they represent. (These typical examples are also referred to as **anchor papers.**) After reading several benchmark papers and discussing how they relate to the scale, the trainees are then given a mixed set of papers that also include good examples of the various score levels on the scale. The trainees independently read these compositions and score them using the scale descriptors. Then everyone compares the scores they've awarded. Any discrepancies are discussed, another set of papers is read and scored, and so on. This process is known as **norming,** since it is intended to get all the raters working on the same scale.

During actual scoring sessions, raters are typically seated at tables with a "table leader" at the head. This person is a very experienced rater who has previously demonstrated her skill with the rating scale. As the rating proceeds, she reads some of the same papers that are being scored by the people at her table (to make sure the raters are being consistent in their use of the scale) and gives them feedback about their consistency. This process ensures that everyone at the table stays close to the level descriptors in evaluating the students' essays.

There is an important offshoot of holistic scoring that appears to have great washback potential. In this approach to defining scoring criteria, which is known as **primary trait scoring,** a particular functional focus is selected, based on the purpose of the writing. So, for instance, in an essay that was intended to *persuade* the reader of the author's point of view, the scoring criteria, using the primary trait approach, would be based on how compelling and convincing the author's ideas were to the reader, rather than how well organized the ideas were, or how grammatical the structures were (realizing, of course, that grammaticality and good organization may contribute to an essay's persuasiveness). So if you take my context of writing letters during the long, hot, sticky, boring summer of 1974 in Clarksville, Tennessee, the primary trait by which (I assume) my letters were being evaluated (albeit implicitly) was in terms of their "interestingness"—the ability to provoke a written response from my readers. (Pat Bolger's adaptation of the British Council scale for assessing effectiveness of argumentation, which we saw in Table 11.1, provides an example of primary trait scoring applied to speaking.)

ANALYTIC SCORING

The second major approach to rating second or foreign language writing, analytic scoring, involves a different philosophy. In analytic scoring, raters do assess students' performances on a variety of categories. Indeed, an analytic scoring system embodies hypotheses about the underlying constructs that comprise a given skill. One widely used analytic scale for scoring ESL writing (Jacobs, Zingraf, Wormuth, Hartfiel, and Hughey, 1981) hypothesizes that effective writing consists of five components, and that some of these components are more important than others. The weights given to these components follow: Content: 13 to 30 points possible; organization: 7 to 20 points possible; vocabulary: 7 to 20 points possible; language use: 5 to 25 points possible; and mechanics: 2 to 5 points possible. The points awarded in these five categories would then be added to yield a total score. This approach is referred to as **analytic scoring** because the scale designers have analyzed the hypothesized components of the writing skill, and it is these components that make up the categories used in scoring. So what you choose to rate when you evaluate your students' writing with an analytic scoring system, in effect, amounts to the operationalization of your theory of writing.

Some time ago I participated in the development of an analytic scoring instrument for scoring compositions written by university students in an upper-intermediate ESL course. The instrument was developed by a team of teachers who taught at this particular level. One of the course objectives stated that at the end of the course, a student would be able to

> write a precise, convincing and well organized expository
> composition with an introduction, body and conclusion;
> proofread and revise his/her written work; use connectives
> correctly within and between paragraphs; . . . [and] use new
> vocabulary items in compositions (Bailey, 1977, 5).

We needed to devise an assessment process that would systematize the evaluation of students' writing and operationally define this goal. So we decided to develop categories of scoring criteria for use in progress tests and achievement tests. By making these criteria explicit and public, our team hoped to encourage positive washback and to standardize the grading expectations of the various TAs working at the same level. Here's the procedure we followed:

> Four staff members began the instrument development process by
> identifying the areas they felt were most important in teaching and
> evaluating writing skills at the upper intermediate level. These
> teachers then collaborated on writing verbal descriptors of excellent
> to poor performance in each of the five criteria they had identified.
> Revisions of the instrument were based on suggestions from all of
> the TAs who taught this course and input from the department's
> faculty members. Thus the composition scoring grid [was] based
> primarily on the consensus of experienced ESL teachers, rather
> than on explicit theory or research findings as to what constitutes
> effective writing (Brown and Bailey, 1984, 27).

This process was very time-consuming, but since the resulting system would be used by a team of teachers, we felt it was important that members of the group participate in its development.

The outcome was a one-page scoring grid with five criteria listed on the vertical axis. Each criterion had an array of performance levels ranging from excellent to unacceptable on the horizontal axis. Verbal descriptions for each criterion at each level were written in the cells. The criteria were (1) organization, (2) logical development of ideas, (3) grammar, (4) mechanics, and (5) style and quality of expression. Each criterion had twenty points possible and the students' scores on each scale were summed to obtain the total score (100 points possible).

> One assumption underlying the use of this system was that focusing the raters' attention on a number of specifically defined criteria comprising the total score might yield a more precise estimate and more informative diagnosis of second language learners' writing proficiency than would a global score. An administrative purpose for instituting the use of such an instrument was to standardize the grading procedure in all of the sections of the course. The question of standardization was an issue both during the academic term and in scoring the final examination (Brown and Bailey, 1984, 27–28).

In addition to this concern about standardization, our attempts to promote positive washback were ongoing throughout the instructional term. When the semester started, the ESL teachers distributed copies of the grid to the students and discussed the criteria and the rating procedure with them. The teachers also used this grid during the term to score each composition written by the students. The students' scores were reported to them on the completed feedback sheets, which were given to them along with their corrected compositions. Thus the analytic scoring system was meant to supplement, rather than replace, the specific written feedback teachers gave individual students on their compositions. In fact, comments and corrections written on the papers were left entirely up to the teachers. The scores for the analytic instrument were given to the students on a simple form (Brown and Bailey, 1984, 42), which recorded a score for each of the five analytic categories listed above, the total score, and additional comments from the teacher. This process allowed the students to see areas of progress throughout the term.

The scoring grid that the teachers and students had used throughout the term was also used to evaluate the final examination compositions. These essays were read and scored by two teachers (other than the individual student's own teacher) and the average of the two readers' scores was given to the composition. In cases of a discrepancy of twelve points or more (out of 100 possible points), a third reader evaluated the essay and that score was also computed in the average. Both students and teachers could request that a composition be reconsidered. Our hope was that using this system would provide a uniform and fair assessment of the students' exit-level writing and also promote positive washback.

In writing the article from which the above quotations were taken, J. D. Brown and I surveyed the teachers to get their reactions to this system. Although the raters' responses were generally positive, they felt that the criteria were not defined precisely enough, particularly in the category of style and quality of expression. However, you will recall that some of these raters had worked on revising earlier versions of the scoring grid, so it probably embodied many of their ideas about ESL writing. Other teachers who were not involved in the instrument development might find such a scoring grid less useful. I have not included a copy of the grid here due to space limitations and because my intended purpose is to discuss its development—not to promote its use. A copy of the grid as it was used in the early 1980s is reprinted in Brown and Bailey (1984, 39–41), and also in Brown (1996, 62–63).

This analytic scoring system was a product of our collaborative thinking as a faculty. It fit our needs and our shared understanding of writing at the time. But if I were to design an analytic scoring grid today, it would be quite different. For example, our scoring system did not refer to the *author's voice*, or *awareness of audience*, which are now recognized as essential elements of successful writing.

As I mentioned above, specifying scoring criteria in an analytic approach to evaluating writing, is, in effect, a statement about what constitutes effective writing. As those ideas change, so must our scoring systems. Indeed, Henning and Davidson (1987) conducted research on a much simpler and clearer version of the instrument described above. Although people want stability and continuity in assessment systems, it is important that evaluative criteria develop apace with our theoretical and practical knowledge of the constructs we are measuring. In other words, as our understanding of writing changes, so should the procedures by which we evaluate writing.

OBJECTIVE SCORING

The third major approach to scoring writing is called **objective scoring.** As the name suggests, this approach relies on quantified methods of evaluating students' writing. However, as attractive as objectivity may seem, there are many drawbacks to this approach, as we shall see.

Here is an example of how teachers at one school, the University of New Mexico, devised an objective scoring system for use in making placement decisions. The following descriptions are taken from an article by Dean Brodkey and Rodney Young (1981). Although this article is somewhat dated, I use it because it gives such a clear description of an objective scoring system developed for a particular language teaching context. In the quote below, the authors describe the general administrative framework of their curriculum, as well as the student population involved.

> We needed a simple and quantitative measure of achievement level and progress in writing skill: a measure which would allow us to place students in classes along a continuum from Intensive English through two to three subsequent semesters of freshman English classes geared to both foreign and remedial American students. . . . Upon graduation from Intensive English, students attend a series of freshman composition classes, . . . which carry university credit, and which permit simultaneous enrollment in other university classes. In general, foreign students and those who clearly use English as a second language are taught in a separate stream from American students. The program includes bilinguals and quasi-bilinguals such as Native Americans or Chicanos, recent immigrants who graduat-

ed from American high schools, and some entirely mono-lingual English speakers with remedial writing problems (Brodkey and Young, 1981, 159–160).

Given this complex context, the faculty set about devising an assessment system whose purpose was accurate and fair placement of these various kinds of students into the writing courses. The teachers had been dissatisfied with standardized tests, cloze procedures, and impressionistic scoring systems in the past. For these reasons, they were very clear as to the goals the new procedure would need to accomplish:

> The test we had in mind needed the following features: (1) it had to be a reliable and valid measure of writing performance for college work; (2) it had to be easy and natural for any English teacher to administer and score; (3) it needed to provide a numerical index rather than an impressionistic comment; (4) it had to be a particularly fine-toothed discriminator among levels of instruction which often deceive the naked eye of the grader; and (5) it should help discriminate between ESL students and native-speaker students within our very heterogeneous population of vari-linguals (Brodkey and Young, 1981, 160).

The teachers devised an objective scoring method that emphasized accuracy but accounted for its impact on readability. Here is how Brodkey and Young (160–161) describe the scoring procedure:

1. Count the first 250 words of the essay. (By having students count the words, perhaps exchanging papers, much teacher-work is avoided.)

2. Go through the essay up to the 250th word underlining *every* mistake—from spelling and mechanics through verb tenses, morphology, vocabulary, and logical connectives between sentences. Include every error that a literate reader might note. Entire phrases of five or six words may be underlined where no single source of error is readily analyzable.

3. Assign a weight score to each error, from 3 to 1. A score of 3 is a severe distortion of readability or flow of ideas which throws the reader off the sense of the message through intrusion of an erroneous linguistic element; 2 is a moderate distortion; and 1 is a minor error that does not affect readability in any significant way.

4. Calculate the essay Correctness Score by using 250 words as the numerator of a fraction, and the sum of the error scores as the denominator: The denominator is the sum of all the error scores:

$$\frac{250 \text{ (words)}}{71 \text{ (sum of errors)}} = 3.52 \text{ Correctness Score}$$

You will notice that each composition scored with this particular procedure needs to be at least 250 words long. That number is given to provide a basis for comparison across essays of different length: Someone who wrote a five-hundred-word essay would presumably have more opportunities to make errors than someone who wrote a three-hundred-word essay in response to the same prompt. Unfortunately, using a cut-off point like this may penalize students who write strong conclusions for their compositions. (It has been suggested that we could score the *last* 250 words of our students' essays to overcome this issue, but we're still faced with eliminating from the scoring process some part of what the students have written.)

Brodkey and Young give the following advice about the norming process and the weighting of errors:

> The teaching staff should utilize practice sessions in group-grading at first in order to identify teachers who tend to focus on idiosyncratic scoring. However, one should not overemphasize conformity. No attempts should be made to code or assign standard scores to standard categories of errors. It is not acceptable to say "all spelling errors = 1" since spelling errors differ greatly in their effect on readability of the message (160–161).

Notice that there is thus a fair amount of subjectivity involved in this "objective" error count system. The "Correctness Scores" that were derived from this process were used this way at the University of New Mexico (Brodkey and Young, 161):

Scores	Level
below 3.0 =	Intensive English level, 16 - 32 weeks, 25 hours per week, non-credit
3.0–5.0 =	Low level credit freshman English (ESL), 16 weeks, 5 hours per week, 3 credits
5.0–7.0 =	Intermediate freshman English (ESL), 16 weeks, 5 hours per week, 3 credits
7.0–9.0 =	Advanced level freshman English (ESL), 16 weeks, 5 hours per week, 3 credits
over 9.0 =	English with American students

These descriptions of how to score essays objectively are very clear. However, objective scoring systems are often criticized on two grounds.

The first problem is one that Brodkey and Young allude to when they say that teachers should practice scoring in groups but "one should not over-emphasize conformity" (161) in identifying errors as *severe*, *moderate*, or *minor*. In other words, subjectivity is involved in assigning the gravity weightings to students' errors. This subjectivity may be masked in the subsequent numerical calculations.

A second concern about objective scoring systems is that they often involve some sort of error tally. Many teachers feel this approach accentuates negative aspects of the learners' writing without giving them credit for what they *can* do well. For example, it may be possible to write a coherent well-organized story that has many morphosyntactic errors (as we will see in the "Investigations" section of this chapter). The error-count system seems to work on a deficit model —penalizing the students for problems in their writing without recognizing their strengths. Other teachers feel, however, that alerting students to their errors is one way to help them improve their writing. In the "Teachers' Voices" section of this chapter we will hear how one professional deals with the issue of accuracy in balancing a process approach and a product approach to teaching writing.

Teachers' Voices

In seeking a Teacher's Voice for this chapter, I turned to my colleague John Hedgcock, who had just finished teaching a writing course called "Content Writing." His students were nonnative writers of English who were taking graduate classes in international policy studies or international public administration at our school, the Monterey Institute of International Studies. I asked John about his view of assessment in teaching a writing class, since there has been a historic trend away from an emphasis on the product to an emphasis on process in writing pedagogy. Here is John's reaction:

> **John:** My view of assessment in writing doesn't presuppose mutual exclusivity between process and product—either in assessment or in teaching. The course that I just taught has to give students a strong awareness of product because of the purpose of the class. The content of the course is intended to give students an explicit awareness of the kinds of writing they need to do in their content courses in policy studies and public administration. So product is certainly part of my instructional process, and it's also part of the way in which I assess not only their progress but also how I evaluate their end product.

Where John talks about "content courses" he is referring to the students' classes in their major disciplines, because all the writing the students do in his class is designed to help them succeed in their graduate coursework. He continues:

> **John:** So I don't see that much antagonism between a process orientation and a product orientation, as long as there's explicitness all throughout the teaching cycle, concerning my expectations as a writing teacher and the difference between those expectations and the expectations that the students' content professors might have. In a social constructivist view, I try to give the students a repertoire of skills that they can use to apply to very specific kinds of product expectations within their content classes. So my teaching involves lots and lots of process, but also junctures along the way where the product is evaluated as a reflection of process, and, I hope, progress. Here I mean progress in the global sense of building up skills, but also progress in terms of improving "draft 2" over "draft 1," and "draft 3" over "draft 2," and so on.

I asked John to explain what he meant by a "social constructivist view."

> **John:** The basic premise is that academic writers (native speakers and nonnative speakers alike) have to produce academic texts for an academic audience. That readers in that audience will have cer-

tain expectations that are informed by their discourse communities and disciplines. Social constructivists therefore argue that the texts we teach students to write need to address specific discourse communities, since textual conventions (i.e., rhetorical patterns, etc.) are socially constructed. The general implication for teachers is basically that because student writers may ultimately be judged on the basis of the products they compose within their discourse communities, their ESL instruction should prepare them by giving them tools to generate those products successfully.

I was curious about the types of practical help John had to offer the students, so I asked him about the typical kinds of writing they would do in their content classes:

> **John:** Many of the students really had to write arguments a lot, for example, so many of the microskills we practiced in class were geared toward starting, composing, and revising an argumentative essay.

> **Kathi:** Are argumentative essays the kinds of things they have to write in their content classes?

> **John:** It's one of the genres, among many, particularly in essay exams. So that was one rhetorical mode that we dedicated quite a lot of time to because of the assignments they brought in from their other classes. They had to write things that we called "position papers." They had to write things like "rebuttals," which were genres that had rhetorical characteristics that I was familiar with but I knew by different labels. And these assignments all fit under the large umbrella of argumentation.

I wanted to see how John handled first and second drafts of papers, in terms of evaluation, so I posed a hypothetical situation.

> **Kathi:** Let's say I'm a student in your class and I turn in my first argumentative essay as a draft. What might I expect to get from you when you've dealt with my paper?

> **John:** Lots and lots of narrative and descriptive feedback. I also refrain from putting a score on those papers, but instead I refer to the criteria that we had agreed to at the outset of the assignment. But I didn't rank or score any of those papers unless the student explicitly asked me to do so. This was because they were drafts and because I wanted to make it really clear that what I was looking for was progress from one draft to the next. I wanted to make that [scoring] information available to the students if they wanted it, but I felt that I wanted to leave that up to them. Some students worked well without any kind of quantitative evaluation. In other

words, my narrative and descriptive feedback was enough for them to get a toehold and make changes that I thought were productive and useful for the second draft, or whatever subsequent draft they were working on at the time.

John's students also received input from peer reviewers at the same time they were getting his reactions to their drafts. Thus the sorts of feedback his students received were much richer and more varied than the information they would get from just a holistic score, an analytic score, or an objective score alone.

When the draft submission and review process was complete and students turned in the final versions of their papers, John used the following criteria for grading their work. You will see that this is a holistic scale used for evaluating the students' products, but that the descriptions (which were developed in collaboration with the students and shared with them before the final evaluation) clearly spell out the kinds of steps a writer would take during the process phase of developing a text.

Evaluation Criteria for Revised Writing Assignments in John Hedgcock's Content Writing Class

Characteristics of an 'A' paper: An 'A' paper is admirably thorough and complete. Explicit and clear, the position is strongly and substantially argued with abundant reference to published works. The central issues and their complexity are treated seriously, with alternative viewpoints taken into account. The paper shows rhetorical control at the highest level and displays unity and subtle management. Ideas are balanced with support which is organized according to the content. Textual elements are connected through explicit logical and/or linguistic transitions. Repetition and redundancy are minimal. The paper shows excellent language control, accurate diction, stylistic precision, and meticulous adherence to mechanical conventions.

Characteristics of a 'B' paper: A 'B' paper is thorough and complete. The text deals effectively with the issues, presenting the position clearly and articulating arguments substantively. References made to published works are ample and appropriate. Alternative perspectives are also addressed competently. The paper shows strong rhetorical control and is well managed. Ideas are generally balanced with support; the whole text shows good control of organization appropriate to the content. Textual elements are generally well connected, although rhetorical fluency may occasionally need improvement. Occasional repetitions, redundancies, and missing transitions may occur, but the paper reflects strong language control and reads smoothly. Grammatical well-formedness and accurate diction are apparent, although minor errors might be present. Stylistic and mechanical errors are minor and do not distract the reader.

Characteristics of a 'C' paper: Possibly lacking in thoroughness, a 'C' paper is nonetheless complete. The text discusses the issues but requires more focus, development, and/or synthesis of published works. The position, while thoughtful, needs to be clarified; arguments may require further substantiation. Repetition, redundancy, and inconsistency sometimes compromise the paper's focus and direction. Alternative viewpoints are minimally addressed and developed. Although the essay shows acceptable rhetorical control, competent management, and appropriate organization, ideas may not be balanced with support. The text shows evidence of planning; a lack of connectors sometimes interferes with rhetorical fluency. Language is grammatical but may lack fluidity. Whereas the grammatical structures and lexical choices express the writer's intended meanings, more appropriate choices could have been made. Morpho-syntactic, stylistic, and mechanical errors sometimes interfere with the reader's comprehension. Papers assigned a mark of 'C' should be revised and resubmitted.

Characteristics of a 'D' paper: A 'D' paper lacks both completeness and thoroughness. Although the text may consider the issues, it relies heavily on opinions or claims that lack substantial evidence, sometimes leading the reader to wonder if the writer has come to grips with the complexity of the topic. Synthesis of published works is clearly deficient. Superficial and/or inconsistent argumentation, along with inadequate development, seriously compromises the text's ability to convince the reader. Alternative perspectives are given little or no serious attention. Lacking rhetorical control much or most of the time, the paper's overall shape is difficult to discern. The organization suggests a lack of balance or support, which leads to noticeable breakdowns in rhetorical fluency. Transitions within and across sentences and paragraphs are attempted, with only partial success. Displaying weak linguistic control, the text contains grammatical, lexical, and mechanical errors which are a serious threat to the reader's comprehension. Papers assigned a mark of 'D' must be revised and resubmitted.

Characteristics of an 'F' paper: An 'F' paper is unsuccessful because it is clearly incomplete and fails to develop and support an argument related to the topic. While the topic may be mentioned, the text digresses or does not treat issues of relevance to the assignment. Superficial and inaccurate treatment of published works suggests a failure to read sources carefully and extensively. Demonstrating little rhetorical control, the paper shows virtually no evidence of planning or organization, as exemplified in underdeveloped or nonexistent connections and transitions. The text demonstrates inadequate linguistic control, with morpho-syntactic, lexical, and mechanical errors seriously marring the writer's *intended meaning. Papers assigned a mark of 'F' must be revised and resubmitted.*

You will notice that in the interest of promoting improvement, John's grading criteria state that "C" papers should be revised and resubmitted, while papers receiving grades of "D" or "F" *must* be revised and resubmitted.

Keep in mind that John's students were already enrolled in an English-medium graduate school. They all had *TOEFL* scores of at least 550, and they were all competing with native writers of English in their content courses. These evaluative criteria would probably *not* be appropriate for other students, at different levels of proficiency, writing in different contexts. I am grateful to John for sharing his criteria with me as an example of what one teacher did to meet both the particular needs of his students and the standards of his school. (If you would like to read more about his ideas on teaching writing, see Ferris and Hedgcock, in press.)

---

1 *Compare John Hedgcock's grading criteria with the scoring criteria on the* TWE *scale. Keep in mind that his scoring criteria were used to assess student achievement at the end of a particular course, whereas the* TWE *scale was designed to measure writing proficiency. What similarities and differences do you find? If you are currently teaching adult students in an academic setting, is either scale appropriate for you to use with your learners?*

---

2 *Printed below are two stories written by ESL students in an intermediate writing class in an intensive college preparatory program. The prompt was to write about something memorable. As you read these stories, try to be aware of your own reactions to the text. What features of the writing do you find annoying? Clear? Convincing? Would you say that either composition is better than the other, in your view of what constitutes effective writing?*

Composition 1 was written by a native speaker of Japanese. Composition 2 was written by someone who was raised in Japan, but who was not ethnically Japanese. The two authors were students in the same ESL class in California.

Composition 1

When I was a child, my father was always saying to me "Make friends." so I made many friends.

How? I tell you how.

I had a couple friends. They are still good friend. I was playing with them everyday. Each of them have friends. then They introduced their friends to me. I played with them. Little by little, this group was getting big. We began to play baseball. this group got more big group.

Friends are very important in human life. Even though you are 50 or 60 years old. Why my father said to make friends? I was watching T.V. everyday after school off course I had friends but I wasn't playing with them. Father said "It's OK to watch T.V. but if you want to watch T.V., take some friend's then watch together. It's better than alone.

Now I'm still trying to make many friends.

Composition 1 is 148 words long.

Composition 2

This is very shameful experience to me.

When I visited to KOREA first time in 1980.

I took a taxi from airport. It was rainny night and really hard to cought the taxi. Because there are so many people at the airport.

At last, I cought the taxi after I waited about 40 minutes. Then the taxi was begin to run.

After drove about 5 minutes the driver went to other way that was made me feel some fear.

I asked him "why you going this way?"

He said "Oh, don't worry this is a short cut!!"

After a little while he made stop a car and he said "I think there is some troble with engine."

I was really scared because it was really dark and became terrible rain. He said "I'm sorry but I need your help. Whoud you push my car?"

Then I did. I was of couse leave all of my stuff in the car. At the time, I suspected what I going to happen from now.

I added all of my power and push the car.

Then he has gone. Yes. he steal my all of stuffs. And I never find my stuff again.

I was really sad, but I couldn't tell any my Japanese friends. Because I am KOREAN.

Composition 2 is 224 words long.

Most people who read these two stories find the second one (about the misadventure with the taxicab) to be more compelling, and somehow "better written" than the story about making friends. (Perhaps this is especially the case for readers who understand the peculiar social role of ethnic Koreans raised in Japan.)

If you agree with this assessment—that the second composition is somehow "better written" than the first—what is it that leads you to this conclusion? If you feel the first composition is better, try to determine why you think so. The analysis may be facilitated by a simple compare-and-contrast procedure. What would you say are the three main contrasting features that distinguish composition 1 from composition 2? Use the following grid to help shape the comparison:

	Composition 1	**Composition 2**
Feature 1		
Feature 2		
Feature 3		

3 *Evaluate Composition 1 and Composition 2 using the* TWE *scale (or another age-appropriate and proficiency-appropriate holistic rating scale with which you are familiar). How do the two compositions compare? Does the holistic rating scale provide criteria that are detailed enough to distinguish between the two essays? If so, what features of the scale capture the key contrasts? If not, what features does the scale lack in order to capture the differences?*

4 *Think about the writing demands faced by your own students (or the students you expect to teach). In terms of the usual criteria (validity, reliability, practicality, and washback), which of the three traditional approaches to scoring writing would be most appropriate for your students? The following grid may be helpful. Use a plus ("+"), check ("√"), or minus ("–") to indicate positive, neutral, or negative effects, respectively:*

	Holistic Scoring	**Analytic Scoring**	**Objective Scoring**
Validity			
Reliability			
Practicality			
Washback			

5 *If you were to devise an analytic scoring system to evaluate the essays written by students in an intermediate ESL or EFL course, what categories would you include? What weight would each category receive? It may be informative to compare your categories and weightings with those selected by your classmates or colleagues.*

Imagine that the compositions in Task 2 were submitted to you by students in an intermediate ESL or EFL writing course. Would the analytic categories you have devised be adequate and appropriate for evaluating these two compositions? Try scoring these two compositions using your analytic scoring system. How do you feel about the scoring system after trying it out on these papers?

---

6 *Use Brodkey and Young's system to mark the errors in the two compositions in Task 2. Here's how their error counts were weighted (1981, 160):*

> Assign a weight score to each error, from 3 to 1. A score of 3 is a severe distortion of readability or flow of ideas which throws the reader off the sense of the message through intrusion of an erroneous linguistic element; 2 is a moderate distortion; and 1 is a minor error that does not affect readability in any significant way.

After you have marked and weighted the errors on the two papers, you need to find a way to adjust for the different lengths of the two essays. One way to do that is to divide the error score by the number of words, as follows:

$$\frac{\text{Error score}}{\text{Number of words in composition}}$$

This process should give you ratios of error weightings relative to essay length, which would allow you to compare your assessments of the two papers. (Note that a smaller ratio indicates a better score.)

If you are working with a group of classmates or colleagues, it will be informative for you to compare your assessment to theirs. I think you will find that "severe" and "moderate" distortions will vary from one reader to another.

Suggested Readings

The analytic scale described in this chapter is derived from a U.S. university context. For a discussion of a system developed in the British tradition, you may enjoy Liz Hamp-Lyons' article, "Performance Profiles for Academic Writing" (1987). The system she describes was developed by the British Council for students applying to universities in the United Kingdom. The procedure involves both holistic and analytic scoring.

For a time there was a great deal of concern about whether holistic scoring was valid and reliable. A number of studies were conducted investigating holistic versus objective scoring. These include accessible articles by Homburg (1984) and Perkins (1980).

Grant Henning and Fred Davidson (1987) conducted an interesting study using a revision of the analytic scoring system described in the Brown and Bailey (1984) quotations cited in this chapter. They report on a much simpler and clearer version of the scoring system. The article involves some statistical analyses that have not been introduced in this book, but it is well worth reading.

If you work with tertiary students' writing, you should read *Assessing Second Language Writing*, edited by Liz Hamp-Lyons (1991). A number of chapters in that anthology have influenced my thinking considerably. Chapter 14, "Scoring Procedures for ESL Contexts," written by Hamp-Lyons, is most closely related to the issues raised here. Hamp-Lyons discusses holistic scoring and primary trait scoring but also **multiple trait scoring,** which assigns scores to various hypothesized components of writing (as does analytic scoring) but which, she says, is more context-specific and involves more rater training and more reader involvement in the instrument development process than was the case with the earlier analytic scoring instruments. The chapter by Sara K. Allaei and Ulla Connor discusses **performative assessment instruments,** which combine the focus and task specificity of primary trait scoring with the diagnostic information value of analytic scoring procedures. Finally, the chapter by Daniel Horowitz raises a number of dilemmas and contradictions in writing assessment that are well worth considering if you are concerned with evaluating students' writing.

For a good overview article, see "Issues in ESL Writing Assessment: An Overview," by Liz Hamp-Lyons and Barbara Kroll (1996).

Peter Elbow, whose work is well known in first-language writing instruction, has written an interesting article entitled "Ranking, Evaluating, and Liking: Sorting Out Three Forms of Judgment" (1993). It will provide a different perspective from the one presented here.

13

"ALTERNATIVE" ASSESSMENTS: PERFORMANCE TESTS AND PORTFOLIOS

Many teachers and students think that exam and test scores can never be wrong. However, this is simply not the case. Every test score is surrounded by an area of uncertainty. For example, some students may not be on their best form when taking a test. Moreover, the questions in the test may favour certain students but not others.

Consequently, while a student's score on a good test will result in a fairly accurate assessment, there will always be a slight degree of uncertainty about it. We can usually be sure, of course, about the difference in performance between a student who has scored 60 per cent and one who has scored only 40 per cent. However, we cannot be as certain about the difference in performance between a student who has scored 49 per cent and one who has scored 51 per cent. If the pass-fail mark on the test happens to be 50 per cent, it then becomes very easy to fail a student who may deserve to pass, or to pass a student who really should fail. As a result, crucial decisions affecting students may rest on extremely small or chance differences in test scores.

For this reason, it is always useful to take into account a number of test scores or other factors whenever an important decision is made about a student's ability in English. These other factors may consist of an interview with the student or an examination of the student's work in class (e.g., exercises, homework assignments, and project work).

J. B. Heaton, author of the text from which the above quotation was taken, stresses the "importance of continuous assessment" (Heaton, 1990, 7–8). He concludes that "it is advisable to treat all test scores with caution. There is no such thing as a perfect test" (1990, 7–8).

I agree. One of the disturbing things about tests is the extent to which many people accept the results uncritically, while others believe that all testing is invidious. But tests are simply measurement tools: It is the use to which we put their results that can be appropriate or inappropriate. J. B. Heaton is right: Important decisions should not rest on simple test scores.

As noted in Chapter 10, many language teachers have become dissatisfied with the mismatch between how they teach and how assessment is conducted. In this chapter we will consider some important alternatives to traditional language tests.

Teachers' Voices

This chapter features three different teachers' voices. We will begin with Pete Rogan's introductory comments based on his experiences teaching English in Poland, which were part of the rationale for a language testing ideas file he compiled as a master's candidate in my graduate seminar on language assessment. I think Pete's comments nicely summarize the dilemma that many teachers experience in grading their students' efforts. The "Frameworks" section will introduce two powerful recent developments in language assessment: performance tests and portfolios. Two teachers' voices will illustrate these approaches. We will first hear from Beckie Chase about her efforts to develop a performance test for Arabic-speaking secondary school students. We will also hear from Maricel Santos about her experiences introducing portfolio assessment in an English program at a Japanese university. Pete, Beckie, and Maricel all have valuable insights to offer. Here are Pete's comments (1996, 1).

> My early experience as a teacher, working in English classes in two Polish high schools, provides an interesting anecdote to frame my discussion of assessment. I began the first year of teaching with a hands-off view on assessment, unclear on how to digest the recent writings I'd come across dealing with grade-free education systems and portfolio assessment in light of the situation I was in. Most of my classes were designed as supplemental conversation classes; the students received their core English instruction from a Polish instructor. I viewed my role in these classes as simply providing opportunities for exposure to and use of the language; assessment was not a factor in my design of class activities. I served as an advisor to the main instructor as she conducted final end-of-semester evaluations.
>
> With a few other classes, I was responsible for the full range of course design, including evaluation. Learning that a failing grade in my course (or any one course) would mean that a student would need to repeat the whole year of schooling, I became intimidated by evaluation. For most of the semester, I avoided the issue, freed the students of the anxiety of test-taking and forged ahead. As the semester drew to a close, however, it became clear that I had little evidence to support decisions about course grades. Now I was in the situation that whatever test or task I designed would carry an immense weight by itself in the semester evaluation. This was the nightmare I had dreaded all along—one-shot, indirect, inauthentic assessment.

Pete's concern about "one-shot" assessment echoes J. B. Heaton's caution that we "take into account a number of test scores or other factors whenever an important decision is made about a student's ability" (Heaton, 1990, 7–8). Pete goes on to explain what he learned (1996, 1–2):

For the following school year, I came to grips with my situation and worked within the system. I administered a few more exams each semester, so any one of them was not the "big one." I assigned a number of projects, both individual and group work, to add unspeeded tasks to the pool. I experimented with an idea I'd stumbled across of continual observation and assessment. This process involved concentrating observational energy on one or two students each day, taking notes after class on what evidence they had provided of positive or negative growth, and providing the students with occasional feedback on their progress. These efforts, at the least, helped provide a battery of support for the final grades.

I realize now that a number of issues relevant to language assessment were playing themselves out in my untrained ramblings. I was questioning some commonly used aspects of the testing that I had experienced or witnessed in my years of being a student: speeded exams; indirect, one-shot measurement; decontextualized test tasks; norm-referenced standardized testing. Most of the ideas that were proving interesting lay in the area of "alternative" assessment: portfolios; longitudinal evaluations; direct performance testing; authentic assessment; bias for best; criterion-referenced exams.

Pete wrote that in completing his graduate seminar on language assessment, his focus was on developing his background so he'd have support for his inclinations about "alternative" assessment (1996, 2).

It became clear that an understanding of "alternative" assessment must be based on a background in the traditional assessment concepts which are laid down as a contrast to the alternatives. The seminar activities and texts developed the concepts necessary to critically examine any approach to assessment as appropriate or inappropriate for a given task or course. It was my intention to structure my language testing ideas file to include information expanding on this process of critical discovery.

Pete's dilemma is one that will seem familiar to many teachers. He used the experience to further motivate his own thinking and learning, as we will see in the "Frameworks" section.

Pete's comments set up several possible contrasts that we should examine in thinking about alternative assessment procedures. As he points out, "an understanding of 'alternative' assessment must be based on a background in the traditional assessment concepts which are laid down as a contrast to the alternatives" (1996:2). Let's examine some of these contrasts. As a heuristic device, I will arrange these concepts as if they were polar opposites. The issues Pete raised will serve as a starting point.

Figure 13.1: Contrasting Traditional and "Alternative" Assessment

One-shot tests .... Continuous, longitudinal assessment

Indirect tests .... Direct tests

Inauthentic tests .... Authentic assessment

Individual projects .... Group projects

No feedback provided to learners .... Feedback provided to learners

Speeded exams .... Untimed exams

Decontextualized test tasks .... Contextualized test tasks

Norm-referenced score interpretation .... Criterion-referenced score interpretation

Standardized tests .... Classroom-based tests

In fact, in listing only the opposite poles of these concepts we have probably masked an important point: That is, that there may be many increments between these poles, and that shades of gray are possible. Figure 13.2 shows an example of one such continuum—that of standardized versus classroom-based tests or even individualized assessments—broken down into smaller possible gradients.

Figure 13.2: An Example Continuum of Standardized Assessment to Individualized Assessment

- *Internationally used standardized tests (e.g., the* TOEFL)

- *National standardized tests (such as the Sri Lankan test described by Wall and Anderson [1993])*

- *Statewide or provincial standardized tests (for instance, the* California Achievement Test *discussed by Ellie Mason in her description of Maria (Chapter 3)*

- *Schoolwide tests (such as the* ESLPE, *the placement exam required of all entering nonnative speakers of English at UCLA)*

- *Programwide tests (such as the criterion-referenced final examinations we used in the ESL program at UCLA)*

- *Classroom-based tests (devised by a particular teacher for use with his or her own students)*

- *Individualized assessment (in which the evaluation procedure is designed or selected to be appropriate for the needs of an individual student)*

Three of the variables Pete was concerned with—direct, authentic, and contextualized assessment—are central to an understanding of our next topic, performance assessment. Please keep Pete's concerns in mind as you read through the next section.

PERFORMANCE TESTS

Imagine that you are an airline passenger on a flight bound for an English-speaking country and that the pilot, copilot, and navigator are all nonnative speakers of English. As you begin your descent into a busy metropolitan airport, you may wonder about the flight crew's ability to communicate by radio in English with the ground control personnel. Which of the following situations would make you happiest?

1. Knowing that the flight crew members had all passed a multiple-choice paper-and-pencil test of listening comprehension over topics of general interest;

2. Knowing that the flight crew members had all passed a face-to-face oral interview in English on general topics (such as the *ILR OPI*); or

3. Knowing that the flight crew members had all passed an authentic test of oral English communication in an air-to-ground radio setting using topics based on recordings of actual conversations between air traffic controllers and airline pilots

If you fly as much as I do, I think you'll say the third situation is preferable. The difference between the first and second situations is one we've already discussed: indirect versus direct assessment. The third situation goes a step further, however. Given the contextual variables (e.g., the static associated with radio transmissions) and the authentic discourse basis of the test (derived from actual professional communications), the third situation typifies what is sometimes called a **performance test** because the learner's response involves comprehending and producing language under the types of contextual constraints that would be involved in performing one's job. There is some potential for confusion here. In first language assessment of native speakers, the term performance assessment is sometimes used to refer to the performance of a skill (e.g., a "performance test of writing" would involve the students in writing)—what we would think of as a direct test. In second language assessment, however, the term performance testing is often associated with the performance of a particular job or set of situated functions. For this reason, second language performance testing is typically found in LSP (languages for specific purposes) programs. The authenticity of the stimulus material and the task posed to the learner are central concerns in designing performance tests, a practice that has been heavily influenced by our understanding of sociolinguistic variables (e.g., genre, audience, register, setting, etc.).

Beckie Chase wanted to develop an authentic performance test for secondary school students based on a situation that learners might encounter outside the classroom. Her special interest is in students who are native speakers of Arabic.

Beckie called her assessment mechanism the "Cultural Bridges Test," because of the thematic content (Chase, 1996, 1–2):

> This test is a performance test that is designed for secondary ESL students at the intermediate level. The focus of this type of test is to predict how the test-taker will be able to communicate in the target language. "In performance tests, language knowledge must be demonstrated in the context of tasks and situations which represent or simulate those for which examinees are preparing to use their second language" (Wesche, 1985, 1). In this test, the topic is the application process to a hypothetical job situation.

> This test needs to be sensitive enough to determine the English communicative abilities of the students in this context. The practical focus of the test tries to encourage positive washback where students will be using the language in a practical way. This could also help motivate the students by having them feel that learning a language is useful and relevant to their lives.

Here Beckie has explicitly linked her performance test with positive washback. The following description gives more information about her pilot test and about her plans for future test development (1996, 2).

> The texts are based on a written advertisement for a summer job, a job application form and a short essay question that is part of the application. The student is also asked to write a letter of inquiry. Since the theme of the test is based on a hypothetical job situation, an oral "job interview" will eventually be included. The addressees are prospective job employers who are older than the students.

> The topic of this test is a hypothetical summer job situation for non-native speakers of English to travel around the United States and visit communities to talk about their native cultures. The examinees have to go through the process of inquiring about the job, filling in the application, writing an essay [about some aspect of their own culture], and then having a job interview.

> This is an integrated test of reading, writing, and eventually speaking. Students will have to read the text in order to comprehend the tasks and advertisement. Reading is also necessary for understanding the job application. In the written activities, students will be expected to write a letter of inquiry, the answers to a job application, and an essay. The abilities tested will be organization, cohesion, grammatical accuracy and appropriate sociolinguistic use (i.e., correct register). The test-takers will be allowed to use dictionaries.

The stimulus material for the Cultural Bridges Test begins with the following job advertisement. After reading the job announcement, students write a business letter requesting an application and then fill out the application, using the forms that follow.

*Would you like to travel around the
United States and get paid for it?*

Are you interested in meeting other people?

*Are you from another country
or cultural background?*

*If you answered yes to all of these
questions then . . .*

Cultural Bridges

wants

You

If you are a high school student in the United States and
are from another country and/or were raised speaking a
language other than English, you could be eligible for the trip
of a lifetime! Cultural Bridges is a nationally known organization
that is designed to introduce Americans to other cultures.
As a representative of this organization, you would travel
around the United States explaining what your culture is all
about. This organization is involved in building understanding
about other countries and cultures through the use of theater,
cultural workshops, and discussions.

> Requirements: full-time high school student
> able to communicate in spoken and written English
> ability to speak in a language other than English
> from another country

Eligible participants will have all travel expenses paid,
free room and board, and a weekly salary of $200.

For more information and a job application write to:

Cultural Bridges

*Ms. Ima Busybody (Director)
57 State Street
Anywhere, NY 11111*

Using the information from the advertisement, write a business letter to the Director of CULTURAL BRIDGES. In this letter, ask for a job application and give two reasons why you are interested in applying for this job. Make sure that the letter is in business letter format. Write the letter in the space below.

_____

_____

_____

_____

_____

_____

_____

_____

_____

_____

_____

_____

_____

_____

_____

_____

_____

_____

_____

_____

Your letter was successful! Here is the job application. Fill in the information that is requested in the blanks provided. Make sure to print clearly and fill in every blank space.

Cultural Bridges Application

Print in clear block letters

---

1) Name (Family Name)   (Given Name)

                                                           Male   Female

2) Birth date (Month, Day, Year)   3) Sex (check one)

4) Birth place (City and State or Country)

Current Mailing address:

5) Street (including apartment number, if any)

6) City   State   ZIP Code   7) Home Phone

8) School Name

9) What is your current grade in high school? (check the one that applies)

_____ Ninth Grade (freshman)   _____ Tenth Grade (sophomore)

_____ Eleventh Grade (junior)   _____ Twelfth Grade (senior)

10) Country of origin   11) Native language

12) List your hobbies or interests

I hereby certify that, to the best of my knowledge and belief, all of my statements are true, correct, and complete and made in good faith.

13) Applicant's signature   14) Date

In terms of the polar opposites listed in Figure 13.1, Beckie was striving to create a contextualized and authentic test. She did this by examining typical job application forms for young people, and by trying to make the stimulus material, the task posed to the learner, and the learner's response interesting and appropriate (in terms of the ages and levels of English proficiency of the learners). She describes her scoring criteria and the interrater reliability on the subjectively scored section (1996, 7, 9).

There were two different methods of scoring. The job application was objectively scored. "Objectively scored items are those which have only one correct response" (Turner, 1992, 54). In the job application, one point was given for each item. Incomplete answers were treated as incorrect, but spelling errors (such as Pebel Bech) were accepted as long as the item was in the correct spot. Both the letter and the essay sections were subjectively scored using the *Test of Written English* (*TWE*) scale.

"Establishing the reliability of the scoring procedure is especially important for tests that are subjectively scored" (Turner, 1992, 54). Two raters read and scored the essay and letter portions of the section using a modified version of the *TWE* scale. After reviewing the *TWE* scale and what the criteria were, the two raters scored the test independently. Using Cronbach's alpha, inter-rater reliability was very high and identical for both the essay and the letter sections (alpha = .98). The high reliability could be due to the fact that the two raters spent a long time reviewing the *TWE* scale and they knew each other.

Beckie piloted the Cultural Bridges Test in California and Saudi Arabia with twelve students who volunteered to take the test. Afterward she analyzed the relationships among the students' scores on the various parts of the test. Here's what she found (1996, 9).

Using Pearson's *r*, the internal consistency was calculated to find the strength of the relationship between each sub-test. . . . The weakest relationship was between the application section and the business letter section (*r* = .55). This indicates there is a moderate correlation between performances on the application and the letter. There is only a 30 percent variance overlap between the two subtests (r^2 = .30). This means that the two sections are mainly measuring two different things. This result is not surprising, due to the different activities in the two sections.

The relationship between the application and the essay section is stronger (*r* = .66). There is slightly more variance overlap between the two sections (r^2 = .44). This indicates that something similar is being measured in these two parts of the test.

The biggest surprise is the moderately strong relationship between the essay and the business letter and that it is the same strength of relationship between the application and the essay (*r* =.66). I thought that the relationship between these two sections would be higher because the tasks are similar. The variance overlap between them is also the same as the application and the essay (r^2 = .44). This indicates that there is some similarity between what these two subtests are measuring.

Here are some examples of the business letters written by the test-takers when Beckie piloted the Cultural Bridges Test. Remember that these students were volunteers who had not taken any sort of course to prepare them for this task. The letters are reproduced with the original vocabulary, spelling, and grammar the students used.

The Director
Dir Sir

I so happy when I read this application because Really I would like
take this job because I love culture also I so happy when I read about cluture.

Thank You

[Student's name]

Student 1 did not include the address or Ms. Busybody's name. In addition, the salutation is to "Dir Sir" even though the job announcement indicates that the director is a woman. Nor does the letter request the application form.

Student 2 began his letter by putting his return address where the addressee's information should have been. He too disregarded the "Ms." in the job announcement:

Dear Sir.

I like this job because
(i) I like to know about other countries culture.
(ii) previously I heard the culture of other countries by cinema,
Books like that.
I think this job will help me to listen the other countires cultrue
directly.

Thankyou

[Student's name]

Although Student 2 does give two reasons for wanting the job, he does not request an application.

Student 3's business letter reveals more understanding of the expected format than the other two. Although he requests an application, he does not offer two reasons why he'd be interested in applying for the job. The tone of the letter is sociolinguistically appropriate, but the leave-taking that precedes his signature is a bit unexpected.

April 15th, 1996

Ms. Ima Busybody (Director)
51 State Street
Anywhere, N.Y. 11111

Dear Ms. BusyBody,

Hello, My name is [student's name]. *I am from Sudan. I read your Advirtisment and was very interested. I was wondering if you would send me a job application.*

I would be very grateful.

Peace Out,

[Student's name]

As you can see, the use of the simple business letter format to request a job application reveals a great deal about the students' linguistic and sociolinguistic competence. In addition, the task posed to each learner (in the instructions) provides clear criteria for scoring the content of these letters. The requirement that students (a) include specific information, and (b) use the appropriate form for a business letter illustrates the importance of authentic contextual variables in performance testing.

Keeping the Cultural Bridges Test in mind as an example, let us return to Figure 13.1 and try to locate performance tests along the various continua listed there. Performance tests can be administered on a one-shot basis, or they can take the form of more continuous assessment, depending on the program. The learners' responses may include either individual or group projects (though the example here was clearly individual). Performance tests may be either speeded or untimed. Feedback may or may not be provided to the learner, although the washback potential of such a test is certainly enhanced if detailed feedback is given.

The strength of performance tests, by definition, lies in the fact that they are direct, authentic, and highly contextualized. This is because their very design depends on using stimulus materials and posing tasks to the learners that are based directly on the learners' intended (or hypothesized) use of the target language—whether the learners are high school students who want to join the Cultural Bridges organization or pilots who will fly commercial airliners in international airspace. Because performance tests are written for specific purposes, an audience and a purpose need to be widely distributed to justify developing a standardized test to assess learners' performances in any given profession. Thus classroom- or program-based tests may be sufficient, depending on the assessment context. (One example of a performance assessment context that has seen much activity in recent years is the oral proficiency testing of international teaching assistants in the United States, which we discussed briefly in Chapter 8. Both program-based and standardized tests are used to assess the speaking skills of international TAs.)

An additional continuum, which we have not previously addressed, is whether the individual language learner has some control over the assessment procedures. In totally standardized international, national, provincial, or statewide tests (especially indirect paper-and-pencil tests) the student has virtually no control (except in the decisions of whether to try his or her best, skip over items, or cheat) and no direct influence on the test. In more interactive assessment procedures, such as the *ILR OPI* and some forms of computer-administered tests, the individual student's input helps to shape and direct the assessment to some extent.

We will now examine another interesting form of "alternative assessment" that takes as its starting point the idea that learners should, in fact, have a great deal of influence over the assessment process—that they should select (or have a major say in selecting) which samples of their work are evaluated. This approach is known as *portfolio assessment*. In fact, portfolio assessment has become so important in recent years that it is practically a mainstream assessment procedure in some places.

Portfolio Assessment

What exactly is a **portfolio**? I find the following definition works well:

> A portfolio is a purposeful collection of student work that exhibits the student's efforts, progress, and achievements in one or more areas. The collection must include student participation in selecting contents, the criteria for judging merit, and evidence of student self-reflection (Paulson, Paulson, and Meyer, 1991, 60).

Mary Schafer, writing in the newsletter of TESOL's Elementary Education Interest Section, provides this description (1993:1):

> A portfolio is a collection of student work that tells the viewer about the student. It is important that the student be a participant in the selection of his/her work. In looking over an ESOL portfolio, a student, a parent, or a teacher will not only see the student in light of her/his language development, but also in terms of his/her cultural background, personality, special abilities, and talents (or, perhaps, limitations).

> An ESOL portfolio is valuable to a student. It helps a student see all the positive growth that is taking place during the learning process, thus enhancing her/his self-esteem and nurturing further growth.

> An ESOL portfolio is valuable to a parent. It provides a portrait of the student's learning and helps the parent to better understand his/her child. It gives the parent cause for pride in the abilities, interests, and development of her/his child.

> An ESOL portfolio is extremely valuable to teachers, both ESL and content-area teachers. It not only traces the language growth of the student so that the teacher knows where to pick up in terms of continuing instruction, but it can also reveal much about the student as a person, thus helping teachers to know their students early in the school year.

Schafer's comments reflect a growing interest in portfolio assessment among ESL and EFL teachers.

In a letter to the *TESOL Journal* (1995, 44–45), Teddi Predaris wrote about the use of portfolios in elementary and secondary schools in Fairfax County, Virginia:

> The ESL assessment portfolio will accompany students throughout their tenure in the ESL program. ESL teachers incorporate alternative assessment techniques as part of their classroom instruction to students. Several core elements are required for every ESL student portfolio as well as optional elements that the ESL teacher and student select to include in the portfolio. The core elements include a beginning and end-of-year writing and oral sample, a reading log, and the *DRP* [*Degrees of Reading Power*] test (for secondary school students). In addition, teachers are encouraged to include other selected alternative assessment techniques, such as anecdotal records, checklists, and cloze tests that give additional assessment information regarding the students' progress.

Predaris notes that teacher development opportunities are an important part of promoting the use of portfolios. For example, in Fairfax County a group of twenty teachers called the "ESL Portfolio Interest Group" meets every month to work on these issues.

What happens if we try to use Wesche's (1983) four-part framework to analyze portfolios? I will apply the framework to the generic portfolio concept, but let me stress that the various components of the framework might change, depending on the assessment context.

First we must ask what the stimulus materials are in using a portfolio as an assessment device. It is possible that the stimulus material would be simply the instructions to the students about compiling their portfolios. On the other hand, all the items included in the portfolio might be based on different stimulus materials (e.g., the assignment for a term paper the student includes is the stimulus material for that particular component).

The task posed to the learner is what unifies the portfolio concept as an assessment device. The learner's task is typically some variation on the idea that the individual is to demonstrate progress by compiling a collection of his or her work, which represents both the breadth and the depth of learning. The task also typically asks the learner to document development over time. (So, for example, a writing portfolio might include several drafts of a major paper a student had written.) The task may also require that the student analyze his or her own work, as a self-assessment of progress. However, the task is usually posed in broad enough terms for the learner to respond in a way that uniquely represents his or her own development and accomplishments.

One of the strengths of the portfolio concept is that acceptable learner responses may be tremendously varied. This allows the learner a fair amount of leeway in selecting the items that will be included in the finished product. As we will see from Maricel Santos's experience introducing portfolios in a Japanese university, a portfolio can even include a section designated "Personal Information," which might include photographs, artwork, letters, journal entries, test score reports, and so forth.

It is the last category of Wesche's framework, the scoring criteria, that distinguishes assessment instruments from other learning activities. (For instance, when we considered dictocomps in Chapter 10 we saw that the procedure can be used as a classroom activity, but that if it is to serve as a test, the teacher [or whoever is scoring the learners' responses] must decide how to evaluate the students' output.) In this regard, portfolios are problematic as assessment devices when used on a large scale. An individual teacher may value (and rate) creativity, organization, evidence of progress, and so on. But if a department, a program, or school chooses to use portfolios as an exit mechanism, for example, then it is necessary to (1) articulate the criteria by which they will be judged; (2) agree on those criteria and establish the reliability with which various readers use them; and (3) determine to what extent products as unique as an individual's portfolio can be evaluated equitably with any single set of criteria.

Liz Hamp-Lyons and Barbara Kroll explain the dilemma this way (1996, 67):

> The first requirement of any assessment measure is stability: The goalposts, whatever they may be, must be the same for all persons

being assessed and for all persons asked to make judgments. But a portfolio by its nature permits each writer to create a personal portrait, a personal record, which is in important ways different from the portrait or record created by every other writer. The force of the portfolio is in the sense of uniqueness it gives each writer.

In other words, wide variation in the learners' response is inherent in portfolios, due to the fact that students self-select much of what will be included. This intentional uniqueness is thought to contribute to the high validity and washback potential of the procedure. However, the diversity of the products to be evaluated can also create problems in terms of practicality and reliability.

Teachers' Voices

Maricel Santos told me that she was using portfolio assessment in her English classes for undergraduate students at a Japanese university. I was very curious about what she was able to accomplish, since the Japanese university context seems to be exam-driven in terms of evaluation. So Maricel and I had an e-mail "conversation" about her use of portfolios. The exchange is reprinted below.

> **Kathi:** What do you mean when you say you use portfolio assessment in your EFL classes in Japan? I mean, what do you do exactly with portfolios during the course of a term?
>
> **Maricel:** I used portfolios with a group of twenty-eight freshmen in an integrated skills English course. I was with this group for two semesters, so their first semester portfolio was a "progress portfolio" (one which shows improvement over their first semester) and the second semester portfolio was an "achievement portfolio" (one which showcases their best works over the past two semesters). Throughout the two semesters, the students are taking quizzes, doing projects, giving presentations, etc., all of which becomes the stockpile of work to select from to place in their portfolios.
>
> A typical portfolio contains four sections: first, an introductory section which includes an overview of the portfolio contents and a reflective essay; second, an academic works section for demonstrating the students' improvement or achievement in the major skill areas; third, a personal section, which can include the students' journals, *TOEFL* score reports, photographs—anything related to their individual achievements and interests in English; and finally, an assessment section, which includes evaluations from the students themselves, from peers and from me.

Introducing the notion of portfolio assessment to her students involved some background conceptual work that Maricel had to do to help them learn a new way of thinking and working. This preparation included helping the students learn how to be reflective.

Maricel: The area which I tried to work on the most was familiarizing them with the task of reflection. Our operative definition right now is that reflection means "serious thinking." When we worked on progress portfolios, I told the students that the portfolio process could help them think about realistic goals in English and ways of meeting those goals. For the achievement portfolio, I encouraged them to focus on the choices they have made in English learning (for example, choosing to spend either thirty minutes or two hours on an essay assignment) and to think of ways that good choices have led to great achievements in English.

If I could improve one area in my portfolio approach, I would focus more on getting the students to engage in reflective activities as part of a weekly practice of class activities. Right now, I have a hard time squeezing in reflection tasks into the already packed curriculum. I think that the students would be less confused by the reflective component of the portfolio if we were frequently reflecting throughout the semester.

There is often a need to lay the groundwork when you are trying to implement an innovation in assessment. Maricel realized that getting her students to reflect on their own work would take time and practice—especially because the students had been "raised" (intellectually speaking) in a context in which most evaluation was externally conducted.

Maricel: I think of Donald Schon's thoughts on reflective practice in *Educating the Reflective Practitioner* (1987). After struggling to articulate the task of reflection to my students, I can relate to his description of the predicament in teaching reflection. The students are often unsure about what is involved in reflection for the portfolio, and my explanations are sometimes not useful since it is not until the students actually start working on the portfolio and answering reflective questions that they slowly begin to understand what I am talking about.

Schon refers to Plato's question, "'How will you look for something when you don't in the least know what it is?'" I smile now when I remember my students asking me, "What do you mean by reflection?" The same questions we, as graduate students, asked of our professors my students now ask of me.

Given these questions, I wondered how Maricel's students had reacted to their portfolio assignment in the long run, and to the portfolio concept in general.

Maricel: Their reactions were generally positive. In their course evaluations, they told me that they would recommend making a portfolio to other students because, for instance, as one student said, "It was a good chance to reflect and I could be sure of my goal." Many of the students felt that it was a lot of hard work and very time-consuming, but in the end, I think they felt a great deal of satisfaction.

I also remember a student telling me that "making a portfolio makes me feel I accomplished a lot, but it is not so valuable in terms of academic perspective. I do not think the portfolio would be interesting [in typical Japanese English classes]."

As this student's comment reminds us, any educational innovation takes place in a wider context. I was curious about how the portfolio idea was received by Maricel's coworkers.

Kathi: Any reactions from your colleagues or the administration?

Maricel: From the administration, I think there's a genuine interest to know what goes on in classrooms which use portfolios. But it still is a foreign concept at the Japanese university, so the amount of interest which translates into active application of portfolio theories and concepts is not so great. In our program, we are lucky in that our classes are limited to 25-30 students, whereas in other departments, there are 50-60 students in a class. I imagine that sitting down to read 60 student portfolios at the end of the term is hardly appealing to the other teachers. I'm also lucky in that I have had the experience of making my own portfolio, so I feel more at ease in presenting the idea to the students. There is now this new research committee on alternative assessment here which may help to familiarize other departments with the concept.

As Maricel points out, the number of students involved may make the use of portfolios as assessment devices prohibitively expensive in terms of time (the practicality criterion again). I asked Maricel about this issue, but her concern was not the time constraints so much as the official grade issue.

Kathi: Is it a lot of work for you? If so, is it worth the effort?

Maricel: Yes and yes. The work in reviewing the portfolios was enjoyable and enlightening. But it was also frustrating at points because in the end, I felt so torn that I had to assign a number grade to the student.

I felt defeated at times when I realized that in the end, there still was the grade to contend with. During the week I was reviewing the portfolios, I would walk around my apartment demanding of the furniture to tell me, "Who owns learning anyway?" I gave out a lot of A's last term; I had heard that there is an unspoken opinion in Japanese universities that teachers who give out too many A's are too easy and ineffective, but I tried to set that "rumor" aside as I confidently turned in my grade sheets. I knew that my students had done good work. Now, as I look back, I am not confident that the number grade I assigned them was accurate, fair, or informative, but I am confident that the portfolio provided a lot of "assessable information"—information which was recognized as "real" by the students and by me.

As a teacher, I feel that the portfolios provide me with so much feedback about my own teaching. I find out what projects and assignments had the greatest impact on the students, and I find out how their confidence levels are rising. I find out how their interests and goals are shifting. The experience is also valuable in that I put myself through the process of having to explain the portfolio concept and process, having to articulate my values about assessment, and saying all this in ways which make sense to non-native speakers.

Maricel's comments echo Mary Schafer's (1993) ideas about how portfolios are useful to teachers. I asked Maricel if she had any other ideas about portfolios to share with other teachers.

Maricel: I still feel like I'm on proving ground right now with regard to portfolios—still trying to convince myself that the approach I take to portfolios WORKS (which I guess is a simple way to refer to validity). I'm also trying to understand what went right during the portfolio process, since it feels like a successful tool.

Here at my university I have found it challenging and sometimes frustrating to sustain enthusiasm about the validity of portfolios if the teacher is working within a system which is still heavily grade-oriented and test-based. The attitudes which hold together much of what is still considered "VALID" in the Japanese education system often seem to work against me when I try to explain portfolio systems to the students. I don't necessarily view this struggle as an obstacle—just a reality to contend with and work through. After all, I think that most teachers working toward alternative assessment probably face the same kind of struggle with questions of validity.

As you can see from Maricel's reflections, portfolios are an interesting assessment format. They are cumulative in nature and demand a great deal of input and responsibility from the language learner, as well as a tremendous time commitment from teachers. However, their potential for positive washback and validity makes portfolios extremely promising as an assessment tool. The "Investigations" in this chapter are designed to give you more personal and practical experience with portfolios and performance tests, and to interest you further in alternative assessment.

Investigations

1 *If you are teaching now, find out from your students what it is they ultimately want to do* with *the language they are studying. Try to identify a measurable construct related to their goals. For example, imagine that an EFL student wants to work in the tourist industry in his or her home country, either as a tour guide or as an information booth attendant. What would be the specific uses of English associated with those jobs?*

Once you have generated a list of the functions your students would need to be capable of to meet their own goals in the target language, think about how you would design a performance test to assess their abilities. It may be helpful if you first specify the purpose of the test and then use Wesche's framework to identify the stimulus material, the task posed, the learners' responses, and the scoring criteria. In what way(s) would your proposed performance test differ from a more general test of the target language?

If you are not yet teaching, try imagining the language needs of a student with the same goal—wanting to work in the tourist industry. If you were to draft a performance test of oral English for tour guides and information booth attendants, what would it be like? It may be helpful to compare your response to this question with the responses of your classmates.

2 *Following are two more examples of the business letters written by students in the pilot-testing of Beckie Chase's Cultural Bridges Test. Keeping in mind the task posed to the learners, write specific scoring criteria and evaluate these two letters. Which is better, according to your criteria?*

> Culture bridges
> Ms Ima Busybody Dir
> 57 state street
>
> Dear Sir
>
> I have learned that your company is searching for some one who have an other langage bisides his. And that he can speak and write in this language therefore I am for this job. I came from Araibian background and studied the English Language for ten years.
> I am sue that I will meet your requirements. Please call me at
> [student's phone number].
>
> Senserly.
>
> [Student's name]

Ms Ima Busybody
57 State Street
Anywhere, NY 11111

Dear Ms Ima Busybody:

I am interested in Cultural Bridges, and I would like
you to send me an application. I am interested in applying
for this job because I would like to travel around the
United States explainig what my culture is all about,
and I would like to introduce Americans to other cultures.
If you send me the application, I would be very proud to
attempt to getting this job.

Yours truly,

[Student's name]

If you are working with a group of classmates or colleagues, it may be useful to agree on a set of scoring criteria that you could use independently. Then compare and discuss the scores you award based on those criteria.

---

3 *Imagine that you are about to teach a course in business English that includes a unit on writing business letters. If the five student letters reprinted in this chapter had been part of a diagnostic test, what information would they provide that would be helpful? Try to state three objectives for a lesson on business letters based on this diagnostic information.*

---

4 *Imagine that you are a new teacher and you are just completing your first two years of service in a particular program. Or perhaps you are a more experienced teacher who has changed jobs in the past two years and has begun teaching in a new program. Regardless of which context seems closer to your reality, let us further imagine that you are now about to undergo the evaluation process that will determine whether you are to be retained and promoted in the program. How would you react to the following memo from your headmaster, dean, coordinator, or department chair?*

Memo to: Teachers in line for retention/promotion decisions

From: Your headmaster/dean/coordinator/department chair

Re: The promotion process

Based on the outcomes of the recent discussions between the Faculty Evaluation Committee and the administration, it has been determined that retention and promotion decisions for faculty will be based on the model of portfolio assessment.

It is your responsibility, as a teacher scheduled for review, to produce such a portfolio and submit it to me within one month of receipt of this memo. If you have any questions about what should be included in the portfolio or how it will be evaluated, please feel free to contact me.

1. What questions would you have for this administrator about the expected contents of your portfolio?

2. What questions would you have for this administrator about the criteria that would be used to evaluate your portfolio?

   Or, taking a more proactive stance, you could address these issues this way instead:

3. Given your experience as a teacher, what items (both in terms of categories of submission and particular examples) would you want to include in your portfolio?

4. Given your experiences as both a teacher and a learner, by what criteria would you want your portfolio to be evaluated?

Remember Mari Wesche's point (1983) that the term *scoring criteria* can mean two things: (1) It can refer to the content areas identified as important (in this case, perhaps professionalism, teaching effectiveness, productivity, collegiality, etc.), and (2) it can specify how values are assigned to those areas (i.e., ways to distinguish "very effective teaching" from "moderately effective teaching" and "ineffective teaching").

---

5 *Find a teacher who has been involved with portfolio assessment—someone like Maricel—and who is willing to discuss with you the advantages and disadvantages of using portfolios. Ask him or her the kinds of questions I asked Maricel, as well as your own additional questions. How do the two sets of responses compare? Which teacher's situation most closely parallels your own?*

---

6 *Try to locate a language program in your area that does use portfolio assessment. Find out if you can examine some students' portfolios to see what they included. It would be ideal if you could actually talk to the students about what they learned in compiling their portfolios.*

7 *If you are working with a group of classmates, it might be informative to stage a debate about the advantages and disadvantages of portfolio assessment, performance assessment, or other forms of "alternative" assessment. You could take either of the following prompts as a starting point:*

> **Resolved:** Language learners should have major control over the selection of the products on which they are evaluated.

> **Resolved:** Learners' target language abilities should always be evaluated in assessment situations that closely parallel the actual situations in which the learners will use the language to meet their own goals.

If you are not working with a group, it may be helpful to generate a list of the advantages and disadvantages of portfolio assessment and/or performance assessment.

Suggested Readings

At the Second National Research Symposium on Limited English Proficient (LEP) Issues, Russell L. French (1992) presented a position paper about portfolios and LEP students. (A quotation from that paper was used to open Chapter 3.) His discussion raises a number of issues that we, as teachers considering the use of portfolios, should keep in mind. The conference proceedings include two very interesting responses to his paper. The first is Alice J. Kawakami's (1992) insightful discussion of the use of portfolios in the Kamehameha Elementary Education Program (KEEP) in Hawaii. Her paper stresses the importance of teacher support and development in the implementation of portfolio-based assessment. It is followed by commentary from Daniel Koretz (1992) about the use of portfolio assessment in Vermont schools. I recommend this set of papers as an interesting example of three concerned professionals bringing different experiences to bear on a discussion of portfolio assessment.

If you would like to know more about individualized assessment, you may find two books useful. One is *Self-Instruction in Language Learning* (1987), by Leslie Dickinson. The other is an anthology edited by John H.A.L. de Jong and Douglas K. Stevenson entitled *Individualizing the Assessment of Language Abilities* (1990).

For information about assessment at the opposite end of the standardization-individualization continuum, another volume edited by John de Jong is useful: *Standardization in Language Testing* (1990).

A number of clear references about portfolio assessment are now available. These include Margo Gottlieb's (1995) article in the *TESOL Journal,* and several articles in Volume 49 (No. 8) of *Educational Leadership.*

Recently portfolio assessment has been widely used in writing programs. Two helpful articles on this topic are by Denise Murray (1994) and Liz Hamp-Lyons and William Condon (1993).

The Northwest Regional Educational Laboratory has produced a booklet entitled *Bibliography of Assessment Alternatives: Portfolios.* For information, e-mail the compilers at testcenter@nwrel.org.

If you are interested in how portfolios can be used in teacher assessment, you may wish to read Peter Seldin's book *The Teaching Portfolio* (1991) or Kenneth Wolf's article, "Developing an Effective Teaching Portfolio" (1996).

An interesting anthology of articles about performance testing was edited by Phil Hauptman, Ray LeBlanc, and Mari Wesche (1983). Beckie Chase's work with the Cultural Bridges Test was influenced by two of the papers in that collection: by Peter Tung (about secondary students in Hong Kong) and Daina Green (about *A Vous La Parole,* the test for secondary students of French in Canada).

14

SELF-ASSESSMENT IN LANGUAGE LEARNING

Informal self-assessment is a natural part of language learning.
Formalising self-assessment should help focus the learners'
attention on their strengths, weaknesses, and further needs.
If used continuously throughout a course, self-assessment has
been shown to be of great value to both teacher and learner. . . .
    Arguments in favor of self-assessment have concentrated not
only on the value to the learner of the feedback provided, but on
the benefits of involvement in the process itself. Learners gain
a better understanding of the criteria used in assessment, which
promotes greater involvement in development of those criteria. . . .
(Lewis, 1990, 187–188)

The earlier chapters in this book focused primarily on assessment conducted *by* one individual (a teacher) or group (a school district or an international testing organization) *on* another individual (a student) or group (a class or applicants for admission to a program). However, an increasingly important form of assessment that may not involve any testing at all is gaining recognition among both teachers and researchers (Oskaarson, 1988). The trend to which I am referring is **self-assessment**—procedures by which the learners themselves evaluate their language skills and knowledge. This development is consistent with a trend in language education in general—that of more emphasis on learner responsibility and learner-centered curricula (Brindley, 1988). The information students can provide through a systematic self-assessment process is potentially valuable, not just to testers and teachers, but also to the students themselves.

For instance, based on their research in Canada with university students of French and English, LeBlanc and Painchaud (1985) see the ability to assess one's own performance as an integral part of language learning. They discovered that the use of a self-assessment questionnaire as a placement instrument offers several advantages over standard placement tests, including reduced time for testing; elimination of the need for proctors; and safeguards against cheating, scheduling, and facilities problems. They also concluded that self-assessment involves learners to a large extent, since students are responsible for their own placement in such a system. These findings may reflect the learners' sense of "ownership" over placement decisions, rather than (or in addition to) indicating that more accurate placement decisions have actually been made.

From a pedagogic point of view, the most intriguing and potentially most useful aspect of self-assessment as an evaluative procedure is probably the consciousness-raising factor. In completing a self-assessment questionnaire (honestly) language learners have to think about their language skills, and may presumably become aware of what they have reported.

M y colleague, Peter Shaw described an interesting placement process based on his experience at a large multilevel language school in Mexico City (1980, 261–262). A student coming to enroll at the school would undergo an initial counseling session in which he learned about the program. While interacting with the student, the counselor would make an estimate of his abilities, in terms of which of the courses in the nine-level program would be appropriate. The counselor would then direct the student to a package of instructional materials. These could include a reading passage typical of that level, complete with a self-checkable comprehension quiz; a taped listening exercise (again, with an answer key supplied); the textbooks used at that level, along with representative additional materials; a sample of students' writings, including teachers' evaluations; an example of diagnostic or achievement tests often used at that level; and a videotape of classroom interaction typical of that level. The new student would inspect all of these materials to see how comfortable he might be attending a class at that particular level.

The next step in the placement process involved an actual class visit, after which the student would return to the counselor to discuss what he had seen. The counselor and student would then negotiate visits to higher or lower level classes, as needed. After the visits, the student would choose the level he wished to attend.

Peter recommends that a student should be contacted two or three weeks after he actually begins attending class, to see if he and the teacher feel he is in the right place. When this self-placement process was introduced, Peter reports, placement errors dropped from about 16 percent to about 9 percent (Peter Shaw, personal communication). The following are his comments on the benefits of using a self-placement procedure (1980, 261–262),

> The strongest feature [of the self-placement process], I think, is that students have a very major role in deciding the level at which they will work. The process helps the student to become aware of his own needs and to match them with the most appropriate level in the program. In language programs where students pay a lot of money and put in a lot of time, it is of very great importance that they accept the validity of the placement process.
>
> In addition, the student enters the program with a certain amount of information at his disposal. The placement process has been an exchange of information.
>
> Third, the student is less anxious when he goes to class for the first time. He should know more about what is expected of him and what he can expect of the teacher.

Fourth, there is a saving of time and energy, once the [initial counseling] packages have been prepared.

Fifth, learners in EFL situations, perhaps also in adult education in [the United States], sometimes rate themselves too low. I have seen students avoid the placement process altogether by declaring themselves to be completely ignorant of the language. Unless classes are very small, the fact that these students have been placed too low because of a lack of self-confidence may not be detected for some time. By giving such students a clear idea of what happens at a given level, the self-placement process might avoid this problem.

Finally, it is much easier, in an open enrollment situation, to modify the self-placement package than to construct separate placement tests for different points in the semester. Again, the package will give the entering student an idea of what has happened in the class and what he can expect.

Of course, self-assessment can be used both independently of or in conjunction with a testing program. In the "Frameworks" section of this chapter we will consider data on the relationship between self-assessment mechanisms and more formal tests.

One of the intriguing questions about self-assessment is the extent to which learners can accurately judge their own language abilities. As a result, one common research design used by people interested in this topic is to ask a group of learners to assess their own skills and then to compare those self-assessments to some external evaluation. (This is an example of what is called **criterion-related validity:** One measure is considered valid to the extent to which it correlates with another, more widely accepted measure—the criterion.) Thus, for example, a student's estimate of aspects of her speaking proficiency can be compared with a sample of that performance on tape, with oral proficiency interview data, or with scores from paper-and-pencil tests.

Some years ago I helped design an oral communication course for the international teaching assistants (ITAs) at the University of California at Los Angeles. These were people who had been awarded teaching positions while they were graduate students at the university. Their jobs involved conducting laboratory sessions or teaching classes (e.g., in physics, math, chemistry, engineering, and the like) in English, which was not their native language.

As part of the research contributing to the course design, several colleagues and I interviewed a group of nonnative speaking ITAs in English using the procedure that is now called the *ILR OPI*. (We had been trained and normed with the procedure by certified government language tester-trainers.) Forty-five of the ITAs whose English we evaluated with the *ILR OPI* also completed a self-assessment form in which they evaluated their own use of English. They were asked to categorize their mastery of English as poor, fair, good, very good, fluent, or native-like, which was glossed as meaning "without an accent" (Bailey 1982, 170). These categorical values were quantified as one through six respectively, and correlated with the trained raters' assessments of each ITA's English, using both the overall (holistic) and the componential (analytic) ratings from the *ILR OPI*. The results are shown in Table 14.1.

Table 14.1: Correlation of ITAs' Self-ratings with External Ratings by *ILR OPI* Testers

Overall ability	0.63
Grammar	0.64
Pronunciation	0.61
Fluency	0.62
Vocabulary	0.58

In other words, there was a moderately strong correlation between the ITAs' self-assessments and the evaluations conducted by the trained interviewers.

LeBlanc and Painchaud (1985, 679), working in Canada, also calculated the correlation between students' self-assessments of their language skills and their scores on a proficiency test. The correlations they obtained were somewhat lower than those in my data, and are shown in Table 14.2.

Table 14.2: LeBlanc and Painchaud's Correlations Between Total Test Scores and Learners' Self-assessments

Listening	0.43
Reading	0.53
Speaking	0.39
Writing	0.50
Total	0.53

As with Peter Shaw's data from Mexico, the Canadian team noticed a reduction in the number of changes resulting from the initial placement when a self-assessment mechanism was introduced. The percentage of course changes after placement dropped from an average of 15.7 to an average of 12.8. (These means were calculated from the data given in Table 5, LeBlanc and Painchaud, 1985, 685.)

Some years ago, as part of a study on a new content-based curriculum that was being introduced at our school, Peter Shaw, David Tsugawa, and I undertook a similar investigation (1989). Native speakers of English whose target languages were French, German, and Spanish were interviewed using the *ACTFL Oral Proficiency Interview*. (ACTFL stands for the American Council of Teachers of Foreign Languages. The *ACTFL OPI* procedure was adapted for academic settings from the U.S. government's *ILR OPI* discussed in Chapter 11.) The *ACTFL* ratings for these students separated into language groups are shown in Table 14.3.

Table 14.3: Numbers of Students in the Three Language Groups Rated at the Four *ACTFL* Levels (n = 33)

ACTFL Level:

Language:	Novice	Intermediate	Advanced	Superior
French	0	3 (17%)	12 (66%)	3 (17%)
German	0	0	2 (25%)	6 (75%)
Spanish	0	0	3 (43%)	4 (57%)

The *ACTFL OPIs* were administered at the beginning of the semester by external *ACTFL*-trained personnel who were unaware of the purpose of the evaluation. On the first day of class, students from each language group also responded to a brief self-assessment questionnaire, the items for which were based on two broad domains: (1) general oral/aural target language use, and (2) academic target language use. The seventeen items about general target lan guage use were designed specifically to tap those communicative skills and functions assessed in the *ACTFL OPI*. The twelve items on academic target language use were written by consensus of the research team, based on our understanding of the academic demands faced by students at the Monterey Institute.

In the questionnaire, which is reprinted below, learners responded to affirmative statements on a five-point Likert scale format, with "1" representing "Never" or "Strongly disagree" and "5" representing "Always" or "Strongly agree." In each case the term *target language* refers to the language the learners were studying. We worded our statements in terms of what the students felt they could do in the target language. Later, however, Bachman and Palmer (cited in Bachman, 1990) found that self-assessment statements about each learner's perceived difficulty with a particular task provided more effective measurement than did the "can do" format for self-assessment statements.

PART I: GENERAL USES OF THE TARGET LANGUAGE

When speaking in the target language, I can—

1. use and correctly interpret numerals (telling time, giving dates, reading statistics, etc.). 1 2 3 4 5

2. carry on a casual conversation. 1 2 3 4 5

3. accomplish basic social conventions (such as greetings, introductions, etc.) correctly and appropriately. 1 2 3 4 5

4. ask questions correctly and appropriately. 1 2 3 4 5

5. talk about past events using correct grammatical structures. 1 2 3 4 5

6. talk about future events using correct grammatical structures.	1	2	3	4	5
7. deal with routine situations related to daily life or traveling (e.g., shopping, getting reservations, mailing packages).	1	2	3	4	5
8. provide basic biographical information about myself.	1	2	3	4	5
9. confidently discuss current events.	1	2	3	4	5
10. participate actively in conversations on unknown topics or in unfamiliar situations.	1	2	3	4	5
11. correctly describe people, objects, or places.	1	2	3	4	5
12. confidently and correctly use all the basic grammatical structures.	1	2	3	4	5
13. support my opinions, even in the face of opposing views.	1	2	3	4	5
14. use even infrequent grammatical structures correctly and confidently.	1	2	3	4	5
15. speak in connected discourse, joining several sentences together with appropriate linking words.	1	2	3	4	5
16. handle social situations even if something unexpected happens (e.g., if the hotel has no rooms available and no record of reservations made earlier).	1	2	3	4	5
17. discuss abstract topics and talk about hypothetical situations using correct grammatical structures.	1	2	3	4	5

PART II: ACADEMIC USES OF THE TARGET LANGUAGE

In using the target language, I can—

18. use and correctly interpret numerals (telling time, giving dates, reading statistics, etc.).	1	2	3	4	5
19. confidently seek clarification if I don't understand something in class.	1	2	3	4	5
20. make generalizations confidently during class discussions.	1	2	3	4	5
21. appropriately challenge another person's position during class discussions.	1	2	3	4	5
22. confidently read journal articles and textbooks written for native speakers of the target language.	1	2	3	4	5
23. understand technical material I read, without referring to a dictionary.	1	2	3	4	5
24. read academic materials as fast as I can read in my native language.	1	2	3	4	5
25. confidently approach the task of writing an academic graduate level paper in the target language.	1	2	3	4	5
26. confidently follow both the main points and the important details of a lecture delivered in the target language.	1	2	3	4	5

27. confidently follow the discourse in group discussions.	1	2	3	4	5
28. express myself confidently in a face-to-face discussion on an academic topic.	1	2	3	4	5
29. express myself without groping for words or asking for translations.	1	2	3	4	5
30. write an academic graduate level paper in the target language (with time to prepare outside of class) without making serious errors in grammar or vocabulary.	1	2	3	4	5
31. plan and appropriately organize a graduate level academic paper in the target language as well as I can in my first language.	1	2	3	4	5
32. confidently discuss political issues.	1	2	3	4	5
33. confidently discuss economic issues.	1	2	3	4	5

In addition, students were asked to place an "X" along a sixteen-centimeter line above which were written the words *Novice, Intermediate, Advanced, Superior*—the cover terms for the increments on the *ACTFL* scale—and *Native-like*. This procedure was intended to get the students to indicate their general proficiency levels in a way that would allow us to create interval data (centimeters on the line) from the categorical data headings of *Novice, Intermediate*, and so on. Students were also asked to make any further comments that would be helpful to us in understanding their language learning. These open-ended comments were optional.

One of the key questions raised about self-assessment is whether students overrate, underrate, or accurately assess their own abilities, when self-assessment outcomes are compared to the results of some external evaluation procedure that is used as the criterion measure. (That is, we are posing a question about the criterion-related validity of self-assessment.) Table 14.4 provides a quick visual answer to this question in terms of our data.

Table 14.4: Intersection of External *ACTFL OPI* Ratings and the Students' Overall Self-assessments (n = 32)

Students' Self-Assessments	External *ACTFL* Ratings		
	Intermediate	Advanced	Superior
Intermediate	2	1	0
Advanced	1	10	6
Superior	1	5	6

Those numbers on the diagonal (running from the upper-left corner to the lower-right corner) may be considered to represent "accurate" self-raters. (Here *accuracy* represents a match between the self-assessment and the external assessment.) For instance, two people who were deemed to be "intermediate" by the

ACTFL raters also considered themselves intermediate. There were ten accurate self-assessors in the "advanced" category and six in the "superior" category.

The diagram also shows that seven people out of 32 (those below the diagonal) overrated their abilities, with the largest group being five speakers who were evaluated as "advanced" by the *ACTFL*-trained raters, but who thought of themselves as "superior" speakers of the target language. Another group of seven people underrated their abilities. One person considered "advanced" by the *ACTFL* raters evaluated himself an "intermediate" learner, while six people rated "superior" on the *ACTFL* scale evaluated themselves "advanced."

Another way to look at these self-assessment data is to use the *ACTFL* designations (Intermediate, Advanced, and Superior—there were no Novices in this data set) as group labels and see what the average self-ratings were for each group. This has been done in Table 14.5.

Table 14.5: **Mean Self-assessments for the Various *ACTFL OPI* Levels in the Sample (n = 32)**

Self-rated Items	*ACTFL* Ratings		
	Intermediate [n = 3]	*Advanced* [n = 17]	*Superior* [n = 13]
Total items [1–32]	3.26 (0.74)	3.74 (0.38)	4.08 (0.50)
General items [1–17]	3.30 (0.37)	3.93 (0.33)	4.37 (0.44)
Academic items [18–32]	3.22 (0.65)	3.51 (0.56)	3.74 (0.61)

(Standard deviations are given in parentheses.)

The striking feature of these data is that for every category and at every level, the students' self-assessed mean scores increase with each step on the *ACTFL* scale. This pattern obtains whether the self-assessment data cover the general domain, the academic domain, or a combination of the two. However, we can also see that at each *ACTFL* level, the students' self-ratings were somewhat higher for the general questions (items 1-17) than for the academic items (18-32). This finding suggests that—as teachers—we may find domain-specific questions to be more informative than general self-ratings on the four skills.

We can also use these data to look at the average overall self-ratings of the people in the three designated *ACTFL* categories. (This is the information we got when we asked the learners to place an "X" along the sixteen-centimeter line representing a language proficiency continuum from "novice" to "native-like.") These data are displayed in Table 14.6.

Table 14.6: Overall Mean Self-ratings[8] (n = 33)

Intermediate (n = 3)	Advanced (n = 17)	Superior (n = 13)
6.87	8.34	10.04
(4.14)	(2.05)	(2.20)

Once again, there is a marked increase in self-ratings (in the predictable direction) across the three *ACTFL* categories. There are only three people who were designated by the *ACTFL* raters as "Intermediates" and the standard deviation for that small group is about twice as large as the standard deviations for the "Advanced" and "Superior" groups.

Self-assessment has often been used for placement purposes as described above, but it is not restricted to this function. John Hedgcock, the teacher whose voice we heard discussing writing in Chapter 12, designed a self-assessment mechanism as an achievement measure for his advanced writing students at the end of their course. Here are the instructions:

End-of-term Self-Assessment

DIRECTIONS: This instrument is designed to help you and your instructor understand the ways in which you feel you have improved as a writer of academic English. It is also designed to assess the extent to which you feel this course has met its stated goals. For these reasons, you are asked to refer to the course syllabus, which outlines our general learning objectives. For each of the specific statements below, place an 'X' in the cell that most accurately describes your progress in this course. Please be frank: Your honest responses will give your instructor valuable information.

The cells on John's questionnaire used the familiar Likert scale format, but notice that the numbers on his scale read in the reverse order from the scale Peter and David and I used:

1 = Strongly agree   4 = Somewhat disagree
2 = Agree   5 = Disagree
3 = Somewhat agree   6 = Strongly disagree

Figure14.1 lists the self-assessment items John wrote, along with a tally of how his students responded. (There were ten students in the class, nine of whom responded to the self-assessment questionnaire.)

---

8. These means are derived from students' self-ratings on the sixteen-centimeter scale. Standard deviations are given in parentheses.

Figure 14.1: John Hedgcock's Academic Writing Self-assessment Instrument

	1	2	3	4	5	6
1. I am becoming a more skilled writer of academic English.	2	4	3			
2. I am gaining confidence as a writer of academic English.			6	2	1	
3. I have developed new ways of using source material (e.g., textbooks, scholarly books, journal articles, newspaper and newsmagazine articles, etc.) effectively in my writing assignments.	1	6		1	1	
4. I am getting better at producing interesting and original ideas.		2	5	2		
5. I am gaining skill at organizing my ideas and putting them together logically.	1	4	4			
6. I am more comfortable rearranging ideas and paragraphs as I plan and revise my work.	1	5	3			
7. I have developed new strategies for composing thesis statements and arguments.	2	6	1			
8. My reading in this course and my major courses has helped me to see new ways of organizing text and using language.	2	5	1	1		
9. My typing and computer skills have become more efficient.	4	1	3	1		
10. As I revise my papers, I am now more likely to add new material.		6	2	1		
11. When I write and revise a paper, I think more carefully about what my reader wants to know from me.		7	1			
12. I am more comfortable about getting feedback from my peers.	1	4	1	2		1
13. I am more likely to support my claims with examples and explanations than I used to be.	3	2	2	2		
14. I now try to make clear and succinct transitions between paragraphs.	1	4	4			
15. I have developed strategies for linking my paragraphs to my thesis.	1	4	2	2		
16. In my concluding paragraphs, I understand the need to synthesize my thesis and the evidence I've presented in the body of my paper.		7	1	1		
17. The paragraphs of my papers usually contain plenty of examples and/or explanations.			6	3		

18. When I turn in papers, they have fewer grammatical errors than they did before this course.		4	3	1	1
19. My use of English vocabulary has expanded in my writing over the course of this semester.	1	3	2	2	1
20. My papers now contain fewer errors in spelling and punctuation than they did previously.	1	5	1	1	1
21. When I write an academic paper, I am now comfortable using references, quotations, footnotes, bibliographic sources, etc.		3	3	2	1
22. When I turn in papers, they have fewer errors of spelling or punctuation.		4	4		1
23. I am better able to understand and incorporate the instructor's comments into my revised writing.	3	4	2		
24. I have acquired useful and efficient strategies for writing under timed conditions.	1	5	2	1	

John was able to use these self-assessment data from his learners in at least two ways. First, he could compare the students' self-assessments to his own evaluations of their achievements in the course. Second, he could use these data to help him focus on areas to improve the next time he taught the class.

The "Investigations" in this chapter are designed to encourage you to think about using self-assessment in your own work with language learners. In addition, Task 5 is intended to help you think about what you have learned in reading this book.

1 *Think of a test you have written (or would like to write) for your own students (or future students). What was your purpose (or what would your purpose be) in designing the test? Using Wesche's framework, how would you describe your test in terms of the stimulus material, task posed, learners' responses, and scoring criteria?*

Now let's consider the possibility of devising a self-assessment mechanism for your learners that would evaluate the same constructs. What would it look like? What questions would you ask and in what format? What would you do with the information once the learners had supplied it?

2 *You may want to try writing a self-assessment mechanism for your students. (John Hedgcock's writing questionnaire is a fine illustration of a self-assessment mechanism used to gauge end-of-term achievement.) If you do devise an original self-assessment mechanism and if you also have a test for your students over the same topic, it would be fascinating to compare their self-assessments and their responses on the test. If the two procedures generate interval or ordinal data, you could even correlate the scores on the two measures to find out the relationship between the two methods of measuring the same construct.*

3 *As an alternative to writing a self-assessment questionnaire based on a test, it is worthwhile to devise one based on the objectives of a course you are teaching or planning to teach. After you have drafted the self-assessment mechanism, ask a colleague to read it for any possible ambiguities and compare it to the stated course objectives to see if they have all been covered.*

I have written simple self-assessment mechanisms for my lower-intermediate speaking and listening classes at the Chinese University of Hong Kong, as well as for my introductory research and statistics course and for my language assessment seminar at the Monterey Institute. I ask the students to complete the appropriate questionnaire at the beginning and end of the course. For me, as the instructor, the instruments serve four very useful functions. First, they alert the students at the beginning of the term to the amount of material we will cover during the class. (Some students are flabbergasted initially to see how many difficult tasks and unfamiliar concepts are listed on the questionnaire.) Second, after the students have completed the same questionnaire at the end of the term, I return their originals to them so they can compare their responses, to see how much progress they've made during the course. (This comparison invariably provokes comments of amazement and self-congratulation as they realize what they have accomplished.) Third, I collect the before-and-after questionnaires so that I can make the same comparison and see where the class members felt they did or did not make gains. Finally, I keep a copy of the self-assessment questionnaire attached to my syllabus, to keep me on track: I mark off the objectives as they are stated on the self-assessment form when I feel we have completed them.

4 *If it is age-appropriate and suitable for your students' proficiency levels, you could ask them to complete the 32-item questionnaire that Peter Shaw, David Tsugawa, and I used in our research (pages 230–233). You may find it interesting to compare your students' responses to the items about general target language use (items 1-17) with their responses to those about academic uses of the target language (items 18-32).*

If you are a student in a language teacher preparation program, or if you are teaching a language that is not your mother-tongue, you may find it worthwhile to respond to our self-assessment questionnaire yourself. If you are working with classmates or colleagues, you could compare your responses on the two parts of the questionnaire with those of your peers.

5 *Following is a simple self-assessment mechanism based on the concepts presented in this book. (The chapter in which the information was originally covered is given in parentheses after each item, in case you would like to review.)*

How would you evaluate your own understanding of the concepts we have covered?

Directions: Please complete each of the following items by writing a "Y" for yes, an "M" for maybe, or an "N" for no in front of each statement.

1. I understand the concepts of validity, reliability, practicality, and washback in the context of language assessment. (Chapter 1)

2. I could explain the concepts of validity, reliability, practicality, and washback to my colleagues. (Chapter 1)

3. I can analyze a test using the professionally accepted criteria of validity, reliability, practicality, and washback. (Chapter 1)

4. In analyzing a test, I can identify the stimulus material, the task posed, the learner's response, and the scoring criteria. (Chapter 2)

5. I understand and could explain to my colleagues the differences among standard dictations, partial dictations, and graduated dictations. (Chapter 2)

6. I am able to develop, administer, and score standard dictations, partial dictations, and graduated dictations. (Chapter 2)

7. I understand and can explain the difference between dictations and dictocomps. (Chapters 2 and 10)

8. I understand and can explain the difference between norm-referenced and criterion-referenced tests, in terms of interpreting learners' scores. (Chapter 3)

9. I understand and can explain the varying purposes underlying the following types of language tests: (Chapter 3)

Proficiency tests	Achievement tests
Diagnostic tests	Dominance tests
Placement tests	Admissions tests
Progress tests	Aptitude tests

10. I understand and can explain to my colleagues the differences between content schemata and formal schemata. (Chapter 4)

11. I understand the importance of background knowledge in tests of listening and reading. (Chapter 4)

12. I understand and can explain to my colleagues the differences among fill-in items, cloze passages, and C-tests. (Chapter 5)

13. I am able to develop a cloze test using either the nth word deletion method or the rational deletion method for mutilating the text. (Chapter 5)

14. I am able to develop, administer, and score cloze tests, using either the exact word or the acceptable word scoring method. (Chapter 5)

15. I can develop, administer, and score a C-test. (Chapter 5)

16. I understand and can explain the difference between direct, indirect, and semi-direct tests. (Chapter 6)

17. I understand and can explain the difference between objectively scored and subjectively scored tests. (Chapter 6)

18. I understand and can correctly compute mean scores. (Chapter 7)

19. I understand and can correctly compute standard deviations. (Chapter 7)

20. I can interpret mean scores and standard deviations in looking at my students' test results. (Chapter 7)

21. I can interpret and compute z scores and T-scale scores. (Chapter 7)

22. I understand and can explain to my colleagues the differences among interval data, ordinal data, and categorical data. (Chapter 8)

23. I understand the basic principles of correlation. (Chapter 8)

24. I can explain to my colleagues what magnitude and directionality mean in interpreting correlations. (Chapter 8)

25. I understand and can explain the differences among Pearson's correlation coefficient, Spearman's rank-order correlation coefficient, and the point-biserial correlation coefficient, and know when it is appropriate to use each. (Chapter 8)

26. I can correctly compute and interpret overlapping variance. (Chapter 8)

27. I understand the parts of a multiple-choice item and can develop multiple-choice items. (Chapter 9)

28. I understand the pitfalls associated with multiple choice items. (Chapter 9)

29. I can use item analyses to assess the effectiveness of test items I have written. (Chapter 9)

30. I can construct a distractor analysis and a response frequency distribution to see how well my multiple-choice items are working. (Chapter 9)

31. I can correctly interpret and compute item facility statistics. (Chapter 9)

32. I can correctly interpret and compute item discriminability statistics. (Chapter 9)

33. I understand and can explain the following principles of communicative language testing: (Chapter 10)

  Start from somewhere Concentrate on content
  Bias for best   Work for washback

34. I understand the concept of propositions. (Chapter 10)

35. I am able to develop, administer, and score dictocomps. (Chapter 10)

36. I am able to develop and administer a strip story. (Chapter 10)

37. I understand the meaning of coherence and cohesion. (Chapter 10)

38. I can develop, administer, and score a test of speaking using a role play as the stimulus material. (Chapter 11)

39. I can correctly interpret inter- and intrarater reliability indices. (Chapter 11)

40. I can correctly compute inter- and intrarater reliability indices. (Chapter 11)

41. I understand and can explain the difference among holistic, primary trait, analytic, and objective scoring. (Chapter 12)

42. I can score a writing sample using holistic, primary trait, analytic, or objective scoring. (Chapter 12)

43. I understand how performance tests differ from other direct tests of language ability. (Chapter 13)

44. I understand what portfolios are, as well as some of the advantages and disadvantages of using them for assessment purposes. (Chapter 13)

45. I understand and can discuss a number of issues related to self-assessment procedures. (Chapter 14)

46. I think I can now critically and confidently read many articles on language testing.

Suggested Readings

Geoff Brindley's book Assessing *Achievement in the Learner-Centered Curriculum* (1989) contains a very useful chapter on self-assessment. It includes information on and examples of virtually every self-assessment mechanism (for learners of English) available when the book was published.

 Teaching How to Learn (1989) by Ken Willing contains some excellent self-assessment mechanisms geared for low-level adult learners of English. Although the content is geared toward immigrants to Australia, Willing's materials could provide useful models for teachers working with similar learners elsewhere.

 The article by LeBlanc and Painchaud (1985) provides a clear discussion of the development of a self-assessment system for placement purposes with university students of French and English in Canada.

Nic Underhill's book *Testing Spoken Language* (1987) contains ideas about self-assessment related specifically to oral interaction. Leslie Dickinson's book, *Self-instruction in Language Learning* (1987), also includes a useful discussion of the topic.

Terence Rolfe (1990) has written an interesting comparison of self-assessment and peer-assessment as he used these procedures with a group of adult learners in Australia. His article includes sample rating scales, a good review of the literature, and data analyses in the form of means, ranges, correlation coefficients, and scatterplots—all of which you can now read with ease!

Building on work by Oskaarson (1989), Joanna Lewis (1990) has written a delightful article about the use of self-assessment, also based on adult learners in Australia. It includes numerous clear examples of self-assessment procedures, as well as detailed information about the learners' reactions to those processes.

If you would like more information about the *ACTFL Oral Proficiency Interview,* please write to ACTFL, 6 Executive Plaza, Yonkers, New York, 10701-6801, USA.

Glossary

Acceptable word method: A procedure for scoring cloze tests in which any response which (a) is grammatically correct, and (b) makes good sense in the context is given full credit as an acceptable answer.

Achievement tests: Assessment instruments or procedures based on the objectives of a course, used to determine how much of the course content students have learned.

Admissions test: An instrument or procedure used to provide information about whether or not a candidate is likely to succeed in a particular program. (These tests are sometimes referred to as screening tests.)

Analytic scoring: A scoring system in which the hypothesized components of the skill (often writing) have been analyzed, and it is these components that make up the categories used in scoring.

Aptitude tests: Assessment instruments which do not test someone's skill in a particular language—rather they are intended to assess a person's ability to learn any language.

Benchmark papers: Classic examples of papers typical of the levels they represent in a holistic scoring system. (These typical examples are also referred to as anchor papers.)

Bottom-up processing: Focusing on small components of the language (individual sounds, morphemes, or words) in order to interpret the message.

Bursts: Utterances spoken aloud in phrases when teachers break a paragraph into sense groups, phrases, or clauses while reading a dictation.

Categorical data: Characterizations that divide people or things into groups (such as "limited English proficient students" and "fluent English proficient students"). This type of data is also sometimes referred to as nominal data, because the labels serve to name the classes or groups of people or things.

Central tendency: The patterns of how scores in a data set group together, often with some cluster of scores in the middle. The three measures of central tendency are the mean (the average), the median (the middle score in a data set), and the mode (the most frequently obtained score in a data set).

Conversational cloze test: An indirect test of speaking in which a cloze passage is created from the transcription of an actual conversation

Criterion-referenced testing: An approach to testing in which a given score is interpreted relative to a pre-set goal or objective (the criterion), rather than to the performance of other test-takers.

Degrees of freedom: "The number of quantities that can vary if others are given" (Hatch and Lazaraton, 1991:254).

Descriptive statistics: The measures of central tendency (mean, mode and median) and the measures of dispersion about the mean (the standard deviation, the range, and the variance). These procedures are called descriptive statistics because they describe a set of data.

Diagnostic test: An assessment instrument or procedure that attempts to diagnose, or identify, a learner's strengths and weaknesses, typically so that an efficient and appropriate course of instruction can be presented.

Direct tests: Those assessment procedures in which the learners' response involves actually doing the skill being assessed (writing an original composition as opposed to locating errors in an existing composition, as a task for assessing writing skills).

Directionality: The direction of language used relative to the learner—either receptively (in reading and listening) or productively (in speech and writing).

Discrete-point tests: Assessment instruments in which each item is intended to measure one and only one linguistic element.

Exact word method: A procedure for scoring cloze tests in which the test-takers get credit for a correct answer if and only if the word they write in any given blank is the exact word that was deleted from the original text in that space.

Field independence: "The extent to which a person perceives part of a field as discrete from the surrounding field as a whole, rather than embedded, or ... the extent to which a person perceives analytically" (Witkin, Moore, Goodenough, and Cox, 1977:7).

Fixed ratio deletion (or nth word deletion): When deleting words from a text to create a cloze passage, regardless of its part of speech or the semantic load it bears within the text, every nth word is omitted (every 5th word or every 7th word or every 9th word, etc.) and a blank line is inserted in its place.

Frequency polygon: A line graph that represents the frequency with with each score or rating was received in a set of data.

Graduated dictation: A dictation in which the bursts at the beginning of the text are rather short, but successive bursts gradually increase in length until they become quite challenging.

Holistic scoring: A scoring procedure (typically used in writing assessment) in which the reader reacts to the student's composition as a whole; a single score is awarded to the writing.

Histogram: A bar graph displayed in a matrix in which the vertical axis represents the number of scores and the horizontal axis represents the value of those scores. A vertical bar is drawn above each score value to the point that represents the number of people who got that score on the test.

Indirect tests: Procedures designed to tap into the enabling skills underpinning the macro skills (e.g., locating errors in an existing composition, as opposed to actually writing an original composition, as a test of writing skills).

Integrative tests: Tests that assess one or more levels of language (phonology, morphology, lexicon, syntax, or discourse) and/or one or more skills (reading, writing, speaking, and listening).

Interval data: Measurements derived from scales in which the intervals between one unit and the next unit on the scale are equal for the entire length of the scale.

Language dominance test: An instrument or procedure used to assess potentially bilingual children in both languages they have been exposed to, in order to see which is their stronger (dominant) language, for purposes of instruction.

Learner's response: The test-taker's actions in response to the task that is posed by a prompt or an item; the observable manifestation that he or she can indeed do the mental task that has been set for him or her.

Mean: The mathematical average in a group of scores. It is often represented by an "X" with a bar over it ($\bar{x}$) which is sometimes called "X-bar."

Measures of dispersion about the mean (or simply *"measures of dispersion"*): Statistics that provide information about how spread out the scores are in a given data set (usually the standard deviation, the range, and the variance).

Modality: The channel of language used (spoken or written).

Multiple-choice items: Test items that consist of a stem (the beginning of the item) and either three, four, or five answer options (with four options probably being the most common format). One, and only one, of the options is correct, and this is called the key. The incorrect options are called distractors.

Multiple trait scoring: A system for scoring writing that assigns scores to various hypothesized components of writing (as does analytic scoring) but which is more context-specific and involves more rater training and more reader involvement in the instrument development process than is the case with the earlier analytic scoring instruments.

Mutilation: The processs of deleting words from a text to create a cloze test.

Negative correlation: A situation in which as the scores on one variable increase, the scores on the other variable decrease (and vice versa). This term refers to the direction of the relationship between the two variables in a correlation analysis.

Norming: A process by which raters are trained to score speech or writing samples using a set scale. The raters independently read the compositions and score them using the scale descriptors. Then everyone compares the scores they've awarded. Any discrepancies are discussed, and then another set of papers is read and scored, and so on.

Norm-referenced tests: Tests associated with the familiar bell-shaped curve, which is referred to in the phrase "grading on a curve." In this approach, grades or scores are based on a comparison of the test-takers to a "norming group" carefully selected to be representative of those expected to take the test.

Objective scoring: Scoring procedures that attempt to eliminate the subjectivity involved in rater judgments and therefore reduce the possibility of unreliability of the sort introduced via the scoring process.

Ordinal data: Data in which a series of items or scores are rank-ordered in terms of some quality or attribute (e.g., most fluent to least fluent speaker in the class).

Outliers: Data points that fall outside a clear pattern of correlation on a scatterplot.

Overlapping variance: The extent to which two tests being correlated measure the same construct (sometimes called "shared variance" or "shared variance overlap").

Paradigmatic competence: The part of our internalized grammar that tells us the semantic features required of an item in discourse, based on the surrounding words.

Pearson's correlation coefficient: A correlation formula that uses two sets of interval data; (also called "Pearson's r" or "Pearson's product-moment correlation coefficient").

Percentile: A particular place in a distribution of many scores on a norm-referenced test. (If your score report tells you that you scored at the 96th percentile, this means that you scored better than 96 percent of the people who took the test.)

Performative assessment instruments: Tests that combine the focus and task specificity of primary trait scoring with the diagnostic information value of analytic scoring.

Performance test: A test in which the learner's response involves comprehending and producing language under the types of contextual constraints that would be involved in performing one's job. The authenticity of the stimulus material and the task posed to the learner are central concerns in designing performance tests.

Phoneme-grapheme correspondence: The extent to which the actual sounds of a language are represented by the written symbols of that language.

Placement test: An assessment instrument or procedure used to determine a student's language skills relative to the levels of a particular program he or she is about to enter.

Point-biserial correlation coefficient: A correlation coefficient that uses one set of interval data (e.g., test scores) and one set of dichotomous categorical data (that is, categorical data with only two categories—hence the "bi" in biserial).

Portfolio: "A purposeful collection of student work that exhibits the student's efforts, progress, and achievements in one or more areas. The collection must include student participation in selecting contents, the criteria for judging merit, and evidence of student self-reflection" (Paulson, Paulson, and Meyer, 1991:60).

Positive correlation: A situation in correlation analyses in which, as scores on one variable increase, so do the scores on the other variable. Likewise, as scores on one variable decrease, the scores on the other variable also decrease.

Practice effect: A threat to validity caused when test-takers repeat a test or take two very similar tests within a short period of time; the results on the second test may be inflated by the fact that the experience of taking the first test has provided practice.

Pragmatic expectancy grammar: The portion of our internalized language competence that enables us to predict likely sequences of incoming language, whether we are reading or listening.

Pretest: To try out test items with native speakers, proficient non-native speakers, and/or students like those whom we actually plan to test before the items are deployed in a real test, the results of which will be used for decision-making purposes.

Primary trait scoring: An approach to scoring (especially writing) in which a particular functional focus is selected, based on the purpose of the writing. So, for instance, in an essay that was intended to persuade the reader of the author's point of view, the scoring criteria, using the primary trait approach, would be based on how compelling and convincing the author's ideas were to the reader.

Progress tests: Tests or quizzes used as part of an ongoing assessment procedure during the course of instruction. Progress tests must be very closely tied to the course content.

Prompt: The topic for an essay task (or a speaking task).

Proposition: "The basic meaning which a sentence expresses. Propositions consist of (a) something which is named or talked about (known as the argument or entity) and (b) an assertion or predication which is made about the argument" (Richards, Platt and Weber, 1985:233).

Rater drift: A situation in which two or more raters' scores can be identical, or can demonstrate high interrater reliability, but are nonetheless off scale—that is, the raters have "drifted" away from the scale together.

Rater reliability: The consistency with which raters use a scoring system. There are two main types of rater reliabilty:

1. Intrarater reliability is determined by having the same person evaluate the same data (usually writing samples or recordings of students' speech) on two different occasions and comparing the results to see how similar they are.
2. Interrater reliability refers to the consistency with which two (or more) raters evaluate the same data using the same scoring criteria.

Rational deletion: Deleting words from a text to create a cloze passge on the basis of some rational decision. This process is sometimes refered to as "selected deletion."

Raw data: Records or measurements that have not yet been processed or statistically manipulated in any way—in our case, usually test scores or raters' assessments of students' work.

Reliability: The extent to which a test measures consistently.

Schema activator: Something that triggers the use of existing knowledge structures; also called an "advance organizer" because it helps the listener/reader prepare to test hypotheses about the nature of the incoming text.

Self-assessment: Procedures by which the learners evaluate their own language skills and/or knowledge.

Spearman's rank order correlation coefficient: A correlation statistic that utilizes two sets of ordinal data (or one set of ordinal data and one set of interval data, the latter of which can easily be converted to ordinal data) to determine the relationship between two rankings; also called "Spearman's r" or "Spearman's rho").

Standard deviation: A statistic that summarizes the average amount of difference from the mean in any given data set; also the square root of variance. Since variance is symbolized by "s^2," standard deviation (being the square root of s^2) is symbolized by lower case "s."

Statistic or statistics: The procedures, the actual mathematical formulae, that are used to manipulate raw data; also, the results of applying those formulae (i.e., the outcome of the calculations).

Stimulus material: Whatever linguistic or non-linguistic information is presented to the learners in a test to get them to demonstrate the skills or knowledge we wish to assess.

Strip story: A speaking/listening activity in which every student is given a strip of paper with one sentence (or sentence part) from a story written on it. Each student receives one and only one sentence or sentence part, which are given out in a jumbled sequence. The students' task is to sort out the sentences into their proper order.

Subjective scoring: Scoring procedures that involve raters making value judgments about texts produced by the test-takers.

Syntagmatic competence: That part of our internalized grammar that tells us what part of speech to expect next in an ordered sequence of words. (The word *syntagmatic* comes from syntax—having to do with the rules of word order.)

Task posed to the learner: That which must be done by a test-taker to demonstrate his skill and/or knowledge, thereby successfully completing a test item or prompt.

Think-aloud protocol: A transcript of a person's thoughts that were articulated while doing a task. Think-aloud protocols provide data on what is going on in the minds of learners, including test-takers.

Top-down processing: Using the big picture, the contextual features, to help interpret incoming language.

Validity: The extent to which a test measures what it is supposed to measure.

Variance: The technical term that captures the collective amount of the "differentness" in any given set of scores. Variance (usually symbolized by a lower-case "s^2") is defined as "a measure of dispersion around the mean" (Henning, 1987:198). Or as Jaeger puts it (1990:384), "Variance is an indicator of the spread of scores in a distribution" (a distribution being a set of scores).

Washback: The effect a test has on teaching and learning.

References

Abraham, Roberta, and Carol Chapelle. 1992. The meaning of cloze test scores: an item difficulty perspective. *Modern Language Journal* 76 (4): 468–479.

Alderson, J. Charles, Caroline Clapham, and Dianne Wall. 1995. *Language test construction and evaluation*. Cambridge, UK: Cambridge University Press.

Alderson, J. Charles, and Dianne Wall. 1993. Does washback exist? *Applied Linguistics* 14: 115–129.

Anderson, Jonathon. 1971. Selecting a suitable "reader": Procedures for teachers to assess language difficulty. *Regional English Language Centre Journal* 2: 35–42.

Bachman, Lyle F. 1985. Performance on cloze tests with fixed-ratio and rational deletions. *TESOL Quarterly* 19 (3): 535–56.

Bachman, Lyle F. 1990. *Fundamental considerations in language testing*. Oxford, UK: Oxford University Press.

Bachman, Lyle F. and Adrian S. Palmer. 1982. The construct validation of some components of communicative competence. *TESOL Quarterly* 16 (4): 449–465.

Bachman, Lyle F. and Adrian S. Palmer. 1996. *Language testing in practice*. Oxford, UK: Oxford University Press.

Bachman, Lyle F. and Sandra J. Savignon. 1986. The evaluation of communicative language proficiency: A critique of the ACTFL Oral Interview. *Modern Language Journal* 70 (4): 380–390.

Bailey, Kathleen M. 1977. The ESL service courses: A progress report. In John Povey (ed.), *Working papers in teaching English as a second language* (vol. 11). Los Angeles: English Dept. (ESL Section), University of California at Los Angeles. 11–16.

Bailey, Kathleen M. 1982. Teaching in a second language: The communicative competence of non-native speaking teaching assistants. Unpublished doctoral dissertation. University of California at Los Angeles.

Bailey, Kathleen M. 1996. Working for washback. *Language Testing* 13 (3): 257–277.

Bailey, Kathleen M., Peter A. Shaw, and David Tsugawa. 1989. Assessment implications of a content-based curriculum: The role of self-assessment. Paper presented at the Eleventh Annual Language Testing Research Colloquium in San Antonio, Texas. March 5, 1989.

Bilingual Syntax Measure. 1975. New York: Harcourt Brace Jovanovich.

Bolger, Pat. 1996. Review of the *Readiness Test for Content-Based Instruction*. Unpublished Paper. Monterey Institute of International Studies, Monterey, California.

Bowker, David. 1984. The information gap in placement testing. *ELT Journal* 38 (4): 248–255.

Brindley, Geoff. 1989. *Assessing achievement in the learner-centered curriculum*. Sydney, Australia: National Centre for English Language Teaching and Research.

Brodkey, Dean, and Rodney Young. 1981. Composition correctness scores. *TESOL Quarterly* 15 (2): 159–167.

Brown, David. 1983. Conversational cloze tests and conversational ability. *ELT Journal* 37 (2): 158–161.

Brown, James Dean. 1980. Relative merits of four methods for scoring cloze tests. *Modern Language Journal* 64 (3): 311–317.

Brown, James Dean. 1981. Newly placed students versus continuing students: Comparing proficiency. In Janet C. Fisher, Mark A. Clarke, and Jacqueline Schachter (eds.) *On TESOL '80 Building bridges: Research and practice in teaching English as a second language.* Washington, D.C.: TESOL.

Brown, James Dean. 1983. An exploration of morpheme-group interactions. In Kathleen M. Bailey, Michael H. Long and Sabrina Peck (eds.), *Second language acquisition studies.* Rowley, MA: Newbury House, 25–40.

Brown, James Dean. 1988. *Understanding research in second language learning: A teacher's guide to statistics and research design.* Cambridge, UK: Cambridge University Press.

Brown, James Dean. 1991. Statistics as a foreign language—part 1: What to look for in reading statistical studies. *TESOL Quarterly* 25 (4): 569–586.

Brown, James Dean. 1992. Statistics as a foreign language—part 2: More things to consider in reading statistical studies. *TESOL Quarterly* 26 (4): 629–664.

Brown, James Dean. 1995. Differences between norm-referenced and criterion-referenced tests. In James Dean Brown and Sayoko Okada Yamashita (eds.), *Language testing in Japan.* Tokyo: The Japan Association for Language Teaching.

Brown, James Dean. 1996. *Testing in language programs.* Upper Saddle River, NJ: Prentice-Hall Regents.

Brown, James Dean, and Kathleen M. Bailey. 1984. A categorical instrument for scoring second language writing skills. *Language Learning* 34 (4): 21–42.

Brown, James Dean, and Sayoko Okada Yamashita (eds.). 1995. *Language testing in Japan.* Tokyo: The Japan Association for Language Teaching.

Buck, G. 1988. Testing listening comprehension in Japanese university entrance examinations. *JALT Journal* 10 (1): 15–42.

Canale, Michael, and Merrill Swain. 1980. Theoretical bases of communicative approaches to second language teaching and testing. *Applied Linguistics* 1 (1): 1–47.

Carrasco, R. L. 1981. Expanded awareness of student performance: A case study in applied ethnographic monitoring in a bilingual classroom. In H. T. Trueba, G. P. Guthrie, and H. P. Au (eds.), *Culture and the bilingual classroom.* Rowley, MA: Newbury House, 153–177.

Carrell, Patricia L. 1984. Evidence of a formal schema in second language comprehension. *Language Learning* 34 (1): 87–112.

Carrell, Patricia L., and Joan C. Eisterhold. 1983. Schema theory and ESL reading pedagogy. *TESOL Quarterly* 17 (4): 553–573.

Carroll, Brendan J. 1980. *Testing communicative performance.* Oxford, UK: Pergamon Press Ltd.

Carroll, Brendan J., and Patrick J. Hall. 1985. *Make your own language tests: A practical guide to writing language performance tests.* Oxford, UK: Pergamon Press.

Chase, Beckie. 1996. Cultural bridges test. Unpublished paper. Monterey Institute of International Studies, Monterey, California.

Clark, J. L. D. 1983. Language testing: Past and current status—directions for the future. *Modern Language Journal* 67 (4): 431–443.

Cleary, Christopher. 1988. The C-test in English: Left-hand deletions. *Regional English Language Centre Journal* 19 (2): 26–38.

Cohen, Andrew D. 1984. On taking language tests: What the students report. *Language Testing* 1 (1): 70–81.

Cohen, Andrew D. 1993. The role of instructions in testing summarizing ability. In Dan Douglas and Carol Chapelle (eds.), *A new decade of language testing research*. Alexandria, VA: TESOL Publications. 132–160.

Cohen, Andrew D. 1994. *Assessing language ability in the classroom* (2nd ed.). Boston, MA: Heinle & Heinle.

Cronbach, Lee J. 1951. Coefficient alpha and the internal structures of tests. *Psychometrika* 16: 292–334.

Cumming, Alister, and Richard Berwick. 1996. *Validation in language testing*. Clevedon, UK: Cromwell Press.

Davis, Paul, and Mario Rinvolucri. 1988. *Dictation: New methods, new possibilities*. Cambridge, UK: Cambridge University Press.

De Jong, John H. A. L. (ed.). 1990. *Standardization in language testing: AILA Review*. Amsterdam: Free University Press.

De Jong, John H. A. L., and Douglas K. Stevenson (eds.). 1990. *Individualizing the assessment of language abilities*. Clevedon, UK: Multilingual Matters.

Dickinson, Leslie. 1987. *Self-instruction in language learning*. Cambridge, UK: Cambridge University Press.

Educational Testing Service. 1996. *TOEFL Test of Written English Guide* (4th ed.). Princeton, NJ: Author. 23.

Elbow, Peter. 1993. Ranking, evaluating, and liking: Sorting out three forms of judgment. *College English* 55 (2): 187–206.

Erickson, Melinda. 1990. A role for dictations in writing classes. Paper presented at the 1990 CATESOL Conference, Los Angeles, California.

Ferris, Dana, and John Hedgcock. In press. *Purpose, process and practice: A manual for teachers of ESL writing* (working title). Hillsdale, NJ: Lawrence Erlbaum.

Flanagan, J. C. 1939. General considerations in the selection of test items and a short method of estimating the product-moment coefficient of correlation from the data at the tails of the distribution. *Educational Psychology* 30: 674–680.

Freeman, Donald. 1996. Redefining the relationship between research and what teachers know. In Kathleen M. Bailey and David Nunan (eds.), *Voices from the language classroom*. Cambridge, UK: Cambridge University Press. 88–115.

French, Russell L. 1992. Portfolio assessment and LEP students. *Proceedings of the Second National Research Symposium on Limited English Proficient Student Issues: Focus on Evaluation and Measurement*, (vol. 1). Washington, D.C.: U.S. Department of Education, Office of Bilingual Education and Minority Language Affairs, 249–272.

Gardner, David. 1996. Self-assessment for self-access learners. *TESOL Journal* 5 (3): 18–23.

Genesee, Fred, and John Upshur. 1996. *Classroom-based evaluation in second language education*. Cambridge, UK: Cambridge University Press.

Gibson, Robert E. 1975. The strip story: Catalyst for communication. *TESOL Quarterly* 9 (2): 149–154.

Gottlieb, Margo. 1995. Nurturing student learning through portfolios. *TESOL Journal* 5 (1): 12–14.

Green, Daina Z. 1985. Developing measures of communicative proficiency: A test for French immersion students in grades 9 and 10. In Philip C. Hauptman, Raymond LeBlanc, and Marjorie Wesche (eds.), *Second language performance testing*. Ottawa, Canada: University of Ottawa. 215–228.

Griffee, Dale T. 1995. Criterion-referenced test construction and evaluation. In James Dean Brown and Sayoko Okada Yamashita (eds.), *Language testing in Japan*. Tokyo: The Japan Association for Language Teaching.

Grotjahn, R. 1996. The C-test bibliography: December 1995. In R. Grotjahn (ed.), *Der C-test. Theorietische Grundlagen und praktische Anwendungen* 3: 435–457. Bochum, Germany: Brockmeyer.

Hacker, Tim. 1991. A teaching technique for raising grammatical consciousness: The C-test. Paper presented at the WAESOL Conference, University of Washington, Seattle, Washington.

Hamp-Lyons, Liz. 1987. Performance profiles for academic writing. In Kathleen M. Bailey, Ted L. Dale, and Ray T. Clifford (eds.), *Language testing research: Selected papers from the 1986 colloquium*. Monterey, CA: Defense Language Institute. 78–92

Hamp-Lyons, Liz (ed.). 1991. *Assessing second language writing in academic contexts*. Norwood, NJ: Ablex Publishing.

Hamp-Lyons, Liz, and William Condon. 1993. Questioning assumptions about portfolio based assessment. *College Composition and Communication* 44 (2): 176–190.

Hamp-Lyons, Liz and Barbara Kroll. 1996. Issues in ESL writing assessment: An overview. *College ESL* 6 (1): 52–72.

Hart, Doug, Sharon Lapkin, and Merrill Swain. 1987. Communicative language tests: Perks and perils. *Evaluation and Research in Education* 1 (2): 83–94.

Hatch, Evelyn, and Anne Lazaraton. 1991. *The research manual: Design and statistics for applied linguistics*. New York: Newbury House.

Hauptman, Philip C., Raymond LeBlanc, and Marjorie Bingham Wesche (eds.). 1985. *Second language performance testing*. Ottawa, Canada: University of Ottawa Press.

Heaton, J. B. 1988. *Writing English language tests (new edition)*. London: Longman.

Henning, Grant. 1983. Oral proficiency testing: Comparative validities of interview, imitation, and completion methods. *Language Learning* 33 (3): 315–331.

Henning, Grant. 1987. *A guide to language testing: Development, evaluation, research*. Cambridge, MA: Newbury House.

Henning, Grant and Fred Davidson. 1987. Scalar analysis of composition ratings. In Kathleen M. Bailey, Ted L. Dale, and Ray T. Clifford (eds.), *Language testing research: Selected papers from the 1986 colloquium*. Monterey, CA: Defense Language Institute. 24–38.

Hinofotis, Frances B., Kathleen M. Bailey, and Susan L. Stern. 1981. Assessing the oral proficiency of prospective foreign teaching assistants: Instrument development. In

Adrian S. Palmer, Peter J. M. Groot, and George A. Trosper (eds.), *The construct validation of tests of communicative competence*. Washington, D.C.: TESOL, 106–126.

Homburg, Taco Justice. 1984. Holistic evaluation of ESL compositions: Can it be validated objectively? *TESOL Quarterly* 18 (1): 87–107.

Houba, Christine. 1996. Original test project. Unpublished paper. Monterey Institute of International Studies, Monterey, California.

Hudson, Thom. 1993. Testing the specificity of ESP reading skills. In Dan Douglas and Carol Chapelle (eds.), *A new decade of language testing research*. Alexandria, VA: TESOL Publications. 58–82.

Hughes, Arthur. 1981. Conversational cloze as a measure of oral ability. *ELT Journal* 35 (2): 161–168.

Hughes, Arthur. 1989. *Testing for language teachers*. Cambridge, UK: Cambridge University Press.

Jacobs, Holly L., Stephen A. Zingraf, D. R. Wormuth, V. Faye Hartfiel, and Jane B. Hughey. 1981. *Testing ESL composition: A practical approach*. Rowley, MA: Newbury House.

Jaeger, Richard M. 1990. *Statistics: A spectator sport* (2nd ed.). Beverly Hills, CA: Sage.

Johnson, Donna M. 1992. *Approaches to research in second language learning*. New York: Longman.

Johnson, Harvey L. 1949. *La América Española*. New York: Oxford University Press.

Johnson, Keith. 1982. Five principles in a "communicative" exercise type. *Communicative syllabus design and methodology*. Oxford, UK: Pergamon Press.

Johnson, Patricia. 1981. Effects on reading comprehension of language and cultural background of a text. *TESOL Quarterly* 15 (2): 169–181.

Johnson, Patricia. 1982. Effects on reading comprehension of building background knowledge. *TESOL Quarterly* 16 (4): 503–516.

Jonz, John. 1990. Another turn in the conversation: What does cloze measure? *TESOL Quarterly* 24 (1): 61–83.

Kawakami, Alice J. 1992. Response to Russell French's presentation. *Proceedings of the second National Research Symposium on Limited English Proficient student issues: Focus on evaluation and measurement*, (vol. 1). Washington, D.C.: U.S. Department of Education, Office of Bilingual Education and Minority Language Affairs. 273–279.

Keller, Helen. 1902. *The story of my life*. Garden City, NY: Doubleday Publishers.

Kenny, G., and B. Tsai. 1993. Teachers speak out: Test case. *Practical English Teaching*, December, 16–17.

Keuneman, H. 1983. *Sri Lanka*. Hong Kong: Apa Productions.

Klein-Braley, Christine. 1985. A cloze-up on the C-Test: A study of the construct validation of authentic tests. *Language Testing* 2 (1): 76–104.

Klein-Braley, Christine, and Ulrich Raatz. 1984. A survey of research on the C-Test. *Language Testing* 1 (2): 134–146.

Koretz, Daniel. 1992. Response to Russell French's presentation. *Proceedings of the second National Research Symposium on Limited English Proficient student issues: Focus on evaluation and measurement*, (vol. 1). Washington, D.C.: U.S. Department of

Education, Office of Bilingual Education and Minority Language Affairs. 281–285.

Law, Barbara, and Mary Eckes. 1995. *Assessment and ESL*. Winnipeg, Manitoba: Peguis Publishers.

LeBlanc, Raymond, and Gisèle Painchaud. 1985. Self-assessment as a second language placement instrument. *TESOL Quarterly* 19 (4): 673 687.

Lewis, Joanna. 1990. Self-assessment in the classroom: A case study. In Geoff Brindley (ed.), *The second language curriculum in action*. Sydney: Macquarie University, National Centre for English Language Teaching and Research 187–213.

Lin, Nien-Hsuan Jennifer. 1982. Developing integrative language testing techniques: The graduated dictation and the copytest. In Yamana Kachru and J. R. Cowan (eds.), *TESL Studies* (vol. 5). Urbana, IL: University of Illinois. 108–129.

Llewelyn, Susie. 1990. Learner language and the cloze procedure. In Geoff Brindley (ed.), *The second language curriculum in action*. Sydney, Australia: Macquarie University, National Centre for English Language Teaching and Research, 128–162.

Lugton, Robert. 1978. *American topics*. Englewood, NJ: Prentice-Hall, 221.

Lynch, Brian K., and Fred Davidson. 1994. Criterion-referenced test development: Linking curricula, teachers, and tests. *TESOL Quarterly* 28 (4): 727–743.

Mackay, Ronald, and Maryse Bosquet. 1981. LSP and curriculum development— from policy to practice. In Ronald Mackay and Joe Darwin Palmer (eds.), *Language for specific purposes: Program design and evaluation*. Rowley, MA: Newbury House, 1–28.

Madsen, Harold S. 1983. *Techniques in testing*. Oxford, UK: Oxford University Press.

McNamara, Tim. 1996. Interaction in second language performance assessment. Plenary presentation at the Association for Applied Linguistics Annual Conference, Chicago, Illinois.

Munby, John. 1978. *Communicative syllabus design*. Cambridge, UK: Cambridge University Press.

Murray, Denise E. 1994. Using portfolios to assess writing. *Prospect: A Journal of Australian TESOL* 9 (2): 56–69.

Nevo, D. 1986. Comments on Stansfield: A history of the *Test of Written English*: The developmental year. *Language Testing* 3 (2): 235–236.

Nunan, David. 1988. *The learner-centered curriculum*. Cambridge, UK: Cambridge University Press.

Nunan, David. 1989. *Understanding language classrooms: A guide for teacher initiated action*. New York: Prentice-Hall.

Nunan, David. 1992. *Research methods in language learning*. Cambridge, UK: Cambridge University Press.

Oller, John W., Jr. 1979. *Language tests at school*. London: Longman.

Omaggio, Alice C. 1986. *Teaching language in context: Proficiency-oriented instruction*. Boston: Heinle & Heinle.

Oskaarson, Matts. 1978. *Approaches to self-assessment in foreign language learning*. Oxford, UK: Pergamon Press.

Oskaarson, Matts. 1984. *Self-assessment of foreign language skills: A survey of research and development work*. Strasbourg, France: Council for Cultural Cooperation.

Oskaarson, Matts. 1989. Self-assessment of language proficiency: Rationale and applications. *Language Testing* 6 (1): 1–25.

Palmer, Adrian S., Peter J. M. Groot, and George A. Trosper (eds.). 1981. *The construct validation of tests of communicative competence*. Washington, D.C.: TESOL.

Parry, Thomas S., and Charles W. Stansfield (eds.) 1990. *Language aptitude reconsidered*. Englewood Cliffs, NJ: Prentice-Hall Regents.

Paulson, Leon F., Pearl R. Paulson, and Carol A. Meyer. 1991. What makes a portfolio a portfolio? *Educational Leadership* 48 (5): 60–63.

Pearson, Bethyl, and Cathy Berghof. 1996. London Bridge is not falling down: It's supporting alternative assessment. *TESOL Journal* 5 (4): 28–31.

Perkins, Kyle. 1980. Using objective methods of attained writing proficiency to discriminate among holistic evaluations. *TESOL Quarterly* 14 (1): 61–67.

Perkins, Kyle, and Sheila R. Brutten. 1988. An item discriminability study of textually explicit, textually implicit, and scriptually implicit questions. *RELC Journal* 19 (2): 1–11.

Quick Start in English Assessment. 1983. Los Altos, CA: Quick Start in English Co.

Richards, Jack C. 1983. Listening comprehension: Approach, design and procedure. *TESOL Quarterly* 17 (2): 219–240.

Richards, Jack, John Platt, and Heidi Weber. 1985. *Longman dictionary of applied linguistics*. London: Longman.

Rogan, Pete. 1996. Testing file rationale. Unpublished paper. Monterey Institute of International Studies, Monterey, California.

Rolfe, Terence. 1990. Self- and peer-assessment in the ESL curriculum. In Geoff Brindley (ed.), *The second language curriculum in action*. Sydney, Australia: Macquarie University, National Centre for English Language Teaching and Research, 163–186.

Roller, Cathy, and Alex R. Matambo. 1992. Bilingual readers' use of background knowledge in learning from text. *TESOL Quarterly* 26 (1): 129–141.

Ross, Steven. 1987. An experiment with an on-line narrative discourse test. In Kathleen M. Bailey, Ted L. Dale, and Ray T. Clifford (eds.), *Language testing research: Selected papers from the 1986 colloquium*. Monterey, CA: Defense Language Institute. 60–69.

Savignon, S. J. 1983. *Communicative competence: Theory and classroom practice*. Reading, MA: Addison-Wesley.

Schafer, Mary B. 1993. Portfolio assessment in ESOL. *Elementary Education Newsletter* 16 (1): 1.

Schon, Donald A. 1987. *Educating the reflective practitioner*. San Francisco: Jossey-Bass.

Schutz, Noel W., and Bruce L. Derwing. 1981. The problem of needs assessment in English for specific purposes: Some theoretical and practical considerations. In Ronald Mackay and Joe Darwin Palmer (eds.), *Language for specific purposes: Program design and evaluation*. Rowley, MA: Newbury House, 29–44.

Seldin, Peter. 1991. *The teaching portfolio: A practical guide to improved performance and promotion/tenure decisions*. Bolton, MA: Anker Publishing.

Shavelson, Richard J. 1988. *Statistical reasoning for the behavioral sciences* (2nd ed.). Boston, MA: Allyn & Bacon.

Shaw, Peter A. 1980. Comments on the concept and implementation of self-placement. *TESOL Quarterly* 14 (2): 261–262.

Shohamy, Elana. 1982. Predicting speaking proficiency from cloze tests: Theoretical and practical considerations for test substitutions. *Applied Linguistics* 3 (2): 161–171.

Shohamy, Elana. 1993. A collaborative/diagnostic feedback model for testing foreign languages. In Dan Douglas and Carol Chapelle (eds.), *A new decade of language testing research*. Alexandria, VA: TESOL Publications. 185–202.

Short, Deborah J. 1993. Assessing integrated language and content instruction. *TESOL Quarterly* 24 (4): 627–656.

Stansfield, Charles W. 1985. A history of dictation in foreign language teaching and testing. *Modern Language Journal* 69 (2): 121–128.

Stansfield, Charles W. 1986. A history of the *Test of Written English*: The developmental year. *Language Testing* 3 (2): 224–234.

Stansfield, Charles W. 1991. A comparative analysis of simulated and direct oral proficiency interviews. In Sarinee Anivan (ed.), *Current developments in language testing*. Singapore: Regional English Language Center, 199–209.

Stern, Susan. 1983. Why drama works: A psycholinguistic perspective. In John W. Oller, Jr., and Patricia A. Richard-Amato (eds.), *Methods that work*. Rowley, MA: Newbury House, 207–225.

Sturman, Peter. 1996. Registration and placement: Learner response. In Kathleen M. Bailey and David Nunan (eds.), *Voices from the language classroom*. Cambridge, UK: Cambridge University Press, 338–355.

Swain, Merrill. 1984. Large-scale communicative language testing: A case study. In Sandra J. Savignon and Margie Berns (eds.), *Initiatives in communicative language teaching*. Reading, MA: Addison-Wesley, 185–201.

The top censored stories of 1993: Big news you didn't hear. *Utne Reader* 63: 42–47.

Tung, Peter. 1985. Designing oral proficiency tests in EFL for Hong Kong secondary schools. In Philip C. Hauptman, Raymond LeBlanc, and Marjorie B. Wesche (eds.), *Second language performance testing*. Ottawa, Canada: University of Ottawa. 229–242

Turner, Jean L. 1992. Creating content-based language tests: Guidelines for teachers. *The CATESOL Journal* 5 (1): 43–58.

Turner, Jean L. 1995. Testing preparation. Presentation at the TESOL convention, Long Beach, California.

Underhill, Nic. 1987. *Testing spoken language: A handbook of oral testing techniques*. Cambridge, UK: Cambridge University Press.

van Lier, Leo. 1988. *The classroom and the language learner: Ethnography and second-language classroom research*. London: Longman.

van Lier, Leo. 1989. Reeling, writhing, drawling, stretching and fainting in coils: Oral proficiency interviews as conversation. *TESOL Quarterly* 23 (3): 489–501.

Wajnryb, Ruth. 1990. *Grammar dictation*. Oxford, UK: Oxford University Press.

Wall, Dianne, and Charles Alderson. 1993. Examining washback: The Sri Lankan impact study. *Language Testing* 10 (1): 41–69.

Wesche, Marjorie B. 1983. Communicative testing in a second language. *Modern Language Journal* 67 (1): 41–55.

White, T. H. 1939. *The once and future king.* New York: Putnam.

Willing, Ken. 1989. *Teaching how to learn.* Sydney, Australia: Macquarie University, National Centre for English Language Teaching and Research.

Wishon, G. E. and J. M. Burks. 1968. *Let's write English.* New York: American Book Company.

Witkin, H. A., C. A. Moore, D. R. Goodenough, and P. W. Cox. 1977. Field dependent and field independent styles and their educational implication. *Review of Educational Research* 47: 1–67.

Wolf, Kenneth. 1996. Developing an effective teaching portfolio. *Educational Leadership* 53 (6): 34–37.

Woods, Anthony, Paul Fletcher, and Arthur Hughes. 1986. *Statistics in language testing.* Cambridge, UK: Cambridge University Press.